LIFE OF MORAVIA

LIFE OF MORAVIA

Alberto Moravia
AND ALAIN ELKANN

Translated by William Weaver

STEERFORTH ITALIA
AN IMPRINT OF STEERFORTH PRESS
SOUTH ROYALTON, VERMONT

Library of Congress Cataloging-in-Publication Data
Moravia, Alberto, 1907–1990
[Vita di Moravia. English]
Life of Moravia / Alberto Moravia and Alain Elkann ;
[translated by William Weaver]. —1. ed.
p. cm.
Includes index.
ISBN 1-883642-50-7 (alk. paper)
1. Moravia, Alberto, 1907–1990 2. Authors, Italian —20th century—
Biography. I. Elkann, Alain, 1950– II. Title.

PQ4829.062 Z46813   2000
853'.912 — dc21
[B]
00-044539

Manufactured in the United States of America

FIRST EDITION

CONTENTS

Translator's Note

*P*ERHAPS BECAUSE of his lonely childhood, when his early illness separated him for long periods from his family and from coevals, Alberto Moravia (1907–90) in later years relished conversation. And if conversation is an art, as some have suggested, then he was its Titian, its Caravaggio, or — depending on the situation — its Hogarth. Before he actually began writing novels (and he began young, in his teens), he would tell himself stories or plays, aloud, fabulizing, dramatizing the life around him or the life he imagined beyond the walls of his sanatorium.

And if ever a writer had a distinctive voice, Moravia was that writer. Friends, reading his works, could actually hear his accent, his slightly husky tone, his private chuckle as he recalled a particularly sapid detail. And yet he was not garrulous; indeed, he was an excellent, alert listener. It was an inspired idea for him to present his autobiography in the form of an interview, by the writer Alain Elkann, a novelist and close friend of Moravia's during the last decade of his life. Composed of recorded conversations dating largely from 1989 and the early months of 1990, the book must not give the mistaken impression that Moravia was logodiarrheic or egocentric. His affectionate and justified admiration for the works and words of other writers, including those of his first wife, Elsa Morante, are an indication of his curiosity, his perception, his generosity; and — as I can testify — he was as receptive to the opinions of a callow youth as he was to those of the great and famous, many of whom he met. Though he was the most professional of professional writers, he was not concerned only with writing; among his close friends and interlocutors he could number many artists and people from other worlds, especially the theater and the exciting Italian film industry (he even wrote a deft little pamphlet on the actress Claudia Cardinale, at about the time that Simone de Beauvoir wrote her essay on Brigitte Bardot).

Like all storytellers, Moravia repeated himself; but the repetitions never sounded like set pieces, and if he retold a story, it was likely to appear in a different context. An example: Elsa Morante was very fond of parlor games, whether conventional ones of the twenty-questions variety or others of her own invention. Often the game would consist simply of Elsa's asking everyone an embarrassing question and demanding an honest answer. I remember an evening at their apartment in Rome when, after dinner, all of us were asked to recount the greatest sacrifice we had ever made for love. At twenty-four or twenty-five, I did not have a great experience of love, or, fortunately, of sacrifice; but I managed to give some kind of answer. Moravia told a complex and amusing story about making a trip from Rome to Berlin with the aim of completing a seduction he had failed to accomplish during an encounter with a German girl on Capri. Years later, I recognized this story as the germ of his novel 1934, one of his best late works and the only novel that I translated. To Elkann he tells the story again, but with quite a different hue. For his Roman after-dinner audience he had emphasized the discomfort of the train journey, in third class (to those of us old enough to have made long journeys in Italian third-class carriages, the very recollection was excruciating). Then, when the seduction again failed in Berlin, Moravia — who had brought a supply of money along with him, imagining smart Berlin cafés and the usual seduction expenses — found himself flush, and for the return to Rome, changed his ticket to first class. Retelling the story to Elkann twenty years later (and fifty years after the journey), Moravia emphasizes its historical context, its sinister atmosphere, associated with the early days of Nazism. During the years of his marriage to Dacia Maraini, Moravia fell in love with Africa, and he and Dacia made many extended trips there (his travel books, by the way, are a major part of his oeuvre, and perhaps the least known outside of Italy). It was a special treat to spend time with him when he had just returned from one of these journeys, for he loved reliving his adventures. Once an American magazine had asked me to interview him, I believe on the subject of Italian politics. We arranged to meet for lunch in Piazza Navona, but instead of politics he wanted to talk about Africa, and as I was enjoying my pasta, he told me about a boat trip he had taken. Shortly after he had come aboard, he was invited to the captain's cabin to settle some trivial matter, and on opening the door, he immediately was confronted by a dead crocodile, propped upright against the wall. "That's our dinner," the captain said. And with his characteristic repressed laugh, Moravia repeated, "Our dinner," then added, "and it was!" The pasta suddenly seemed culpably prosaic.

Though he had opinions and expressed them readily, Moravia was not opinionated. Still, whenever something apparently important happened in the world, the Italian newspapers regularly called him and asked him for a statement. To outsiders he could occasionally give the impression of glibness, but even his most spontaneous declarations were never ready-made. He liked questions, and — as readers of the present book will see — he often questioned himself, eager to delve into his own past, his own thoughts, to examine, to weigh and ponder. He wrote copiously: fiction, travel articles, reviews. For years he was the film critic of a leading Italian magazine, and even in those rapidly written notices there are always, unfailingly, some original, thought-provoking aperçus.

He was a man who thought his own thoughts, in other words; and he was not afraid to contradict received ideas. He got into trouble, for example, when, after the death of Ernest Hemingway, he wrote a kind of obituary expressing some reservations about Hemingway's achievement. Italian admirers of the American novelist seized the occasion to attack Moravia for what they considered not only a piece of bad taste but also an erroneous estimate of the dead writer (though, in the years that followed, the position of Hemingway was drastically reevaluated in Italy as everywhere else).

At dinner once, with some friends, Elkann among them, somebody mentioned Thomas Mann; and Moravia, in his blurting way, asserted that *The Magic Mountain* was vastly overrated. While I was recovering from shock, he then went on to excoriate Aldous Huxley's *Point Counter Point* and André Gide's *The Counterfeiters* as two other contemporary examples of books valued beyond their worth. He, of course, had read these books when they first appeared; reading them a generation later, in boarding school, I had fallen in with the majority opinion, considering them shining, unassailable beacons illuminating the path of literature, which I dreamed of undertaking. Again, in talking with Elkann, he reiterates his harsh but not captious judgment.

Moravia's first novel, *Gli indifferenti* (1929; *The Time of Indifference*) — now a milestone of modern European literature — appeared when he was in his early twenties and won him immediate fame, at least in Europe. Because of that fame he was able, while still a young man, to meet many of the intellectual luminaries of his day (his account of Bloomsbury in this interview is engagingly unencrusted by later, adulatory legend). After World War II he was a kind of Roman landmark: no important writer arrived in Rome without an introduction to him — not that an introduction was necessary; he was eminently accessible, always eager to meet new arrivals. At his house you were likely to encounter interesting people (he once told me that the young Norman Mailer had challenged him to an Indian-wrestling match; Moravia declined).

Thus the pages of this volume are dotted with names, some familiar, some not; and along with the names there are a number of references to events, political and intellectual, not always meaningful to the younger or the non-Italian reader. Thanks to the alert assistance of my former student and present friend Kristina Olson, the volume includes a glossary of names, though some of the references are probably self-explanatory and, like Moravia's real-life conversation, the text should be enjoyable even for the reader too lazy to look up obscure writers or political figures. We have also tried to keep footnotes to a minimum, rather than clutter the pages with numbers and small print and perhaps stem the free flow of Moravia's speech.

In translating these conversations of Moravia's, my chief concern has been to convey their informal, discursive tone. When speaking of his works and the works of others, the author naturally referred to them by their original titles. It is a standard practice to follow foreign-language titles with their English-language translation, however, I depart from this practice for two reasons: first, frequent parentheses would have arrested the natural flow of the talk; and second, there is some confusion about the English titles. Several of Moravia's novels have appeared under more than one title (for example, *La noia* was called *The Empty Canvas* on its first English appearance; more recently it has been given a title closer to the Italian: *Boredom*). Some of Moravia's works have not been translated, so adding an arbitrary translation of the Italian might give the mistaken impression that English-language editions exist. For the reader's convenience, therefore, I have provided a selective bibliography, with some information about the availability (or nonavailability) of Moravia's works in English.

This book is a testament. On the morning of 26 September 1990, Moravia's editor and friend Mario Andreose arrived at the Roman apartment on Lungotevere delle Vittorie with the first bound copy of the Italian edition. Admitting him, the maid said that Moravia was in the bathroom, shaving. When he didn't appear, they opened the door and found him, lifeless. Other works of his have since appeared posthumously, but this interview is the last work supervised by the living Moravia. And like the author himself, it is full of life.

The translation was originally made some years ago for another publisher, who, once the work was completed, raised some questions and insisted on a number of changes that I was unwilling to make (a translator is always, in some ways, the author's vicar, his advocate, his protector). I am grateful to Steerforth Press for having acquired the rights to the book and to the translation. For this edition, I have gone over the English text — largely to decide on matters concerning the glossary and notes — and it has been an incomparable and sometimes eerie process. As I said above, while I worked on Moravia's words, I could actually hear his voice. My hours at the computer were like so many visits with him, an affecting colloquy with a treasured friend and a great writer.

William Weaver
Annandale-on-Hudson/Rome

LIFE OF MORAVIA

PART I

I

ALAIN ELKANN: *Tell me about the birth of Alberto Moravia.*

ALBERTO MORAVIA: I was a healthy baby, and my family was normal. I was the abnormal one, if anything. Abnormal because I was oversensitive. I don't believe everyone is sensitive in the same way. There are dull, stupid, insensitive children. There are others who are very sensitive, oversensitive. The oversensitive ones can become misfits, but they can also become artists.

What is your earliest childhood memory?

My first childhood memory is of Mademoiselle Durand, my French governess. I was five at the time.

What about your parents?

I remember my parents very well, for example, when they went to the opera. My mother, especially, because she would come to give me a kiss before going out, all in evening dress, with many black beads, jet. I also remember that when I was very little, on New Year's Eve, they would bundle me up in blankets and carry me out on the terrace, to look at the fireworks. Then I remember one day in the Borghese Gardens I found a human turd on the ground and, with great joy, I carried it to my governess, who said, "Throw that filth away!" I was convinced it was a precious object.

You were a very healthy child?

Healthy, yes, in the sense of innocent. Like the penguins in the Antarctic who approach humans without fear or distrust and then are probably killed.

You didn't die, however.

No, but at a certain point I fell ill. Physically, and also spiritually. After that I spent a good half of my life trying to recover my health, again not only physical but also spiritual. It must be said that recovering your health is quite different from always having had it, never having lost it.

We were talking about your childhood memories.

I remember only that Mademoiselle Durand read me the novels of the Comtesse de Ségur. We had a complete set, bound in red and gold. She read aloud to me and to my sisters: *Les petites filles modèles, Les malheurs de Sophie, Le généreal Dourakine*. My sister Adriana, who later became a painter, listened with attention. My sister Elena, on the contrary, refused to listen and cried.

What was your life like when you were little?

The life of a little middle-class boy, who plays with his sisters and goes to bed early, speaks French with the governess. The totally normal life of an abnormal child. Abnormal, as I said, because my sensitivity was highly developed. I saw and felt everything on a bigger scale. The roses in my garden to me were big as cabbages, and their perfume made my head spin. The bees buzzing around them looked enormous to me.

But you were a happy, good-humored child?

I've always been good-humored, I must say. I was a very vital child, and hence good-humored. Life exploded in my hands like dynamite.

When did you see your parents?

I saw them at table.

Did you always take your meals with them?

Yes, always. My father sat at the head of the table, my mother at the other end, facing him. Eating together was important, because my father and mother gave the impression, probably correct, that their only relationship existed at mealtimes; away from the table, it seemed, they never met, as their habits were so different.

What was this relationship like?

The usual conjugal relationship, very dialectic, but basically good.

Were you comfortable with your family?

Not very. But I didn't realize it then. The fact that, unconsciously, I didn't like it is proved by my unflattering picture of family life in *Gli indifferenti.*

Your father was an architect. Did his work interest you?

I remember I used to watch him draw at his desk. He had a drawing board with plans pinned to it, and many implements. He drew plans and designed façades of houses.

Did you think you would also become an architect?

Not at all. My mother wanted me to be a diplomat, because that seemed to her a profession with prestige. I wanted to be . . . hm . . . Actually, I wanted to become a writer as soon as possible.

What did they talk about in your house?

Nothing. There was an antagonism between my father and mother. It could be said that in every family there is an antagonistic dualism, the female element and the male element. My father was conservative, my mother tended toward novelty. My father had regular habits; my mother didn't want to have any. My father was a simple man, opposed to social life. He went to a café every evening at the same hour. He did everything by habit. He was a nineteenth-century man; he was born in 1860. My mother was twenty years younger.

Your mother's family came from the Marche region?

My mother's family name was De Marsanich; they came from Ancona and were of remotely Slavic origin. Probably they had come from Dalmatia in the first decade of the ninteenth century. In fact, the founder of the family was named Dominatore, which is the Italian translation of Vladimir. The family was very poor. My grandfather was a government clerk.

What were your parents' names?

Carlo and Teresa, but at home my mother was called Gina. Her second name was Iginia.

What did they look like?

My father was blond, with blue eyes, a curled mustache, medium stature. His hair was white by the time I remember him; he was forty years older than I. My mother was dark, with a broad face, prominent cheekbones, the face of a Slavic peasant woman.

Where did they meet?

I've always wondered. Perhaps in an office where she was working. I don't remember when my parents were married. In any case I was born in 1907 and my sister Adriana in 1906.

How did they get married: he, Jewish, and she a Catholic?

They were married in a civil ceremony.

In those days, when society was much more rigid than today, wasn't a mixed marriage, between a Jew and a Catholic, difficult?

I don't think so. And in any case, you're forgetting something: Rome was a city of immigrants. If you're born in Mantua or in Lucca, everybody there knows you. Rome was like the Far West. There was a restricted group of truly Roman families, aristocratic or bourgeois. The others all came from elsewhere; they had no connections with the city. Even today the Romans don't love their city, they have no roots. My father and my mother were both immigrants.

You were a cousin of the Rosselli brothers, later assassinated by the Fascist police because of their anti-Fascism.

On my father's side. On my mother's side, my uncle De Marsanich was a Fascist member of parliament.

Your name is Alberto Pincherle-Moravia. What sort of family were the Pincherle-Moravias?

An ordinary family. My father had made a bit of money, but not all that much. His sister, my aunt Amelia Rosselli, had a fairly curious and romantic story. She married Rosselli, a rich musician, by whom she had three children. Then he ran off with a cabaret singer. Finally, after many years, he fell ill and came to die in the same street where my aunt lived. Her husband left her in his will some Monte Amiata shares, which at first were almost worthless; then they began to be worth a great deal. And so she became rich. My mother, on the other hand, as I told you, was the daughter of a government employee whose name was Enrico De Marsanich, a very good man whom I remember fondly. My maternal grandmother was a housewife. I can still see her at the sewing machine with a little shawl around her shoulders. Her name was Adelaide.

Do you remember going to their house?

Of course, I do. I remember very well. I went to their house often. It was the house of a poor clerk. Their dining room served also as living room: there were two big photographs, one of Garibaldi and one of Mazzini. They were a patriotic family. My grandparents had had seven children: Belisario, Canzio, Augusto (the one who became a Fascist deputy), Gina (my mother), Jole, Flora, Gualtiero. Every now and then my grandfather would come, on Sundays, and collect me to take me to the park.

Were you very fond of your grandparents?

I felt a certain affection for my grandfather Enrico. He was very kind. Once he gave me a silver coin. He said to me, "Go and buy yourself a cake." I went and bought the cake, and the vendor didn't give me any change. I came back, and my grandfather asked, "Where's the change?" I said I hadn't been given any. So he went and said to the man, "Give me the change!" The man said, "There isn't any change." And my grandfather said in a very loud voice, "You have to give me the change!" But he realized at once that the man didn't want to give him the change, and he resigned himself as if it were something inevitable.

Did you ever see your Pincherle grandparents?

Never. They had died. My Pincherle grandparents were a couple of old mummies from the mid-nineteenth century. I saw a photograph of them: they looked like an early Ottocento couple, from Manzoni's day or thereabouts.

Was your parents' marriage a love match?

Yes. They married for love: I can't think of any other explanation. But it wasn't an entirely happy marriage.

Why not?

Because of the usual unhappiness that is part of every conjugal relationship. My mother wasn't a satisfied wife, but her peasant background saved her.

Nevertheless, marriage had changed her life.

Yes, it had, no doubt. I have only to compare the house where we lived with the house of my De Marsanich grandparents. Theirs represented absolute poverty. My uncles were all unemployed, without a cent; they didn't know what to do. Whereas my father was an architect, he worked and had a handsome house.

Tell me about your father.

He was a solitary man. He whistled when he walked; he flicked cigarette stubs into the air with the tip of his cane. Sometimes he took me to construction sites. Once I remember there was a bricklayer eating a long sandwich with an omelet in it. He said, in the traditional way, "Would you like some?" I answered yes. As I said, I was very ingenuous. But my father, now that I recall him, seems to me a character from Svevo, a provincial from the north, very civil and cultivated, neurotic and introverted.

You are, by definition, the writer of Rome, and yet you are half from the Marche and half from the Veneto.

Yes, from the north and from central Italy.

You spent your childhood in the Alps?

When I was a child they used to take me to the beach, at Viareggio. Then to the Alps. Finally I spent two years, when I was ill, in the Codivilla Sanatorium at Cortina.

Now we're talking about the period before your illness?

The period before my illness was . . . How can I explain? It was the life of a child who sees the world as an ox does, with the eyes of an ox, which, as we know, enlarge everything. Everything awed me.

How old were you when you fell ill?

Eight years old. I was taken to a party, where there was a huge crowd. There was a raffle, I remember still, in which I won two bottles of some liqueur. The next day I had pneumonia. I was cured of the pneumonia, but shortly after that I began to have pains in the hip. I fell down. I became ill with tuberculosis of the bone. I was nine. After that I studied at home. But at eight I had already gone to school, the Crandon School, Italo-English, in Via Nizza. It was 1916, I know, because the headmistress, Signorina Cutica, who was a kind of dwarf, looked in at the door and said, "Children, Cecco Beppe's dead."

She was referring to the Austrian emperor Franz Josef?

Yes. Everybody applauded. Personally, I thought it wasn't right to applaud somebody's death. That year, as I said, I fell down in the street and became seriously ill.

Were you already interested in literature then?

Yes, I read all the time. I read a lot of illustrated serials featuring Tom Mix. Then I was forbidden to read them, because they made me dream and have nightmares. As I said, I was hypersensitive, and things could only end the way they did. I had to fall ill perforce. Illness was in the logic of my physiology, of my life. I saw everything abnormally. I also walked in my sleep; once I woke up to find myself looking out of the window.

How did you happen to fall down in the street?

My father was walking me to school, I fell, I was carried home, and they called a doctor. He declared that I had tuberculosis of the bone, coxitis; in other words, I had a diseased hip. They put me to bed. I spent two or three months in bed. Then I began to walk, and I was taken to Viareggio for a holiday. I was nine years old. In Viareggio many things happened: I found out what sex was, and also what class was. More or less the basic experience I narrated in *Agostino*, though the situations and characters there are the fruit of invention.

Because you saw your mother with a lover?

No. I never saw my mother the way Agostino sees his. But I imagined a family story based on the mother-son relationship and on class distinction.

Did your mother have lovers?

Who knows? Maybe yes, maybe no. That's the title of a novel by D'Annunzio.

But you think she did?

She certainly had one; she may have had two.

And you knew them?

Yes, I remember both of them.

What sort of men were they?

One came from Viareggio. A simple man, kindly, athletic, nothing special. The other was a little man of business, who for many years was her *cavalier servente*. Little, and a bit ridiculous. My sisters and I made fun of him.

Did your father know?

My father was alive, but he was old.

Did he know?

No, I don't think so.

Was your mother a beautiful woman?

Yes, fairly beautiful.

How old was she?

It's easy to calculate. We went to Viareggio for the first time when I was nine. So it was 1917. I remember how, from the beach, they pointed out to me the English submarines that were patrolling the Mediterranean. She must have been about thirty.

Didn't the fact of her having lovers bother you?

She didn't have lovers, in the plural. She had one. No, it didn't bother me.

You considered it normal?

I've never known what "normal" means. For me, nothing is normal. Or rather, to my sensitivity, everything is abnormal, even the color of a flower.

All right, but let's skip forward about seventy years: the theme of the mother appears also in your latest novel, Il viaggio a Roma.

It would seem that you suffered the trauma of the child who sees his mother with a lover.

No, that's not the question. You're talking about a primal scene. But remember: whereas Freud at one time declared that the primal scene is always witnessed directly by children, at a later time he admitted that it could also only be imagined. In this second case, it is a phantom scene. I didn't know anything about sex, but I imagined the primal scene all the same. Then, twenty-five years later, I told the story of Agostino.

Did your father come to Viareggio?

He came for weekends. Then he went back to Rome, where he had some projects under construction.

What sort of relationship did you have with your father?

None, because he was too curt and uncommunicative. But he was unquestionably a good father, especially at crucial moments. Not at all authoritarian. He saw that I had the best treatment possible, and he supported me until I was married and left home. Until I was thirty-three, in other words. If anybody was authoritarian, it was my mother.

Were you intimate with your parents?

No.

Not even with your mother?

Not at all.

Was there any affection between the two of you?

Perhaps, but it never emerged.

Did you feel a lack of affection?

Perhaps. It's possible. But I wasn't aware of it. My mother was a woman who wanted to improve herself, to learn; she wanted many things. My mother was ambitious and fundamentally discontent. My father was the ordinary, average man of the time. Like many Italians, he spoke in dialect.

What dialect did he speak?
Venetian. He had a morbid devotion to his native city.

This father of yours held no fascination at all for you?
No, I saw him as he was.

Did he ever take you to Venice?
Only once. He went there twice a year and spent his time painting. He used to meet a friend there, a man named De Witt. He always stayed at the Hotel La Fenice. Then, with canvases and brushes, he would find a place near a bridge and paint. He painted only in Venice and only during vacation. In Rome he never did any painting. Painting, in other words, was his hobby.

And in the afternoon, in Rome, what did he do?
Nobody ever found out. He walked around the city, carrying a cane with a horn handle, tapping the ground with the tip. He had many canes. All through those years he carried a cane.

Do you resemble your father?
I resemble my mother; I have her square face. My sister Adriana, on the contrary, resembles my father.

Was your father tall and thin like you?
He wasn't tall. Average height, thin.

What did you eat, at home?
We ate Roman cuisine. For example, pasta as a first course, then a big breaded cutlet, with lots of vegetables, sautéed in a frying pan, and then fruit. My father, I don't know why, was very stingy about fruit. He would take an orange, slice it, and give one slice to each of us. Otherwise, however, the food was plentiful.

At table, were they the only ones who spoke?

They quarreled, mostly. Not a lot, but they quarreled. As I told you, their relationship was dialectic; they had completely opposite views of life. My father was a man of habit and avoided company. My mother would have liked an elegant, social life. She went often to the dressmaker's; she had beautiful dresses. It was the first thing you noticed about her.

Then you resemble your mother. You like fine clothes, too, don't you?

In a way, yes.

And your father?

My father didn't care much. He wore dark gray. If it was windy, he would put on an overcoat with a fur lining.

Are you a man of habit like your father?

No, as little as possible, except for my stint of work in the morning. Every day, like clockwork, my father did the same thing at the same hour. Whereas, after my morning's work, I do whatever I like, without plans, as the occasion arises. Often I go to the movies. For the rest, it's chaos.

Were there any Jewish objects, symbols, in your house?

No, there were Catholic symbols, because my mother and we children were Catholics. As for my father, I know for certain that he wasn't religious. He never discussed anything, least of all religion. As I told you, my father was a typical Svevo character. He had some Svevo-like refinements, some curious aspects.

What?

For example, though he painted, he never wanted to part with his pictures. He would make a copy whenever he gave one away. And he kept them all for himself.

Why?

He was a bit obsessive. Nowadays he would be described as a very private person.

What have you done with his pictures?

I don't have any. My sisters have a number of them.

Were you fond of your father?

Yes and no. We weren't a sentimental family.

Did he ever talk about his parents?

No.

Did you know his sister well, Amelia Rosselli?

I must say that my aunt Amelia Rosselli was very important for me. She saved my life.

How?

She persuaded my family to send me to a sanatorium when I became gravely ill, after four relapses. The disease had begun in 1917 in a mild form. Then, over the years, it grew progressively worse, until in the winter of 1923 I was almost on the point of death.

Do you think it was a psychosomatic illness?

Almost certainly. Perhaps I was overwhelmed by the revelation of sex and class that I had had at Viareggio. In the wider sense, I encountered decadentism.

What do you mean by "decadentism"?

Something that was in the air, the habits of the bourgeoisie, the books they read. I was fifteen, I was about to die, and my favorite writers were Dostoyevsky and Rimbaud.

Was your mother concerned about your illness?

Yes, but in a simple, peasant way. She wanted me to eat as much as possible.

What actually happened? Why do you say you were about to die?

I was in dreadful pain and had a high fever. The doctor had my leg put in a cast, but first he had two orderlies twist it so it would be in the correct position inside the plaster. Then they gave me chloroform, which makes you feel as though you're dying of suffocation, and then they applied the plaster. I woke up an hour later, all in a cast, and because of the chloroform I started vomiting. Unfortunately the plaster, which was all wet, didn't harden enough, and the leg turned inside the cast. Then the doctor had the plaster removed, had my leg twisted again, and made them give me more choloroform and apply the plaster once more. I suffered terribly; I was absolutely without strength; I couldn't even lift my hand. Still I continued reading Dostoyevsky. I remember I was reading *The Idiot*. This was the situation when my aunt Amelia Rosselli came to Rome. I didn't know her. In our family she was spoken of with great respect because she was a writer of some renown. She had written plays in Venetian dialect, as well as books for children. *Topinino* and *Topinino garzone di bottega* (*Mousekin* and *Mousekin the Apprentice*).

What sort of personality did she have?

She seemed very sweet, but in reality she had a strong character. She belonged to the enlightened bourgeoisie, the progressives of the time. She was a socialist, the middle-class socialism of the Turati sort.

Her sons, the Rosselli brothers, were about ten years older than you. Did you consider them men to be admired?

No, not at all. I considered them otherworldly. Without realizing it, I was cynical, perhaps because I had never been to school. Life had tested me. I was very realistic. I thought they were visionaries, something out of the ninteenth century, their heads crammed with generous but impractical ideas. If I really have to say what I thought, when I went to Florence to stay at my aunt's, I found myself in a rather romantic atmosphere that, privately, I considered ingenuous. An atmosphere of other days, pre–World War I, at least.

Did your parents read?

My father owned the complete works of Goldoni in the splendid 1900 edition, and also Shakespeare, Molière, Ariosto, Manzoni, and so on. My mother for the most part read modern books, but without any specific direction: in bookshops she would ask the shopkeeper's advice. They gave her D'Annunzio, and she read D'Annunzio. Then they gave her, say, Gotta or Brocchi, and she read Gotta and Brocchi. Without making many distinctions. I remember she said to me once, "I've brought you a book the bookseller recommended. A man named Klipping." She meant Kipling! In other words, my mother was ignorant, but with a strong desire to better herself. My father had degrees in architecture and engineering and had no desire to know more than he already knew. He was a man — how shall I put it? — of a certain distinction, but a professional man, not an intellectual.

Were you and your sisters taught foreign languages?

French. I learned English on my own.

Did your mother also speak French?

Yes, my mother spoke French.

And your father?

He also spoke it. There's no doubt that my mother spoke French. I remember she read French novels, for example a book called *L'amour est mon péché*, by an anonymous author. It was a book that enjoyed a certain success among the middle-class ladies of Rome. My mother to some extent moved in the middle class, and she knew everything that happened in our neighborhood. She spoke of certain women who lived nearby, saying, "She's a dreadful woman!" Because my mother was a moralist, like all simple and unintellectual people.

Was she a gossip?

No, she wasn't at all a gossip. If anything, she was naive, very naive. The family's naïveté all comes from the De Marsanich side. All of us, I, my mother, my sisters, have a basic naïveté, freshness, which perhaps derives from the Slavic origin of the De Marsanichs. My mother saved herself from unhappiness, though she was often unhappy, thanks to her common sense, that common sense that Madame Bovary, her romantic ancestor, didn't have. She spoke often in proverbs, or in proverbial expressions. She was fond of her children, even too fond, in a passionate but not intelligent fashion. Sometimes she lost her patience and then revealed a certain stupidity. I remember that, after the first time I fell ill, I limped very badly, and she impatiently said to me one day, "Shut up, cripple!" This was on the beach at Viareggio.

It made you suffer terribly?

Of course! It was very unpleasant, wasn't it? To hear that said by your own mother!

And did you really feel you were a cripple?

Not at all. I limped, and that was that. For many years I was almost normal; I hardly limped at all. It's only since 1982, when I was in an automobile accident, that I use a cane and am forbidden to carry anything heavy.

How did your parents behave toward you when you were ill?

How? They did what they had to do, as if the illness were basically a normal misfortune, whereas for me it was terribly abnormal.

Did you cause a lot of bother?

No, I was always alone in the house, in bed. My parents went out. My father went out, and when he came home, from a distance he flung the *Corriere della sera* on my bed, or the *Messaggero*. He also subscribed to the *Gazzettino di Venezia*, where everything was written in dialect, even court proceedings. I still remember a photograph in the *Messaggero*, with lots of people running in a big square: it was the attack on the Winter Palace in Saint Petersburg.

What effect did it have on you?

It had a certain effect. In fact, I remembered it. Then I read an absurd report. The correspondent went on about the Russian revolution, about Lenin. An American woman journalist had gone to the Kremlin. She wandered around the Kremlin looking for Lenin. At a certain point she entered a room where there was a billiard table, and on the table there was a monkey eating peanuts: it was Lenin!

Did they talk about the revolution in your home?

No, there was no talk about anything. My mother believed she was a socialist, true. It was the time of postwar socialism, and she followed the fashion. Unseen, I witnessed a violent argument between my mother and her father, Enrico De Marsanich, who hated the socialists and considered them subversives and traitors. He was a patriot. As I said before, he had portraits of Garibaldi and Mazzini in his dining room. My mother kept saying, "The socialists are the future." My grandfather was shouting, he was for the Risorgimento, the fatherland. In fact, all three of his sons became Fascists.

What about the Pincherle side? What were they like?

They were all socialists.

Did your mother get along with the Rosselli family?

She had great respect for them, because they were a family with cultural, liberal, and socialist traditions. They had a certain style of their own, bourgeois and respectable, to which she aspired, since she knew she didn't have it herself.

Did your Rosselli aunt come to Rome often?

I remember the first time she looked at me and said, "How comical he is." I was comical in the sense that I was already neurotic. I spent hours saying "Je m'ennuie" in a corner of my room.

What was your aunt's salon like in Florence?

She received cultural figures: university professors, intellectuals, writers. I remember, among others, a writer who wrote under the name of Jack La Bolina: he always talked about the sea. My aunt Rosselli's family gave me a strange feeling, of truly good people and therefore destined to end badly. I wasn't a Fascist at all, but I had the modern sensibility that was shared also by the Fascists and by the younger generation in general.

Were they snobs, the Rossellis?

No, not snobs. They were serious people.

And your father?

My father wanted to be left alone, not go out in society. He was too shy, morbidly shy. In politics he was a Liberal: a conservative, that is. But not ideologically. It was his nature, his temperament.

Did you like your father?

In a way, I did, because I could feel that he was fond of me. He was very, very timid, and probably sentimental. When he kissed a woman's hand, which was the custom then, he turned red. He was also very gruff, brusque. He made excessive scenes over little things, and then wouldn't get angry over big things.

He didn't have a great personality?

I told you: he was someone out of Svevo. Do Svevo's characters have great personalities? No, they don't, but . . .

How did it occur to you to write?

Oh, you might say it was always there. Imagine! I've found some notebooks I had when I was nine, and there is already the outline of *Gli indifferenti*. It was always my ambition to write. Just as certain religious figures are said to have had, from childhood, a religious vocation.

Did you talk with your brothers about your literary ambitions?

With my sisters, you mean? My brother was born in 1914. No, I never talked about anything with my sisters. We did our French homework together for our governess, that was all.

How did your sisters treat you when you were ill?

They were very affectionate, but they had their own lives. They were little girls who began to have their friends, boys and girls their own age.

Did you have the impression that you were a burden on the family?

No, I was simply a person who lived in bed. I was always in bed. I did nothing but read. One day my father gave me a toy theater, with many marionettes that I enjoyed dressing and undressing: I still wasn't capable of making them act. But the illness never ended. Every now and then I would get up, and then I would fall on the ground again. I suffered very much, yes, from pain, from desire for life; I suffered the lack of company. It was really a hard existence to bear, I remember it like a long tunnel at whose end there was supposed to be health.

Did you ever think of killing yourself?

No, not at all, absolutely not. I had a downright morbid desire for life, that's all.

But were you sure that you would be cured?

I tried to get well instinctively. The final relapse was when I was fourteen. That summer we didn't go to Viareggio, but to a place called Siusi in the Alps. My father was gruffer than ever at table;

my mother, on the other hand, wanted to cut a fine figure. It was the familiar story of a middle-class family on holiday.

Why was your father so gruff?

Because he was impatient. He couldn't bear waiting for anything. For example, in Rome, on Sunday he made me go out for a carriage ride around the city. If the carriage didn't arrive promptly, he would begin huffing, paying no attention to me, cursing. He was a choleric man. I also recall how he would fly into a rage if any noise was made after dinner, while he was sleeping in his study. But as I said, he became angry only for trivial reasons. A maid stole all my mother's jewels, including a valuable ring still unpaid for, and my father didn't say a word.

Did you have friends?

How could I have friends? I was always in the house, in bed.

Then going to Codivilla, to the sanatorium, was a liberation?

In the final analysis, yes. That is where my real life began. Immediately after Codivilla, I started writing Gli indifferenti.

How old were you when you went there?

Sixteen. 1924. Just barely sixteen. My birthday is November 28 and I went to the sanatorium in March.

Did your father take you there?

Yes. It was a very unpleasant trip. At that period of my life I was embarrassed by many things. I was embarrassed when my father huffed because the carriage was late. I was embarrassed when a janitor carried me into the classroom to take an examination. But especially I was embarrassed to be seen, ill as I was, in the midst of a lot of healthy people. The trip to Cortina d'Ampezzo proceeded in this fashion: an ambulance came to the house, they put me on a stretcher, and we set off for the station, where they set the stretcher on the ground. Then, with great effort, while a crowd looked on, they hoisted me through the window into the sleeping car. I was embarrassed because everyone was watching.

Who was there? Your father?

Yes, my father, who was constantly losing his temper.

With you?

No, not with me. With the things that were happening.

So you were embarrassed. I understand. How did you deal with this embarrassment?

Mentally. Somehow, I remained always outside myself. I watched myself live. I still do it even now.

But at that time were you already aware of being someone with a special destiny?

No. I suffered terribly. I was in total darkness, because I was trying to write, but I couldn't manage to write anything good, and until I had written something good, all I did was suffer in the dark.

But you knew you were an artist?

No, I knew I was a person who was suffering. That was the only thing I knew.

Did this make you mean?

Not so much mean as neurotic. For example, in the sanatorium I was always alone. One day I flung my breakfast tray on the floor. I was like a mad dog. The doctor, when he heard about it, said I was schizoid. In the end I somehow grew fond of the bed and the illness. Isn't that odd? Later, when I was cured and returned to Rome, every now and then I would go to bed. All this lasted two or three years, even longer. I remember one day I said to my father, "I'm not well, I feel the tuberculosis is coming back." I was homesick for the illness. I was psychologically ill for many years after I was healthy. I regained the mental health I had enjoyed before the illness only very late, and naturally it wasn't the same health, ingenuous and innocent: it was something less one-dimensional and more complicated.

What did you do after you were cured?

I began Gli indifferenti before I was seventeen. In September 1925 I left Cortina and went to Bressanone. One morning in bed (for some years I continued writing in bed, with a pen and inkwell), I began *Gli indifferenti* with the first sentence, which remained there: "Carla entered." I didn't yet know what I was going to write. That sentence indicated my ambition to write a play disguised as a novel. Or rather, to blend theatrical technique with narrative, a bit in the manner of Dostoyevsky, with whom I identified myself then. It has been said that my novel was a criticism of bourgeois society. Maybe it is, but I didn't realize that. I had purely literary ambitions. For the rest, I made use of the material within my reach. That is to say, the generic experience of family life, which I wasn't aware of hating to such a degree.

At what moment did you become independent? How old were you?

Independent in what sense? Economically, I became independent when I was thirty-three, when I married Elsa Morante and left home.

I meant psychologically independent.

Psychologically? At once. When my mother came to Bressanone to tell me I had to go back to studying, I said no. I hadn't yet begun *Gli indifferenti*. I saw total darkness ahead of me. I had written only some terrible short stories and many poems in French, completely academic, Parnassian. I was without an *ubi consistam*, a fixed point. But I knew one thing: I didn't want to go back to school. My mother even started crying, but I couldn't be budged.

What did you want to be?

A writer. But I wasn't at all sure I'd become one.

Meanwhile the Fascist regime was at a critical moment because of the Matteotti assassination. What did you know about that?

In 1924 at the sanatorium my cousins Carlo and Nello Rosselli had come to visit me. I was sixteen and had nothing to do with politics. But I had always felt a dislike for Fascism and, at the same time, in a contradictory way, as I explained before, I felt that the anti-Fascists were losers. Carlo, who was truly the more politically active brother, told me that in the autumn they were sure Mussolini would be brought to trial.

What did you think then?

I thought he was being ingenuous, but I didn't know why I thought that. It was just an impression, nothing more.

Were you fond of your cousins?

No, I hardly knew them. I knew my aunt better because, as I told you, she used to come to Rome occasionally and she took an interest in my health. I was really fond of her.

Did your family come to visit you in the sanatorium?

No. I don't think so.

Not even your mother?

I don't remember. Imagine! As far as my family is concerned, for the whole duration of my stay in the sanatorium, my memory is a kind of blank. In any case, I didn't want to see anybody.

How did you reach the sanatorium? What was your life like up there?

I traveled by train as far as Calalzo, then by car from Calalzo to Cortina. As the car climbed into the mountains, I remember having the impression of beginning a new life also because of the biting air and the beauty of the Alpine landscape. After so many years of being in bed at home, I felt I was experiencing for the first time the joy of being alive. As soon as I arrived at the sanatorium, they took me immediately to the operating theater, removed the cast, and put me in traction with a lead weight of eight kilos. The pain immediately disappeared.

Why hadn't they done that before?

Maybe it was a new method and my Rome doctor was a conservative; it was perhaps risky, or so I heard later. But with diseases, basically, you fall ill by chance, and you die by chance or get well by chance.

What was life there like?

Very disciplined and lonely. At eight, sun therapy, naked on the terrace as the sun began to rise behind Sorapis. At eleven, back to my room, as the sun was too strong. At twelve, examination by Professor Vacchelli, accompanied by a male nurse. At one, lunch. From two to eight, solitude and reading. Then supper. At ten, examination by the nurse, and sleep. It was a life that, in the absence of affection and company, resembled more a punishment than a cure. With a pencil one day I wrote on the glass of my window: *Solo col sole*; alone with the sun.

Did you have friends in the sanatorium?

Yes, I made friends with a Triestine, my neighbor in the next room. I had my wheeled bed rolled into his room, and I would stay there an hour or two to chat. He was the son of a tailor, a fashionable tailor in Trieste. He was a bit Austrian in his manner and in his view of the world: decadent, superficial, in other words. He wore a monocle. Later, when I was cured, I also wore one, to imitate him. My friendship for him involved an unconscious homosexual infatuation. Perhaps he didn't notice it. In any case, it remained a pure and simple friendship.

Were you both ill?

Yes, he was very ill indeed. He went on being ill, moving from one sanatorium to another. In the end, I heard no more of him. But to him I owe my first sexual experience.

Where? How?

In a house of ill fame (as they were called then) in Bolzano, a little bourgeois villa, in a suburb. We took a carriage driven by an elderly coachman with white hair. We both had to walk with crutches, and we must have looked a strange pair. The driver refused to wait for us, but inside the house we encountered no objections: we were customers like all the others. My friend chose for me the woman whom he judged the most suitable: a former schoolteacher, with black eyes, a pair of black braids, and a cotton chemise down to her ankles. I had not only crutches but also a plaster-covered brace. But everything went well just the same, simply and sweetly. It was something "normal," that is, and healthy. On the other hand, a few days later something happened to me that was neither healthy nor normal.

What was that?

Every day I went into Bressanone to a café for an aperitif, then to eat in a restaurant next door. In this way I got to know an officer, who came every day with a woman, a pretty blonde, probably Austrian, all dressed in black; I learned later that her mother had recently died. The man was very handsome, tall, elegant, with small hands and feet. One of those evenings, in a moment when the woman was absent, the officer, without the slightest awkwardness, not even lowering his voice, said to me that if I liked, I could make love with Lizzie, as he called the woman. I was dumbfounded, but I accepted. The girl seemed pretty to me, but no more than that; still, the adventure made me curious. Lizzie arrived. He said nothing to her; obviously all had been arranged in advance. We went outside. It was raining. The officer led the way; the woman and I didn't speak. On foot we reached a little villa, where the officer had a kind of studio on the ground floor. Once we were inside, he told the woman in a brisk but polite tone to undress. For some reason she hesitated; then the officer fell on her and started undressing her himself. She began to run around the studio, with the officer after her, tearing her clothes off her

back: the scene appeared too abnormal not to have been rehearsed. In the end she was completely naked, very white, a little
plump, very blonde. The officer told us to hurry up, that he would
wait in the garden, and he went out. She and I made love in haste
and in silence; I wonder why I didn't ask her any questions about
all these oddities. It was like one of those dreams in which nobody
speaks. Every now and then he yanked on the doorbell cord as if
he were out of patience. We finished; she collected her clothes
and took refuge behind a screen. I was very embarrassed; I didn't
know what to do. I shyly suggested a present and heard him answer haughtily, "This is not meat for sale, Signor Pincherle." The
next day I left for Rome and by chance I saw the girl again, still in
mourning, in the corner of a compartment. I sat beside her I
asked her to explain what had happened the previous evening.
She answered in confusion; or rather, she didn't answer anything.
Then a conductor came; she was in second class, I was in first.
The conductor ordered me to go to my class, and I never saw her
again. But actually, I didn't want to see her again. That's how I
was then: I was satisfied with the germ of life, I wasn't interested
in developments. I fled. I was in Rome for a month; then I went
back to Cortina, but to a hotel. This was my life for several years.
I went from Rome to Cortina and vice versa. In Rome I had a
night life, I stayed out until four in the morning. I went to a place
called Teatro degli Avignonesi. It was a place where they gave very
avant-garde plays, surrealist. Then there was dancing. It all took
place in a basement, which had ancient Roman walls. On my way
home I often encountered sheep being herded through Piazza
Barberini. I was seventeen or eighteen at that time.

Were you afraid the illness might come back?

It wasn't fear. As I said: I was homesick for the disease. Every now
and then I had the firm conviction that I should go to the doctor.
I remember something strange. I had met Bontempelli, who in
those years edited a literary magazine, Novecento, which I later
wrote for. Then I conceived the idea that I was sick and I went to
bed. I told my father to call Bontempelli and ask him to come

visit me. I was in bed. Bontempelli came, sat on a chair, was very ill at ease. He talked for a little while, then left.

Why was he ill at ease?

Perhaps because I was in bed. Or perhaps because I was infatuated with him and didn't hide it: he was a writer who edited a magazine, the leader of a literary movement, he asked me to write for him. Ill at ease as he was, he was very polite. Perhaps he had realized that I was a person with a disturbed, not to say abnormal, psychology.

Was he much older than you?

Bontempelli belonged to a generation two generations before mine. He must have been fifty then. By that time I was a part of the *Novecento* group. Bontempelli's career was typical of that transition period. He had been a professor of literature, a classicist, he had written volumes of verse in the style of Carducci. Then, at a certain point, after the First World War, perhaps under the influence of the surrealists, he realized that he had written a lot of unbearable stuff, trash, and he turned modern. He wrote two novels, *La vita intensa* and *La vita operosa*, which are an ironic and clear mirror of postwar life. Then he became a Fascist and, with Malaparte, founded the review *Novecento*, which launched the formula of "magic realism," something between surrealism and the deco style that was then beginning in France. *Novecento* was bilingual; it appeared in Rome in Italian and in Paris in French. I was introduced to the magazine by Alvaro, who was a friend of Bontempelli and the magazine's editorial secretary. It published, among other things, a piece by Joyce for the first time in Italy. In the end Bontempelli and Malaparte disagreed, and *Novecento* died.

How did you meet Alvaro?

It's a fairly long story. I was fifteen and was coming back from the mountains with my parents. In the train I met a Russian, who introduced himself with the Italian name Cenerini, a powerful

brute with blond hair and blue eyes, who told me he was going to
Rome to volunteer with the Italians and take part in the war against
Greece. It was 1923. Mussolini had fired a few shells at Corfu, and it
was all over. This Russian introduced me to Caffi, who in Moscow,
where the two of them had been at the time, had helped get the
Russian a passport for Italy. Andrea Caffi was an intellectual, the
son of a tailor of the czar and a Russian woman. Caffi was an enormously learned man, perhaps a genius, but totally inconclusive. He
had been sent by the *Corriere della sera* to Moscow, but, a great humanitarian, as soon as he arrived in the city, he distributed the
paper's funds among the starving. Now Caffi, also for anti-Fascist
reasons, knew Alvaro, the secretary of *Novecento*, who in turn introduced me to Bontempelli. Between Cenerini and me a curious fellowship was formed, worthy of Gide's *Faux-monnaieurs*, a book of
the period. He wanted to enter the Italian air force, and I — I can't
remember how — procured some false papers for him. The funny
thing is that he really did join the air force. This period ended with
my last and worst recurrence of tuberculosis of the bone. I went to
bed; Caffi came to see me and gave me Dostoyevsky's *The Idiot*.
Cenerini set off for the Congo, in the pay of a Belgian company,
the Alberta, for the exploitation of ivory. I spent two months in bed
in Rome. Then, as I told you, I went to Cortina, to the Codivilla
sanatorium, spent two years there, then returned to Rome and
found Caffi again, the same penniless, learned intellectual as before. And he introduced me to Alvaro.

*You say that, after your illness, you went to your father and said
to him, "I'm going to die," then said, "Do me a favor: call Bontempelli and ask him to come and see me." There seems to be
some complicity in the relationship.*

It wasn't complicity. It was bullying. I was a bully toward my father: I made him do things for me.

*But in those years you weren't yet the famous Moravia. You were
a boy.*

Yes, a boy.

Did you think you would become Moravia? Or did you already know you would?

I was writing *Gli indifferenti*, but I didn't know anything. I lived from day to day.

But did you think you'd become a famous man, a successful writer, and so on?

No, I didn't think anything. I wanted to write a novel, and that was that. In fact, I'll tell you why. In the *Novecento* group there were many young people, and Bontempelli, who had been a professor and had a professorial demagogy, made each of them promise to write a novel. In Italy then there weren't any novelists, except Svevo, who was unknown, however. A year later, when it was time to deliver the novels, the only member of the group who had written one was me. I took the manuscript to the publisher of *Novecento*, but he handed it back to me saying it was "a fog of words." Then I left for Milan. Before leaving, I had Caffi read the manuscript, and he said he was terrified by the cynicism with which the story was narrated. In reality, Caffi was a nineteenth-century romantic and couldn't understand that *Gli indifferenti* wasn't the least bit cynical; on the contrary, it was the first, ingenuous, and unripe fruit of that modern narrative trend that later was to take the name of existentialism.

How did you happen to be a friend of Caffi?

I was attracted by his culture and also by the oddity of his character.

What was he like?

He was tall, very tall, with a lanky and gawky body, like a camel's. A giant, with bristling hair, a big nose, and a big mouth. He was a homosexual. Actually, he courted me a bit. Every time I went to see him, he would embrace me, enfolding me in a cloud of eau de cologne. He was Russian of the Dostoyevskian kind, generous and inconclusive. He had been sentenced to death in the days of the czar. Much later he became the tutor of the children of the princess of Bassiano, who had founded the review *Commerce* in Paris.

But he came to your house?

He came to my house, yes; as I said, he brought me Dostoyevsky's *The Idiot* as a present. I had a high temperature, and I read that novel in a kind of delirium.

Did your mother allow you to invite anyone you wanted to?

Yes, she was pleased if they provided some company for me.

Basically, did you suffer at the indifference of your parents?

No, I can't say I did. I suffered only from my illness and solitude. Yes: illness, solitude, and desire for life.

What was your sexual life like during your illness? Did you have relations with the maids in the sanatorium?

No, nothing at all.

You were a chaste young man, then.

I was chaste, though I had a violent desire for love. I was chaste and I absolutely rejected masturbation. I tried it a few times, but I refused to accept it; I considered it a defeat.

We have reached your eighteenth year. After the sanatorium, did you have some love affairs?

I courted every girl I met, but it never came to anything: I had no money, I didn't have a place where I could see them. That left only prostitutes, but I didn't want them.

Those were also the triumphant years of Fascism. Were you fascinated by power or not?

I wasn't at all fascinated. I was fascinated by revolt in every form, from criminality to political conspiracy. I was physiologically in revolt.

So, basically, the grand bourgeois aspect of the Rossellis, which your mother regarded with admiration, irritated you. Was it a burden?

Perhaps, but I didn't think about it. I've always aimed at something positive that could change life, and for me then the positive thing was revolt. In fact, my favorite poet was Rimbaud. I have never liked being against something; on the contrary, I was always in favor of something. For example, in favor of revolt in and of itself. You might say I was a revolutionary without knowing it.

What about your brother and your sisters?

My brother, unfortunately, died young. He was a good person. He took a degree in engineering. My sisters were very young. One of them, Adriana, was to become a painter.

Did they suspect the person you were, or not?

They didn't suspect anything. I was an interior person. I had conceived a morbid yearning for revolt as the only method of action. I saw action as the only way of being in rapport with others. I dreamed of perhaps becoming a murderer, but for me crime was simply another infraction, or rather, a rapport that was, in its way, social. At the same time, however, I wanted to become a novelist, perhaps to narrate what I would have liked to do but in reality didn't do. You understand? Revolt and, on the other hand, because of my idleness, living at home, to write novels in a country where there were so few novelists! In Italy, true, there had been Manzoni, and in fact there are even some traces of Manzoni in *Gli indifferenti*.

You mean that you don't have an Italian cultural background?

No, European. Above all, European, and therefore "also" Italian, but the Italy of the classics rather than the moderns, who are so often provincial.

So you come from the Veneto and the Marche, but are Middle-European in background, with an Italo-French culture.

Russian, too, for that matter. And perhaps also English. In Italy, the classic novels are foreign, not Italian.

You've lived in the mountains and at the sea, at Cortina and on Capri. But you talk constantly of Rome.

For me, Rome is only a stage backdrop. You must remember that my literary ideal, thanks to my great love of the theater, was to fuse theatrical technique with narrative. My novels are really plays disguised as novels: few characters, unity of time and place, little analysis, much synthesis, that is to say, action.

With, however, the exception of Le ambizioni sbagliate.

In fact, among my novels it's the only one I shouldn't have written. Perhaps it was necessary for me to write it, if for no other reason, to free myself of Dostoyevsky. But what a job!

Plays disguised as novels. Did you like Pirandello?

There was a moment when I felt Pirandello was very close to me. But the real influence, once again, was Dostoyevsky, whose dialogue and situations are theatrical. And then, naturally, the classics of the theater, especially Goldoni, Shakespeare, Molière.

2

*A*LAIN ELKANN: *While you were writing* Gli indifferenti, *did you know you were writing a great novel?*
ALBERTO MORAVIA: No, I learned to write by writing *Gli indifferenti*. I mean that with *Gli indifferenti* for the first time things turned into words for me, and vice versa.

How did you write?

I wrote in bed; I made a nest for the inkwell among the sheets. I wrote with a pen, holding the nib upside down, and so I made holes in the paper. Now and then the ink spilled over and, as I was often away from home, they made me pay for the ink-stained sheets, which I then took back to my mother. I wrote, leaning on one elbow. Today I couldn't do it. But from the time of the sanatorium, for me my bed was what his shell is for a snail. As I said, I wrote the first version of *Gli indifferenti* on tissue paper because that was all I could find in Bressanone.

Did you rewrite it many times?

Three or four times.

What was your relationship with the novel you were writing?

I told you: I was learning to write.

While you were writing?

Yes, I was actually learning how to write. The strength of *Gli indifferenti* derives from the fact that I didn't know how to write and learned to write with that book.

How did you do it?

First of all, it was oral. I would write a page, then I would read it aloud. I checked it with my ear. This could lead us to talk about the origin of narrative. Namely, that I began by ear, repeating the technique of the primitive bards, and then gradually I no longer relied on hearing and I arrived at sight. *Gli indifferenti* was written exactly like a canto, with dashes instead of punctuation, as if to indicate the transition from one verse to the next. In the end, however, I stopped listening to what I was writing and I began to see it. From then on, unfortunately, I've no longer had that rhythm of the spoken tale that I had when I wrote *Gli indifferenti*. The manuscript of *Gli indifferenti* had no punctuation. I added that afterward, like adding salt to the soup.

When did you add it?

I added it after I had finished. In fact, if you read *Gli indifferenti* you'll see that the punctuation is very irregular.

Did you work slowly?

I was so frail that I would write for ten minutes, then stop, exhausted, and almost fall asleep.

But you thought about it a lot?

I didn't think about it at all. I thought about it only when I was writing. The rest of the time I tried to take walks, back and forth on the snow. I pursued girls. I danced; yes, I danced a lot.

When?

During the winters at Cortina d'Ampezzo I danced from five until midnight, or even until one or two in the morning. Since I couldn't engage in winter sports, I danced. But I danced in Rome, too.

Did you limp badly?

I limped, but not very much. I limp much worse now. One leg was a centimeter shorter than the other. Now the difference is almost five.

Did you ever engage in any sports at all?

I rowed. I walked a lot.

You didn't ski?

I couldn't. Not with that leg of mine!

We haven't yet talked about what society was like then.

Society then was the way I described it in Le ambizioni sbagliate, the only thing that is seen clearly in that novel: an ambitious, ignorant, bovariste society, still bound by the prejudices of the provincial bourgeoisie. It was the petty bourgeoisie of a very, very poor country, which had been starving for centuries. Except, naturally, what today would be called "the right people."

When you went out in society what did you talk about?

I pretended to act like everyone else: I didn't talk about anything. I courted the girls, without much success.

But you must have talked about something. What?

I told you: nothing. I talked a lot of nonsense. I said one stupid thing after another. Probably like everyone at that age, with the difference that I was pretty much aware of it. I had a great vitality, but obviously I wasn't able to express it completely in what I was writing, and so, to go on expressing myself, I found nothing better than to talk foolishness.

With the girls, too?

Yes, with them, too. I wasn't at all serious.

Is that why you felt alien to the society of the Rosselli brothers?

Yes, seriousness has always irked me. We must be serious, but in secret.

But you liked social life?

I found it boring. I liked outsiders, people who lived a bit adventurously, outside society.

Because you were also a bit like that, or what?

Yes, I was, or at least I felt I was, an outsider. But like all the boys of my age I went out in society, looking for girls. In the periods when I was in Rome, as I told you, I would pay attention to three or four girls at a time, though with no success. Once in a while I would have an affair, but nothing important, and never with the ones I was courting.

Did you suffer? Did you have regrets?

Not much. I led a very chaste life then. Often women didn't appeal to me. I found them inferior to my fantasies, which still had nothing romantic about them. I dreamed of women not only beautiful but also interesting psychologically, a kind of woman that in Rome, at that time at least, was nonexistent.

Were you melancholy?

Yes, and this melancholy easily turned into rage. I believe these two feelings are present in the writing of *Gli indifferenti*.

But during your illness you lived through the First World War, the fall of the czars, the end of the Austro-Hungarian Empire, the advent of Fascism . . .

When the First World War ended, in 1918, I was eleven.

Do you remember anything of it?

I remember everybody talked about it a lot. I remember also the day when President Wilson of the United States arrived in Rome. The sky resounded with the engines of many planes. It was also the time of the Spanish flu; many people were dying of it.

And Mussolini? The March on Rome? Do you remember that?

I saw that with my own eyes. I remember it very well, because I went to Piazza del Popolo, I sat down on the rim of a fountain. You couldn't cross the square. The Fascists were marching by, looking like so many hunters, with their black shirts, olive drab pants, and puttees. Many had shotguns. They looked like peasants going out after partridge. Occasionally there was a more decorative Fascist. Ulisse Igliori, for example, on a white horse, a Fascist big shot from Rome. As I said, I was sitting on the rim of a fountain, watching. At a certain point something strange happened: a bee stung me, and before my eyes everything turned black, like the Fascists' shirts. And I also remember that, as I tried to cross the square, I passed through the ranks of the Fascists. One of them said to me, "Clear out, boy!" and gave me a light touch of his lash on my legs. I also heard two elderly people remarking with approval, "They're the Italy of tomorrow."

What was your impression of the Fascists that day?

I had the impression of provincial people.

They didn't frighten you?

No, not at all. I wasn't politicized at the time. I thought about nothing but literature.

As a boy, you said, you were attracted by adventurers, by the poor . . .

I was attracted by outsiders, by irregularity, perhaps even by criminality. But it was all fantasy, literature.

You once told me that in those days you also went to salons.

Yes, that's true. After *Gli indifferenti* I had a moment almost of snobbery. It was very brief.

You weren't a snob before?

No, if anything I dostoyevkyized life. My ideal was to live like the characters of Dostoyevsky, among whom there are many outsiders but also many duchesses and many salons. Dostoyevsky had such influence on me that, while admiring him, I felt I could never write anything original. He had already written everything I could have written.

You wanted to be Raskolnikov?

Yes, something of the sort, Raskolnikov, or perhaps the Raw Youth. I was fascinated by his characters, I wanted to live like them. I felt myself an outsider, and Dostoyevksy was, in fact, the novelist of outsiders.

Did you like gossip or not?

Not in the least. Even now I don't like it. I never gossip.

In your home did they gossip?

No, my mother wasn't a gossip. As I told you before, the most she did was, at table, to raise her eyebrows, "Signora X . . . mmm . . ." as if to say, "What a terrible woman!"

When you were in the sanatorium, did you hate your parents?

No, I didn't hate anyone. I hated family life, yes, but I hated it as a situation, not as people.

Did your parents know you were writing?

Yes, they knew that quite well. In fact, I believe they were proud of it. My father, after all, gave me the money to have the book published.

How much?

Five thousand lire, the equivalent of five million today. I asked him for it and, without hesitation, he gave it to me. It wasn't such a small amount even for a well-off family like ours. Naturally, after the book's success, I paid him back. But the publishing firm, Alpes, gave me only the five thousand I had contributed, without royalties. So I earned nothing. But at this point I'd like to make something clear: the attraction of the world of outsiders and transgressors and rebels wasn't merely a literary infatuation. Dostoyevsky opened my eyes, even if only in the literary sense, to what I was. Or rather what I had become thanks to illness and solitude. So, in a way, it should be said that during the whole period when I was writing *Gli indifferenti* and I considered myself a Dostoyevsky character, I was acting according to the ideas of Dostoyevsky. As you know, these are rather complicated ideas.

When you were writing Gli indifferenti . . .

All through the period when I wrote *Gli indifferenti*, I was writing a novel that wasn't Dostoyevskian: that's the curious thing. But I considered myself a Dostoyevsky character in life, in action. This is so true that in *Le ambizioni sbagliate,* which is a failure as a novel, I made an attempt to write a Dostoyevskian novel, fusing Dostoyevsky with Manzoni, a really overintellectual notion. But as I said, with this novel I finally freed myself from my identification with Dostoyevsky.

You told me that I can't imagine the position Dostoyevsky occupied then in European culture. Why not?

You belong to a different generation, you can't imagine that period because you didn't live in it. If you think how a grand bourgeois like Gide wrote a novel called *The Counterfeiters* only because he had discovered Dostoyevsky, then you can understand that my infatuation with the author of *Crime and Punishment* was rooted in the European culture of the moment. It was the equivalent, in other words, of the fashion of existentialism in the post–World War II period, but a fashion that evidenced a profound confusion, which Dostoyevsky has described better than any other novelist. For that matter, Dostoyevsky was in a sense the creator of existentialism: he took the relationship between individual and society, as it had been in Balzac, Flaubert, Dickens, Tolstoy, and so on, and replaced it with the relationship between the individual and himself. *Crime and Punishment* isn't the story of an ambitious man who fails, as in *Le rouge et le noir* of Stendhal; it's the story of a man who has killed and feels remorse, and remorse is entirely interior, between a man and his self. I was born to literature at that historical moment. Besides Dostoyevsky, I was greatly influenced by the surrealists. I was very sensitive to the discoveries of the surrealists about dreams and the unconscious as sources of inspiration. In reality, my avant-garde was surrealism. And this explains why my novels, even today, are distinguished by an ambiguity: they are realistic, but at the same time symbolic. Somewhat like the surrealists. It's something I have in common with a whole generation, the generation of Buñuel, say, who was exactly my age. I pick Buñuel because he's the film-maker with whom I feel the greatest affinity.

With whom did you talk about literature?

Practically speaking, with nobody. But I read and somehow, without being aware of it, I talked with the authors I was reading. At first, in the sanatorium, reading the books sent me from Florence by the Vieusseux circulating library, to which I had subscribed, and later in Rome, reading anything I could get my hands on. But talking about literature with other people — that's something I've never really done. With my friends, with other people, I talked about the events of life, you might say. It was like having a great love and not talking about it, out of modesty.

We haven't yet discussed the landscapes of your childhood.

In my infancy, the landscape was a well-defined space: in Rome, Via Donizetti (where I lived), the Borghese Gardens, which were very close to Via Donizetti, and that was it. The first vacation I remember was on the Adriatic, in Abruzzo, I believe. My mother used to tell me that I talked about myself in the third person, saying, "Mare bulo, bulo, beto ninna," which presumably meant "mare buio, buio, Berto ninna" (sea dark, dark, [Al]berto sleepy-bye). This the first sentence of mine that I remember, the first palimpsest of my life, the very first. In fact, I couldn't yet talk well.

Do you remember what life was like in those years? The streets? What people were like?

Carriages, many carriages, and everywhere the odor of dung and horse urine. Rome was full of horse-drawn cabs. I remember when we returned from the vacation and took a carriage for the whole family, parents and children, the driver put first the trunk on the box beside his seat, then the valises. They used trunks in those days. Overloaded, the carriage would cross the deserted streets in the night always to the same, reechoing sound of the horse's hoofs on the Roman cobbles. My mother had many trunks, some with leather corners, others of wicker. Those trunks carried an enormous quantity of stuff that was needed for three or four months of holiday.

Weren't there automobiles then?

Very few, and only for the rich.

When did you see your first automobile?

Very early, because my father bought one. He was among the first in Rome to have a car.

What was your impression when you passed from carriages to the automobile?

I remember only that my father had a fifteen-horsepower Fiat and a chauffeur. The chauffeur was named Alberi. My father and mother went to the opera in that car.

Did you describe your father's chauffeur in your novel Il conformista?

I used only his name. You want to hear how we set off for our holiday? In 1916 my father had rented a villa at Olevano Romano, seventy kilometers from Rome. It's a beautiful place. The house had an immense view. It wasn't a villa: it was a big, square house, with rooms simply furnished, but it was all he could find. When we left Rome in the Fiat, I was wearing a sailor suit, dark blue, which my mother had ordered from Paris, from the Galeries Lafayette. It was 1916, and my mother had a wide-brimmed hat, a flouncy blouse with a high collar, and an ankle-length skirt. We set out clean, and we arrived white with dust. I must say that going to Olevano was something of an adventure, both because it was very rural and because of diseases. In fact, in the town that summer many children died of typhoid and other intestinal illnesses.

Was poverty visible in that period?

Yes, very. But what was perhaps most striking was not so much the rustic and somehow traditional simplicity of the poor people, but the narrow-mindedness and meanness of the petty and middle bourgeoisie: in theory, the ruling class. But to get back to the holiday. We stayed at Olevano Romano for four months, until vintage time: there was a smell of must everywhere, and many wasps hovered around the casks. Donkeys came and went, bringing the grapes, which the peasants, rolling up their trousers, then trod with their feet. It was also at Olevano that I saw two peasant women, with similar bundles of dried boughs on their backs, so they couldn't touch each other, cry out together, "They've captured Gorizia! Viva l'Italia!" Because the peasants were very patriotic, poor things. From the unification of Italy onward, they had been stuffed with the myths of the Risorgimento: Cavour, Mazzini, Garibaldi, Victor Emanuel. Those few men who have given their names to infinite streets and squares in Italy. The accent then was more on patriotism than on liberalism. In short, an excellent preparation for Fascism.

Was the pope's presence much felt in Rome?

No. For me it didn't exist, at least not until after the war. This doesn't mean that I didn't practice, however mildly, the Catholic religion, in which I was raised. Every Sunday the current governess took me to Mass with my sisters. I understood little or nothing, but I liked the church and the ritual. I discovered the pope as bishop of Rome, as a Roman personage, only after the

Second World War, with Pope Pius XII. Not exactly a lovable pope, but important for the role he played in the horrible years of Nazism. In reality, the atmosphere in which I grew up was secular. My mother was a Catholic, but her Catholicism was as invisible as my father's Judaism. As the years went by, however, my mother became much more devout, but never a bigot.

Did you ever visit the old city? Piazza Navona? The Pantheon?

No, never. I was controlled by the governesses, who confined themselves to taking me to the Borghese Gardens.

Didn't they take you to see the bagpipers at Christmas and the crèches, to see Saint Peter's and the toy fair at Piazza Navona?

Nothing of the sort. I learned about Roman monuments and customs only in the thirties and after.

Do you like old Rome?

Yes, I like it a lot. I discovered it in a nontouristic way, through the movements of everyday life. I went there often during a period when the bourgeoisie never went there, between the two wars. Nobody went there: it was still a working-class neighborhood. I love it less now, because it's become chic and the traffic is hellish. I remember Piazza Navona with two shabby taverns where, during the winter, you kept your overcoat on while you ate, and your shoes were on a layer of sawdust. Mastro Stefano was already there, with that basso profondo voice of his, suggesting, "What'd you like today? We have oxtail!" Nobody went to Piazza Navona. The bourgeoisie preferred Via Veneto. All of old Rome was totally neglected, except for the nobles in their magnificent palaces. The discovery of old Rome by the bourgeoisie came after the Second World War.

You knew more or less the Rome of D'Annunzio, of his novel Il piacere?

No, I couldn't have known it. That was the Rome of 1880.

In your home did they talk about D'Annunzio?

No, they didn't mention him. My mother had read many of his books. My uncle De Marsanich, the Fascist deputy, loved D'Annunzio. Once I ran into him and he said to me, "You young people are wrong to treat D'Annunzio badly. He's a great poet!" I answered that he was right.

What were the mountain localities like, where you went for holidays?

We went to the Alto Adige, or South Tyrol, which was German, and full of Germans.

Was there an atmosphere like Mann's Magic Mountain?

Yes, but what's the connection? That novel was about a sanatorium. In any case, Mann has never meant much to me. *The Magic Mountain* was a novel of conversation, like *The Counterfeiters* of Gide and *Point Counter Point* of Huxley, three novels I didn't like, that say nothing to me.

But was it the world you had known when you were in the sanatorium?

Yes, it was that sort of thing. Yes. But only because there were doctors and nurses there, too. And besides, in my sanatorium people didn't talk at all about Europe, they thought only about making love and, if possible, getting well. Yes, because tuberculosis, it seems, stimulates sexuality. I've written a story, that has been called, with a bit of irony, "the little Magic Mountain," but its real title is "Inverno di malato," and in it I tell what sanatarium life was really like. I think Mann intended a kind of metaphor: the sanatorium was to be bourgeois Europe, sick with decadentism and ideology. But a metaphor is not reality. Italo Calvino said something quite exact: that Thomas Mann had seen everything, but from a nineteenth-century balcony; we, on the contrary, see everything as we are plunging down the stairwell. I find this observation correct and beautiful: Thomas Mann had sensed how

Europe would end, but from the now-dated point of view of late nineteenth-century bourgeois culture. We, instead, are a bit like that Poe character who plunges into the whirling vortex of the maelstrom.

I haven't asked you if, during your illness, you ever gave way to despair.

No, never. I was always very tense, true, but I have never despaired in my whole life. I have always had a fairly combative and patient spirit. I've never suffered long, deep depression. I can be depressed for a few minutes, maybe for a few hours of the day, but then it passes. Probably thanks to my excessive vitality I have always maintained an attitude that people say is positive and youthful. But leaving my vitality aside, this attitude is due also to the fact that I never had a real boyhood and so it crops up when I least expect it.

Do you think you have allowed your true self to emerge or have you repressed it? You told me that when your illness ended you were a savage, in a condition that was both violent and incapable of expressing itself.

It's true that, though I had the appearance of a well-brought-up bourgeois boy, sorrow and solitude had somehow made me a barbarian. Imagine, I was like someone who has spent years in prison, or on a desert island.

Do you think that the boy you were then and the man you are now are pretty much alike?

Oh, yes. Only today I'm a person who knows how to communicate. Then I unburdened myself by talking nonsense all the time. In those years, just after the sanatorium, as I already explained to you, I was silly.

Did they consider you silly at home?

Not in the least. Because I read a lot and was mostly quiet. They considered me a writer.

Even when you were a child?

As a child I didn't act silly. I started acting silly when I encountered the world outside the family. No, as a child I was serious and very sensitive.

Were you shy?

Yes, morbidly shy. I acted silly out of shyness. When I lived alone, in a hotel, after my illness, I always made them seat me at the table nearest the door so I wouldn't have to cross the room in front of all eyes. The first time I took a tram, at the age of fourteen, my legs were shaking as I paid for the ticket.

But you thought about women a lot?

Not as much as you would imagine. In the final analysis, I've had very few.

Who was the first love of your life?

She was German. She was thirty-six and I was eighteen. It happened in March 1926. We were both living in the Hotel Bellevue in Cortina, which at that season was completely deserted. She was the wife of an actor, who was shooting a film at the Falzarego Pass. I found her alone one evening at the bar, she gave me an encouraging look. I looked back at her, but I didn't have the courage to speak to her. In the end she was the one who spoke to me.

What did she say to you?

The usual things you say to break the ice. Then, still taking the initiative, she invited me to sit at her table and asked me if I planned to offer her a drink. She treated me exactly like a child. The bartender wasn't there and the bar wasn't in operation. Seeing that I hesitated and was embarrassed, she said she knew a beer hall not far from the hotel. Should we go there? Once we were outside the hotel, we realized it was pouring rain. We quickly ran to the beer hall, but before entering, on the threshold, I finally mustered my nerve and gave her a kiss. It was the first kiss of love in my life. I say "of love" because neither the women in the

Bolzano brothel nor the Bressanone officer's Viennese woman had inspired anything beyond desire in me. Perhaps I say it was a kiss of love because later it really became love, but that first time it was only a kiss. Nevertheless, I had the sensation that something important was happening to me. We entered the bar, drank a beer, then came out again, returned to the hotel, and went up to her room. I remember her surprise when she saw me slip my orthopedic device from under my pants. We made love in a normal way. For her it was to have been only a fling; for me, in a word, it was an initiation. Now something happened that derived from my inexperience and my immaturity. I was already in love, I could have stayed longer with her in the hotel, but I couldn't bring myself to postpone my already-set departure, though I kept telling myself the whole time that I was doing something absurd. So I left the next morning, very early, after having arranged to meet her a few days later in a hotel in Merano. But she came to Merano with her husband and consequently I couldn't make love with her. Then the husband went back to Cortina, and the two of us with him, and afterward, for perhaps ten days, we were really lovers. Then she left for Munich, where she lived, and she invited me to join her. I waited a week and then I left for Germany.

This first love is characterized by a number of idiocies due to inexperience and immaturity. First of all, I got off the train at a little station just beyond the German border. I dawdled over a coffee, and the train departed without my noticing. Oddly enough, I had carried my typewriter with me into the station café, but I had left on the train my suitcase with the manuscript of *Gli indifferenti*. In desperation, I had them telephone to the next station, to hold the train, then I rushed out, took a taxi, and chased the train just like a scene from one of the American films of the time. I reached the next station and discovered with joy that the train was waiting for me. Apparently such things could happen in those days. Still carrying my typewriter, I began to run along the tracks under the eyes of the travelers leaning out of the windows. At a certain point the typewriter case came open and ribbons were strung all over the tracks.

The second idiocy was when I finally reached Munich. She
had arranged for us to meet at a specific time in a very elegant
downtown hotel. Consumed with impatience, I turned up half an
hour early. She was seated at a table full of people. I must have
looked comic, boy that I was, asking for her, who could have been
my mother. All her friends realized very well what was going on,
and one after the other, they got up and left. But she wasn't too
angry with me, she scolded me a little, but gently.

Third and worst idiocy. One of those days I went to see her at
her house. She was speaking with the cook about some domestic
matter or other and told me to wait in the living room. I went
there and sat down so that I could see her at the end of a long cor-
ridor, talking in the kitchen with the cook. Maybe she did it on
purpose, or maybe she didn't attach much importance to my presence. The fact is that the waiting continued, and I started
drinking some awful German cognac that was on the table. I
think I must have drunk half the bottle. Suddenly, angry, I left the
house with the intention of going back to my hotel. But as soon as
I was in the street I realized I was completely drunk. I reached to
grab a tram, but the tram kept on going. Between my hand and
the tram there may have been a meter's distance. So I crossed a
street with heavy traffic; far off, at the end of the street, I saw a car,
which in reality was only half a meter from me, and it knocked
me down. The impact was very violent, and the strap of my orthopedic brace snapped in four places. Still drunk, I was taken by the
driver of the taxi that had hit me to the station infirmary. There I
had them telephone my friend, who arrived quickly, breathless,
and once again she was very sweet and hardly scolded me at all.
Two days later she left, I went back to Rome, and never saw her
again. Except once, when she was passing through Cortina. I had
a fever, I was in bed, she came up to my room and said hello.

The whole story of this first love lasted three months, between
Cortina, Merano, and Munich, but I went on loving her for many
years, even after I was in love with another woman. Strangely,
both Franziska (that was her name) and France (the French girl I
loved after her) had basically the same name: in Italian,

Francesca. I also recall that the last time I saw Franziska when, as I told you, I was in bed with a fever, and she came in and said, "You haven't changed. I remember your poor sad eyes" (in German, "Diene armen traurigen Augen").

Actually, you were — and still are — the sentimental type.

Let's say I have sentiment, feelings, which is something quite different. I remember those words particularly because they describe me as I was: a boy made sad by a long illness. Those words are a photograph, one of the few I have left from those years.

Let's go back to your relations with your family. They considered you a writer, but did you consider it normal for your father to go on supporting you, once you were cured of the illness?

Yes, I considered it normal, also because my father never voiced the slightest objection to supporting me. Why? Because during the first years after the sanatorium he understood that first of all I had to recover my health. Then the unexpected success of *Gli indifferenti* probably convinced him that I would find my way. Here are the dates: I left the sanatorium at the end of 1925. My father supported me in the mountains for another four years. In 1928 the novel was accepted. In 1929 it was published with great success but didn't make any money. My father had always been a good father, true, but any father in those circumstances would have realized the propriety of supporting me and letting me work in peace. For that matter, his support was limited to my living at home free and a monthly allowance of five hundred lire. Five hundred lire a month at that time was one fourth of a modest salary. It took two thousand lire even to live simply.

What sort of life did you live with five hundred lire?

I led the life of a student, though I was already a well-known writer. For example, if I took a girl to the movies, I had to walk home because I didn't have the money for a taxi. I began to make money in 1950, after *La romana*. Until I was forty, I earned very little. But my father paid the expenses every time I took a trip. I went to America and to China on my father's money. Now I realize that after *Gli in-differenti* I gave him no further satisfaction. I had no money, I was anti-Fascist, people looked the other way if I passed them in the street. My books didn't sell or else they were confiscated. I worked for the *Gazzetta del popolo*, writing one article a year. What can I say? I must have seemed a real idler to him. I read and read, and I wrote. And I went to salons, yes, but without money.

When?

Between the two world wars. They invited me, I went to their salons: that was the social period of my life. At those parties I encountered aristocrats, Fascist ministers, upper-middle-class men. As usual, I courted the women and they didn't want to make love, they wanted only to listen to what I was saying, or at least they pretended to listen.

Between what dates did you write Gli indifferenti?

Between 1925 and 1928. Two and a half years. In 1928 I left Rome to take the manuscript to Milan.

When did you decide the book was finished?

When I saw that I had nothing more to say and especially that the writing couldn't be altered any more or improved.

Had you already read it to anyone?

Yes, I gave it to a bookseller friend of mine named Dore. He was a Catholic, a dear person. He said it was fine. As I told you, Caffi had already read it, and the publisher of *Novecento*, whose name was Lioncurti; he didn't want to publish it, considering it "a fog of words." So I took the train and went to Milan, to the publisher Alpes.

Why didn't you go to Treves?

Treves no longer existed. They had gone bankrupt. It was a bad time for Italian publishing. Zanichelli published Carducci; Laterza published Croce, Bemporad had almost closed down, and Treves no longer existed. The firm had been taken over by

Garzanti, but it wasn't publishing anything yet. So I went to Cesare Giardini, head of the house of Alpes. Giardini was a likable, civil person. A very sensitive man of letters.

You said you were a shy boy.

Externally I wasn't at all aggressive, but inside, as is often the case with the shy, I was. I was nineteen and I looked very respectable. I remember that I always dressed in an English style, like an Oxford student: tweed jacket, gray flannel trousers, suede shoes.

Did you know you were offering an important book?

Not at all. I knew I wanted to publish it. Somehow I knew I couldn't do without that: it was like a physiological need. So I presented myself at the firm of Alpes as the Signor Moravia who had written *Gli indifferenti.* Giardini took it and put it to one side. Naively, I thought he would give me a prompt answer, so I went to Stresa to wait, I remember, in a hotel opposite the Iles Borromées. A very elegant hotel, perhaps the same one where Hemingway stayed.

Were you alone?

Alone, yes. The hotel was entirely empty, deserted; it was out of season. I waited a month. I took wonderful walks and I wooed, in vain, the barmaid, who was very pretty but didn't take me seriously. Finally I realized the answer wasn't going to come at once. Of those days in Stresa I remember how I was buoyed up by hope: every morning I would row on the lake and go ashore at Isolabella. I didn't realize it, but the waiting was making me happy. Finally I understood that the answer would take time, and I went back to Rome. After two or three months, I received a letter from Giardini, telling me I had written a fine book and he was very pleased to publish it.

What did you do when you received the letter? Did you tell your father at once?

Yes, I told my father.

Were you very happy?

Yes, I was, but I was particularly happy when I received the first proofs. I remember that tears came into my eyes as I looked at that first bundle of printed paper. Once again, however, I had to turn to my father. In fact, three months later I received a letter from Giardini, telling me that the firm had no money and therefore he couldn't go before the board with a new and unknown writer. You see what poor Italy was like then! The board! Imagine nowadays Mondadori rejecting a book, saying he can't present it to the board. To put it bluntly, Giardini concluded by saying I would have to pay the expenses, five thousand lire. Then I went to my father and said, "Look, they want me to pay." He said, "How much?" "Five thousand lire." Wham — he paid up immediately, without another word.

Were you afraid, when you asked him?

No, but he made me give him a receipt.

Why?

Probably so he could include it in the housekeeping expenses. In July I went to Viareggio, and I saw the book in the shop windows. *Gli indifferenti,* by Alberto Moravia. I had a ticket to Zermatt already in my pocket, and I left. There I fell madly in love with a seventeen-year-old French girl and I thought no more of *Gli indifferenti.* It went completely out of my mind. I hadn't even subscribed to a clipping service, so I knew nothing. I remember that, before I left for Zermatt, Giardini said to me, "Do one thing at least. Take the book to G. A. Borgese." G. A. Borgese was the leading literary critic, he wrote for the *Corriere della sera.* He received me very politely, but I made an enormous faux pas, because as I was writing the inscription, I said, "What are your first names? Anton Giulio, or Giuseppe Antonio?" He replied by saying, "Are you such a Futurist that you can allow yourself not to know my name?" I said nothing, but that same evening, perhaps as a reaction to Borgese's literary vanity, I wanted to plunge back into real life. Life, in this case, was a prostitute I stopped in Corso

Vittorio Emanuele. To understand that reaction you have to bear in mind that what I then conceived of as life — and what, in reality, was action — held more importance for me than literature. I left for Zermatt and fell in love with France, the young French girl. A genuine, furious, delicate love. She was seventeen and I was twenty. The sum of our ages was thirty-seven.

An adolescent love then, basically innocent?

No, destructive and very sexual, with a sense of extravagance and melancholy, aware and self-satisfied, because, despite our extreme youth, we had both been tested by life, I by my illness, and she by an unhappy and cruel relationship with her family. We danced the fox-trot every day from five to eight and from ten to midnight. Naturally, always in the presence of her English governess. I met France in a piano bar, I invited her to dance, and she accepted. She came from a rich family, was always well dressed, by Patou or Molyneux. During our dancing she rubbed herself slyly against me, consequently provoking embarrassing erections, then she would brusquely and deliberately step back, so that everybody could see. I didn't know what to do. Or else she would walk with me, pretend to fall backward, against a fence, in a meadow, with her legs spread, and I could see she wasn't wearing any underclothes. She was childishly provocative, but in reality she never wanted to go beyond a certain point. She was wild but clearheaded.

And you were crazy about her?

I'll say I was! She was the greatest love I'd ever had! I read her *Gli indifferenti* aloud in the woods where we took walks, translating it into French as I read. We took long, long walks together, but never ventured beyond kissing. On the other hand, she was a fearless masturbator. She masturbated three, even four times a day. Then she went to her grandmother's, at Coppet, on Lake Geneva, and I went to a little city not far away, called Divonne-les-Bains. There was a border between us. Every day a chauffeur-driven car collected me and took me to Coppet, where she lived with her grandmother in a magnificent chalet, all of wood, typically Swiss. Her grandmother was very devout, but in other ways fairly cynical. She lived alone and a young abbé read her the classics aloud, the memoirs of Saint-Simon, for example. She surely understood that I was making love with her granddaughter, in fact one day she called me and said, "France est toujours excitée, je pense que'lle devrait prendre des douches." And I answered, "Je pense qu'elle faut qu'elle se marie." I quarreled constantly with France. One day I gave her a shove and pushed her into the lake from the boat. Naturally she was a first-rate swimmer. She burst out laughing and swam back to shore. She was very beautiful, petite, with a perfect body, like a character by Watteau; her face had fine features and big eyes, with a deep and melancholy gaze. They were a singular contrast with her way of laughing, at once cruel and provocative. Her father was an automobile manufacturer, whose motto was, "Sa capote est en argent, son silence en or"; in short, a thirties atmosphere, between the upper-middle-class plays of Bernstein and the cosmopolitan stories of Morand. She lived with her mother and boasted, with a kind of sadism, that she had made her mother's lover fall in love with her. Then she went to a convent school in England. There, too, she told how she had made a nun lose her head. She showed me a letter from a girlfriend who had stayed in convent, a French Catholic convent; the photograph of a middle-aged nun was enclosed, and under it was written, "La grande coquette du couvent ne me regarde plus; qu'est-ce qu'elle a contre moi?" I've never understood if this was a childish boast or reality.

How long did your love last?

It lasted all summer. When summer was over, I told her I wanted to marry her, and when this became known, her grandmother wrote her a letter, saying, "Ça peut pas continuer comme ça! L'année dernière c'était un chevalier allemand, aujourd'hui c'est un écrivain italien." In fact, the previous year France had had a crush on a German count who competed in the jumping events at the Geneva horse show. In any case, I went to Rome and told my father I wanted to get married. I asked him if he could give me some money. He said yes, but not much. Then I left Rome to join France in Paris and marry her. She lived in a building at the Trocadero. The old Trocadero, I remember, looked to me like an enormous English pudding, black and grim. It was demolished and replaced by the great deco exposition of 1933. When I went to see France, I had a temperature of 100 degrees, and my head was spinning. She came downstairs and said curtly, "Je ne peux pas devinir ta femme, parce que ma grandmère ne veut pas . . ." I lost my head, partly because of the fever. I gave her a punch in the ribs and, without any further pleading, I left. It was pouring rain and I went back to my hotel, an *hôtel meublé* near the Étoile, in the 16ème, rue Pergolèse. I was so unhappy and chagrined that I stayed there for a month all alone, leaving the hotel only for meals.

What about your parents?

I wrote my parents that it was all off.

Did you see Carlo Rosselli in Paris?

Not that time. It was during another trip. He lived behind the Panthéon. Once he said to me, "Take a letter to Rome for me." To a man by the name of Meloni, I remember. I answered, "Is it dangerous?" "Yes, it's dangerous, and maybe they'll arrest you. If a famous writer is arrested by the Fascists, we can make some good propaganda out of it." Naturally, I agreed and decided to use the Poe method, "The Purloined Letter." I traveled in a sleeping car, with my raincoat hanging in the most obvious place and the letter sticking out of the pocket. Then I went to bed. The Fascist guards came; they made me open my suitcase, but they didn't pay any attention to the raincoat, proving that Poe was right. When I reached Rome I mailed the letter, and a few days later, a bomb exploded in the Vatican wardrobe, destroying various cardinals' hats. I've always wondered if there was some connection between that bomb and Signor Meloni.

To get back to France: I never saw her again. I felt like a widower. I had plumbed the depths of an absolute sadness, as if

France were dead. But instead, I saw her again, as I'll tell you, twenty years later.

What had happened to Gli indifferenti *in the meanwhile?*

I had become famous, and consequently this sort of thing happened: I was strolling with a friend. He met a friend and said, "Let me introduce the author of *Gli indifferenti.*" And the other man immediately answered with an incredulous laugh, "With that face? Oh, come on!" I was famous and without a penny.

Were you still in love with the French girl?

No. It's strange, I was then, and still am, a person who prefers, at least in love, the first, dazzling experience to the opaque developments of everyday life. Many times this leads me to forget completely that the years pass. Take the case of France, for example. More than twenty years later I happened to meet her in a Paris hotel. Well, she — who did have the sense of time passing — called me *maître*; but I, beyond the presence of this woman now forty, saw again the seventeen-year-old and I felt for her again, intact, the feeling I had had twenty years earlier. We went to her house; I tried to make love. For me the years hadn't passed, and this shows, if nothing else, that it hadn't been an infatuation, but real love.

You said you had become famous and had had a big success with Gli indifferenti. *How did the critics receive it?*

I had some reviews with headlines over six or eight columns. I still remember *La tribuna*, a Roman newspaper at that time that paid attention to literature. An eight-column headline, "*Gli indifferenti*, by Alberto Moravia." Many things had been inspired by the article of Borgese. In reality, I owe a great debt of gratitude to Borgese. He published a two-column article, a literary piece entitled "Gli indifferenti," which is a good article even today, and it made me famous. In those days Borgese and Pancrazi, another critic of the *Corriere della sera*, could make or break a writer, for those hundred or so readers who were interested in literature.

Today this is no longer possible; there are more readers, true, but literature is no longer a cultural matter: it's just another industrial product.

What did these critics say?

To understand the success of Gli indifferenti you must remember first of all that the last truly successful novels had been those of D'Annunzio, forty years previously. All the literary movements that had come after D'Annunzio, from the group of La voce to that of La ronda, had been hostile to fiction. On the other hand, however, the great success of the collection of Russian classics brought out by the publishing firm called Slavia had created an almost maniacal expectation: everyone was waiting for a finally Italian novel. Gli indifferenti to many readers seemed to fill a gap, and this explains why it appealed to critics of very different schools. In any case, there was no lack of hostile voices; Italy is still today a country with a moralistic, Catholic mentality. So you can imagine it then! Gli indifferenti is an absolutely chaste book, but it was attacked as if it were pornography. Then there was the political reaction from the Fascists, and this was in a sense more justified than the traditional moralist reaction. Because Fascism affirmed and proclaimed a renovation of Italian society. And here, the long-awaited Italian novel contradicted such affirmations. The core of this Fascist reaction can be found in a public speech made by Mussolini's brother Arnaldo, who was one of the owners of the firm Alpes that had published the novel. He said, "We would like to know if Italian youth must read the books of Dekobra, inventor of easy decadent adventures, of Remarque, destroyer of the grandeur of war, and of Moravia, negator of every human value." The words of this man who, armed with the full force of Fascism, was taking it out on a boy of twenty, show, if nothing else, that literature, even the most remote from social criticism, always goes far beyond the true intentions of the writer. I had simply wanted to write a novel against indifference and instead they saw in it a criticism of the Fascist regime that had not been my intention. There was also a review by Montini, later

Pope Paul VI, in the review *Civiltà cattolica*, very reasonable and measured.

How did you react to success?

I didn't. It immediately bored me, then as it does now. Because I attached more importance to expression than to publication and, somehow, to life rather than to literature. On this score, I recall that the year after the publication of *Gli indifferenti*, an Italian-American girl whom I had been seeing for a few months asked me if she could translate it and publish it in America. I didn't hesitate a moment and accepted her proposal, and immediately afterward forgot all about it. It's true that I didn't have a cent, but I didn't even hope to earn anything. I hoped only to write a second novel, better than the first. *Gli indifferenti* came out in America, almost unnoticed, with the title *The Indifferent Ones*. It was retranslated many years later with a new title, *The Time of Indifference*. I was genuinely indifferent to everything that could be called money and success. This indifference continued for a very long time. In 1935 the Viking Press published *Le ambizioni sbagliate*, which I'll discuss later. They asked me to send some material for publicity. I didn't even answer the letter. Then the Viking Press wrote me a second letter, thanking me sarcastically for the "splendid material I had sent." In other words, I didn't exploit my success in any way.

But you do now?

Yes, sometimes, when the publisher insists. Today, however, with the total triumph of the culture industry, I consider it dangerous both from a literary point of view and — how shall I say? — from a spiritual one.

Still, you've become a professional.

No. Or at least, as little as possible. If I really had become one, I wouldn't be today what they call a controversial author. I would already be forgotten.

Why?

Professionals, as the word itself suggests, are not creative. The majority go on imitating themselves after a first book has had success.

At the time of Gli indifferenti, *were you a dilettante?*

I was less and more than a dilettante: I was an outsider.

But the literary society concerned itself with you.

Yes, that's true, in many ways. There was even a very well-known writer who wanted to promote an appeal against me. I knew nothing about Italy: I was a kind of literary displaced person.

3

ALAIN ELKANN: *When did you meet Bernard Berenson?*

ALBERTO MORAVIA: I met him in 1927.

You once told me you had read Gli indifferenti *aloud to Berenson.*

Yes, that's true. In 1926 I went to live in Perugia in a furnished room in the house of a chauffeur. Somebody introduced me to Umberto Morra. Umberto Morra introduced me to Berenson. I remember that Berenson invited me to spend the summer holidays at the Consuma Pass, a beautiful place above Florence. He spent his vacation there every year, always in the same villa, which didn't belong to him. I went and stayed in a tiny pensione. I remember — to give you an idea of the atmosphere of the pensione — that, just after I had arrived, I was putting away my things when a little girl came in and said, "Come, we'll do a few spins with your gramophone." Now I didn't have a gramophone; it was a typewriter. At mealtimes they put me at a table with a priest, also on holiday. Every day a car came with a chauffeur and took me to Poggio allo Spino, the Berenson villa.

What was Morra like?

He was rather ugly, tall, emaciated, lame. He was a nobleman of Piedmontese origin; his full name was Count Umberto Morra di Lavriano. He was a very refined, exquisite person, an intellectual with a mixture of stiffness and sociability. He lived in a villa full of books; he liked to invite people, to put up intellectuals. He spoke English and French well. Many years later he became director of the Italian Cultural Institute in London. He was the son of a general, Morra di Lavriano, who had distinguished himself for two things in his life. He had accompanied the future king of Italy on a long journey through Russia. Morra still had the imperial court menus. And then general Morra di Lavriano had repressed some uprisings in Sicily, known as the Sicilian *fasci*, a revolt of starving peasants. Perhaps because of his father, Morra had a curious habit: he followed carefully, reading the annual lists, all the movements of the Italian army.

Morra was a friend of Berenson's?

A very close friend. He was one of the faithful. Berenson had a circle of faithful friends who collected around him like a court. So Morra introduced me to Berenson, who, learning I had written a novel, asked me to read it to him aloud every day. This always took place after lunch. Berenson would stretch out, a Panama hat pulled down over his eyes. I read and Berenson listened. On the day I finished reading the book he confined himself to a single phrase which, considering the speaker, was actually rather flattering: "A remarkable achievement."

Did being with Berenson make a deep impression on you?

Only the suffering I had undergone made, as you say, a deep impression on me. There is a story — you might call it a love story — that dates from those days. I'll tell it to you. I went to Florence, where I met a girl named Silvia, of an old noble Tuscan family. Not beautiful, but strange; she slightly resembled Baudelaire's mistress, very dark and slender. I saw her often. In the end we became lovers, and our relationship led on my part to a proposal of marriage.

But hadn't you wanted to get married also the previous year?

Yes. In those days I always wanted to get married. I thought that with Silvia I had what you might call a commitment, a debt of honor, and it seemed my duty not to evade it. Privately, I thought that marriage would be a huge mistake, but I told myself I had to go through with it anyway. In other words, it was the typical situation of the inexperienced man who doesn't know women. In fact, she refused, both because there was no real love between us and because she obviously didn't consider me a good match. But that wasn't the end of it. Morra regarded my marriage proposal very seriously and took it upon himself to tell Silvia, a bit ingenuously, that in view of the nature of our relationship, she couldn't reject me. She in the meanwhile had begun another affair with a Prince B. in Rome, who died a few years later, a volunteer in the Spanish civil war. He had become Silvia's lover and Silvia incited him to challenge me to a duel, because I had told Morra she had lost her virginity to me, and she couldn't understand that I had made this indiscreet revelation only to justify my marriage proposal. So, one day when I was calmly reading all alone on the graveled yard at Poggio allo Spino, an open car drove up with Prince B., whom I didn't know, at the wheel. He made a circle all around me on the gravel and went off. But the next day I was informed that I couldn't fight the duel, as would have been my duty, because B. had come, had given me two slaps, and I hadn't reacted. This was the story that B. had told Silvia, who was waiting for him down at Vallombrosa. Dumbfounded, I said to Morra, "What a tale! He drove around me and didn't even look at me." Then Morra went again to Silvia and told her of B.'s strange behavior. In the end B. confessed, contritely, that he had told her a lie. I've told you this absurd story chiefly to give you an idea of the atmosphere in which I lived then, among customs and habits that were foreign to me, though I had to adapt myself to them the way you observe the customs of a foreign country you are passing through on a journey.

It was after that affair with Silvia that I decided to go to London, and Bernard Berenson gave me various letters of introduction that allowed me to meet many interesting people. I traveled by sleeping car. In London I stayed as a paying guest with the widow of an art critic of the *Times*. I found myself in a fin de siècle atmosphere, old and tired, in a high and narrow house in Oakley Street, in Chelsea. I remember that my hostess would sit in front of the fire and take off her shoes; she wore heavy wool stockings. There was an elderly maid who yelled because she was deaf. They prepared mutton on Monday, then we ate mutton every day until Saturday, and on Sunday they cooked the mutton bone with sausages. And they also made something I hated profoundly, which was bread pudding. It was like being in a Dickens novel! The landlady had two sons: one, a neurotic with a number of nervous tics, let me in the first day and I never saw him again; the other was an aesthete of the pre-Raphaelite variety, with long blond hair and a beautiful wife. Both were in psychoanalysis under a famous analyst, who was the niece of Lytton Strachey. In London I had some odd experiences. For example, I went to a costume party dressed as a telegraph pole. I wandered through the rooms with my arms extended, like wires, and a number of white studs on my chest, meant to be porcelain fuses. During this party I happened to meet a woman in a sphinx costume: she was beautiful, a helmet of black hair and blue eyes. We joked together a lot during the party, and at the end she invited me to come to her house the next day. The next day it was raining hard, a real London rain. I took a taxi and ended up in a very distant suburb. I found the house, rang the doorbell, but nobody answered, nobody opened. In a fury, I plunged into the tube and went home. The next day I telephoned her and spoke with such violence that she took fright and made a new date. I went back to the house in the distant suburb, and this time I found her agreeable, perhaps repentant, but firm. She told me simply that she couldn't make love with me because she was accustomed to doing it by herself. The habit was too strong, and she could do nothing about it. I was amazed at how the true face of life had been suddenly revealed to me, only to become mysterious and enigmatic again.

What was London like at that time?

London was black, totally blackened by smoke, and very foggy. Coming from Italy, I felt I was on another planet. I had never seen anything like it: I was stupefied. Stupefied that London was so black, all black with soot, and there was a thing that you have probably never seen: it was called, in English, "pitch black mist," in other words, darkness at noon: a hood of black fog hanging over the roofs of the houses and, under the fog, a perfect visibility, but like night. The first time I witnessed this phenomenon I thought I was mistaken. I had come out of the house, but I went back inside with the idea of returning to bed. From London I wrote some articles for La stampa that had some success in Italy. Curzio Malaparte, then editor of La stampa, had invited me to contribute and had sent me to London.

You haven't told me when you met Malaparte.

I met him when he was coeditor of Novecento with Bontempelli. Then the two of them quarreled, and Malaparte became editor of La stampa while Bontempelli became a member of the Academy of Italy. Novecento had brought both of them luck. The articles in La stampa, as I said, had success because I managed to express directly in them my amazement at English life, so different from Italian. The two things that struck me most were the fog, as I've mentioned, and English understatement. In Italy there is rarely fog, especially in the south, and conversations are explicit and realistic. Naturally these two impressions did not alter the third and greatest impression: of being in a city whose poetry was strange for me, new and fascinating. I may say that during the whole period of that first visit of mine to London I was in love with the city.

Whom did you see in London?

I tried to make my way with Berenson's letters and by spending time with two friends, Piedmontese painters who lived in the same pensione I did: Carlo Levi and Enrico Paolucci. I was often with them and since, thanks to Berenson, I had met the director of the

Tate Gallery, I tried to make him buy a painting by Carlo Levi and I succeeded. The painting was of a woman seated on a bed. It was the period when Carlo Levi imitated Modigliani. Actually, I have in my house a portrait painted by Enrico Paolucci in the pensione in Upper Bedford Place. Carlo Levi also painted a portrait of me in the same Modigliani-like style as the Tate Gallery picture. Thanks to Berenson's letters, I met also some members of the so-called Bloomsbury set, then approaching its end. I met, for example, Lady Colefax and Lady Ottoline Morrell, who were friends of Berenson and had the two most important intellectual salons of the Bloomsbury set. I also saw a lot of Camillo Pellizzi, who was then the correspondent of the *Corriere della sera.*

How did you go about getting in touch with the people to whom Berenson had recommended you?

I telephoned, though I knew it was very rude to telephone. In fact one lady, to whom I was presented, asked me in a reproachful tone, "You've telephoned?" I replied, "Yes, because I don't know English well enough to write properly." This was my excuse, but I was considered very ill mannered. Telephoning was not done.

The first time you went into those salons, were you a bit intimidated or not?

I was a bit dazed, as if I were two people and were watching myself live. For that matter, this happened to me also in Italy on such occasions. I felt an almost schizophrenic indifference that delegated to my social ego the nuisance of having rapport with others.

At that time was London much more important than it is today?

It was the capital of the greatest empire that had ever existed, and you could see and feel this. I was invited to the Round Table Conference on India, in the house of Lady Astor. It was a great conference with all the Indian potentates. Lady Astor was a teetotaler; she offered only orangeade. There were numerous rajahs, with diamonds, turbans, decorations. On that occasion I also saw Bernard Shaw, in a tailcoat too big for him, its tails hanging to his feet, abundantly stained. I felt as if I were looking at an almost prehistoric character, like the dinosaurs.

Did you see Gandhi?

No, I never saw Gandhi. I was introduced to a rajah. I made a terrible faux pas. I said to him, "I've read Katherine Mayo's book *Mother India*." It was a book that spoke very unfavorably about India. He listened to me and, without a word, turned his back.

What effect did London have on you?

It was strange, very strange. Odd things happened to me all the time. One morning, for example, while I was still asleep, the wife of the brother of Aldous Huxley telephoned me, Mrs. Julian Huxley, whose husband was a famous scientist. She said, "Do you want to come to Stonehenge?" "Yes, gladly." I was always available. She came with a car and we set off for Stonehenge. She drove at a crazy speed, taking the curves headlong, terrifying pedestrians in the villages. Then I said to her, "Excuse me, could you go a bit more slowly?" She said, "Life means nothing to me; my husband left me yesterday evening." I answered, "But life does mean something to me. Nobody's left me." During my London stay I had some dealings with Englishwomen, in the sentimental sense. I think they are the most fascinating women, because they are at once very sensual, very moralistic, and very cynical, a contradictory blend that must correspond to a similar tendency in my own character. Furthermore, they have a sense of humor that at times becomes eccentricity. I was just getting over my great love for France, and I couldn't help saying to myself that a woman's unconscious is like a safe in which, without her awareness, all the treasure of national archetypes is preserved. I mean, I liked Englishwomen because they were so English, as I had liked France because she was so French. During those days another strange thing happened to me. I remember that I went into a stationer's to buy some sheets of paper. When I came out, I saw Carlo Levi, who had left ahead of me. I took him by the arm and began speaking to him in Italian. After a little while I realized the man was English and was terrified.

It wasn't Carlo Levi?

No, but there was such fog! I remember it all happened in an impenetrable fog.

Was the fog really all that bad?

Horrible, it was absolutely beyond belief. You went out and banged your nose against a lamppost because you couldn't see it.

Did you smoke then?

Yes, I smoked. Players, without filter.

How much did you smoke?

About ten, fifteen a day. But I smoked more or less all brands. In Italy I also smoked Giubeks, and the Macedonias of the government monopoly, Abdullah, Melachrino Egyptian cigarettes, the American brands, Chesterfield and Lucky Strike. In Paris I smoked Gauloises. I had a great assortment of cigarettes. I constantly changed brand because I liked the packaging. There's a photograph of me taken by Lady Ottoline Morrell (I'll talk about her in a minute); it shows me at a garden party near London, wearing a gray flannel double-breasted suit, with a cigarette in my mouth. I smoked while I worked, because the smoke would envelop my head, and I liked to believe that smoke isolates you. At times, however, my head would swim, and I would have to lie down on the sofa because I felt sick.

What did you write while you were in London?

I was scribbling *Le ambizioni sbagliate*. During those years I wrote one of the best things of my life, the short story "Inverno di malato." I wrote it at Divonne-les-Bains during the summer when I met France. I sent it to Pancrazi for the magazine *Pegaso*, which was printed by LeMonnier in Florence. It was a conservative literary magazine, edited by Ugo Ojetti. Pietro Pancrazi was the editorial secretary. In "Inverno di malato" I summed up in a novella the two years of my life in the sanatorium. As I believe I've already told you, while *Gli indifferenti* and "Inverno di malato" were written with expressionist features, in *Le ambizioni sbagliate*, on the other hand, the influence of Dostoyevsky emerges, and with it, in another respect, the influence of Manzoni. I had got it into my head to write a novel Dostoyevskian in content and Manzonian in style. Absurd! Result: frightful labor over five years, a downright chore. This chore, nevertheless, contains a fairly successfully drawn character whose name is Andreina. But, all in all, it was a chore: the only positive result was that I liberated myself from *Gli indifferenti*. I didn't know it, but this is what I tried to do for fifteen years: free myself from my first novel and its success.

And while we're on the subject I would like to make an important observation: I was very precocious. At seventeen I expressed myself in a novel that still today is considered one of my best books. After *Gli indifferenti*, except for "Inverno di malato," I never again wrote something so fundamental, until 1942, the year when, at Anacapri, I recovered my original inspiration and wrote *Agostino*. So it was a long travail between experimentation and impotence. Therefore my observation concerning precocity is this: if Rimbaud, instead of roaming around the world after writing his poems, had remained with his mother, don't you think something similar would have happened to him? I mean, wouldn't he have written in another way the same things he had written in the poems? This observation may seem presumptuous, but actually it concerns not talent but precocity. For fifteen years I had nothing more to say. I can't help thinking that Rimbaud's silence is perhaps to be attributed to his extraordinary precocity. Naturally it's just another hypothesis to explain in a psychological way a literary mystery that even today fascinates critics and readers. In short, precocity involves for a certain period the sleep of talent, the lethargy of the spirit.

I also had to overcome something very similar to death: that is, the death of inspiration. I overcame it in various ways, in the literary sense, testing and retesting a number of different approaches to writing. So in the period between 1928 and 1942 I wrote first of all *Le ambizioni sbagliate*, my Dostoyevskian-Manzonian novel;

then some surrealist novellas; then a satirical Stendhalian novel, *La mascherata*; and finally some fairly pompous prose works in the style of *La ronda's* writers. I skirted the problem of writing because it wasn't yet clear to me what I wanted, or rather what I ought, to say. Finally, in 1942, at Anacapri, I wrote *Agostino*, in which I found again the main line of my inspiration, that of *Gli indifferenti*, but with a new dimension gained from fifteen years of literary experimentation.

So in London you were writing Le ambizioni sbagliate?

I may exaggerate in denigrating this novel of mine. You know what Emilio Cecchi said of *Le ambizioni sbagliate*? He didn't speak well of it, but he said, "It has the power of a locomotive that drags uphill a large number of coaches." The opinion is correct, because it expresses the stubborn and impotent determination that dominated me at that time.

In London did you see many English people?

I led a social life for a whole winter. I was a regular visitor to the salon of Lady Ottoline Morrell, who had been an important figure in the then almost defunct Bloomsbury set. She was a friend of Virginia Woolf, Russell, Yeats, Lytton Strachey, Forster, Connolly, the Huxley brothers, and so on. I still remember a lunch at the Travellers Club, where I was invited by Lytton Strachey and Forster. I was silent the whole time with these two whom I considered the highest in every sense. I had already read Forster's *Passage to India* and Lytton Strachey's *Eminent Victorians*. I admired both writers, considering that they had done a great deal through their books to destroy Victorian conventions.

How did they happen to invite you?

Again thanks to Berenson's introductions. All this happened because of the magic wand of Berenson, who made me realize the importance of private life, which in countries like England could also become social and public. In Italy, on the contrary, private life remains private and public life public. The real mainspring of this transformation of the private into the public was nevertheless something I didn't much like: snobbery.

What was this snobbery?

It was a very subtle snobbery. I went to Oxford to see an exhibition of painting. It was simply ridiculous! I understood enough about it to realize it was ridiculous. I remember a painting that depicted a box of matches. I said to a friend of the painter, "Say what you like, all I see is a box of matches." And he said, "Yes, but he painted it so slowly." He was such a snob that it stuck in my mind! Snobbery, you know, is called the English syphilis.

What's the difference between English and French snobbery?

The French kind is linked with culture, the English with social position. Madame Verdurin in the *Récherche* says, "Don't play the *Neuvième* for me, it gives me the most frightful headaches!" — typical of French snobbery. Whereas when the Baroness Blixen mentions in her book on Africa that the Prince of Wales came to dinner at her house: that is English snobbery. In England everything is based on two points: social power and language. There is still today an unbridgeable gap between those who speak Cockney and those who speak Oxonian.

Did this snobbery amuse you?

Yes, it amused me, but I found it absurd, often cruel. The English are like hunters waiting behind a hedge to shoot some poor animal, or some hapless wretch who mispronounces a word, or uses the wrong fork, or wears the wrong clothes. I also felt sometimes that they would gladly have shot at me. What saved me was the fact that I wasn't an animal in their game reserve, but a foreigner and therefore incomprehensible, an outsider, practically of no use. Conversation among the English was a game of dominos; one would put down a piece and the other, another. The only thing that proved forbidden was anything personal. They talked among themselves; I was always a spectator. They would ask me something, then walk off.

And what did you do when you couldn't see the Italian painters or the Bloomsbury set?

When I didn't see these people I had, or tried to have, love affairs. I had a strange affair with a girl who was to be married two days later. My problem, just like any poor student's, was where to go. In my rooming house it was impossible; furthermore, I didn't know London. I invited the correspondent of an Italian paper to lunch and he, not the least surprised, gave me the address of a room off Regent Street. Our lovemaking was all right. But the thing I remember best is that the next day, a day before she was to be married, she wanted to see me again. We met in a bar, and it emerged that she was afraid I would blackmail her into continuing our affair after her marriage. Somewhat taken aback by this low opinion, I swore I wouldn't do it and never saw her again. In that period in London I was living badly: besides being still in poor physical shape, I found the English way of life didn't suit me. Furthermore, I was obsessed with my illness.

You were afraid the illness would come back?

I wasn't afraid of it; I almost missed it. I didn't feel very strong in the face of life. I did everything as if in a dream. And then I would almost feel nostalgia for the illness, because an ill person during his illness is protected by the sanatorium, by the doctors, the nurses. Life, on the contrary, was like a place where I had to make my way on my own strength, which was still scant. It may seem strange, but when a person has been ill for ten years of his life, the illness becomes a second nature.

To conclude, we've talked about two foreign periods, one in London and one in Paris. What difference was there between these two experiences?

In London, the experience of social life; in Paris, of love. In London I loved nobody but saw many people. In Paris I loved one person but, striking a balance, since it was an unhappy love, saw almost nobody.

What was the effect on you of returning from London to Italy?

The effect of going from a place where there was a society to another place where only a family was awaiting me. Actually, I felt a foreigner everywhere, both for social reasons and for reasons of the heart. I was writing a novel that didn't convince me, and yet I felt I had to write it. I was living with my family after having written *Gli indifferenti*, which symbolized a farewell to family life. And I spent my time with women who didn't appeal to me and in salons that didn't interest me.

What salons?

In London I had come to understand a bit the mechanisms of society, and I tried to repeat in Rome the life I had led in London. But what a difference! In the salons of Lady Sybil and Lady Ottoline I had met the cream of the contemporary London crop. But in the salons of Rome, as I said before, intellectuals didn't exist; almost the only intellectual who visited them was I. In the Roman salons you saw only foreign diplomats, aristocrats, upper middle class, and Fascist politicians. As for the intellectuals, they were also divided into two categories. The smaller was that of the Fascist intellectuals, whom I didn't see (only once I went to the Fascist salon of Mussolini's mistress Marghrita Sarfatti, crammed with ambitious painters and academicians, dominated by Panzini, and I heard my hostess say to me, "You're a cousin of that pig Carlo Rosselli!"), or else they were anti-Fascists — and then, since they were for the most part very poor people, I saw them in taverns. But perhaps the word "intellectuals" is not correct. They were instead artists (writers, critics, painters, musicians) who weren't interested in politics and in any event never talked about it. You mustn't think, however, that they remained silent out of fear. It was simply because literature and the arts in general, through the poetics of hermeticism, had turned their back on the political commitment of Fascism: this, too, was a way of being anti-Fascist.

Do you have any memory of Hitler's rise to power?

In that year, 1933, I had a kind of amorous infatuation that, in a remote way, was connected with Hitler.

Connected how?

This is the story: in the spring of 1933 I went to Sorrento for a brief holiday. I lived in a pensione by the sea whose patrons were almost exclusively Germans. Next to my table, in the dining room, there was a young couple that I took for husband and wife; instead they were brother and sister. She was big, shapely, with a beautiful face but with a sleepy air, as if caused by too much repressed desire; he was thin, lanky, with a broad, bald forehead and an aquiline nose. It seemed to me that she looked at me insistently; perhaps it was an illusion due to that gaze of hers, which was at once lascivious and murky.

After two or three days I took advantage of her brother's absence and struck up a conversation. She told me her name was Trude, she was a student of philosophy; her brother's name was Alois and he was a music critic. And when I invited her to go out with me in a boat the next day, she accepted with flattering alacrity. Then the brother arrived and I extended the invitation to him as well. But the next day she arrived alone and so we went out in the boat, me rowing and her seated at the poop. Once we were well away from the shore, I shipped the oars, sat beside her, and told her frankly that I was very attracted to her. She let me kiss her as if it were something foreseen, taken for granted, but then she immediately told me that I should have spoken to her earlier: she was about to leave for Germany. Encouraged by the favorable tone, I said that during the night I would come to visit her in her room. She told me promptly that I was not to do that, she wouldn't open the door, and I then said to her, as if joking, that my room was on the floor above hers, and I would lower myself from my balcony to hers and enter through the French window. She started laughing and said that, like all Italians, I was a braggart but in the end I wouldn't do a thing. I considered these words a kind of challenge and an invitation, and I decided to carry out my joking boast.

When night came, I waited for a long time in my room. The nervous waiting provoked a little ridiculous accident. I went into the bath and picked up a heavy carafe to fill a glass with water. The carafe slipped through my fingers, fell into the sink, and shattered it. A piece of porcelain fell on my foot, wounding me and producing a fair amount of blood. I bandaged my foot as best I could and went out on the balcony. There was a bright moon, like daylight. I went to the railing, looked down, and saw that it wasn't very high, and that I could slip down to the balcony below by sliding down the drainpipe. And so I did. I climbed over the railing and grasped the drainpipe; but it was either rusted or insecurely attached to the wall because, when I was halfway down, it came loose and I fell awkwardly onto the balcony, still clinging to the pipe. I had only scratched my hands and legs slightly. I resolutely entered through the open French window into Trude's bedroom. It was in darkness, and I could discern Trude seated on the bed looking at me without a word. I went over to her and said, "Here I am, I made it," or something of the sort. I sat on the bed and tried to take her into my arms. But I encountered a stubborn, mute resistance. In the end, however, she gave me a kiss and asked me to leave: she wasn't well, it was that time of the month. She said this in the tone of someone telling a lie with no effort to dissimulate it. Disappointed, I said, to be polite, "When will I see you again?" She answered promptly and willingly, "Nothing easier, come see me in Berlin." I asked her to give me her address and she turned on the lamp; she was naked, with her hair undone, and her face more than ever seemed full of desire and sleep. She leaned toward the night table, wrote the address on a slip of paper, then once again asked me to leave.

This time I left, quite sure that I would never see her again. But then, the next day, rowing a boat in the midst of the sea, I thought about her again and decided to go to Berlin. I let a few days pass, then I went back to Rome, packed my suitcase as if for a long trip, and left for Germany. I traveled third class; I wanted to save money so as to stay in Berlin as long as possible. I traveled many hours, day and night, seated on a very hard wooden seat in a compartment crowded with Germans. I remember that I kept falling asleep, then waking up; I would see that it was still night, then fall asleep again. During one of these waking moments, I also took part in the conversation of the other travelers. At a certain moment I was asked about the problem of the Jews. They asked me what the Italians thought about it. I answered curtly that Mussolini had had a Jewish mistress, the Signora Sarfatti, in fact; then I went back to sleep.

At the conclusion of the endless and very uncomfortable journey, I arrived in Berlin, and since I didn't know the city, I took a room in a hotel that was part of the station, the Hauptbahnhof Hotel. I was very tired, but not so tired that I didn't realize there was something strange about the hotel. Everywhere, in the lobby, in the corridors, on the stairs, you could see only men in Nazi uniform, in brown shirts, coming in and out, running here and there, walking, then stopping abruptly to exchange the Nazi salute. There were so many of them, in such a rush, so busy, that the whole hotel suggested a crazed anthill. I realized finally that there was a Nazi Congress being held in Berlin and that my hotel had been virtually requisitioned by the party. It was late by then; I had some cold supper brought to my room, then flung myself on my bed and began reading the only book I had brought with me, the poems and the *Operette morali* of Leopardi. I wonder why that ancient despair of his seemed to me in harmony with the unconscious and unconfessed despair of my absurd journey. I read on, then I became sleepy. I dozed off fully clothed, then I woke up, undressed, and fell asleep again.

The next day I telephoned Trude, who answered me with some amazement and arranged for us to meet that afternoon in the bar of the hotel. Then I busily set about preparing my stay in Berlin. First of all I telephoned an Italian journalist I had known in Italy and made an appointment for lunch. Then I went to a rental agency, where they gave me some addresses of furnished rooms. Finally, I walked for almost an hour. At lunch I met my

Italian friend, who informed me at once about the state of things in Germany. So there was an air of revolution; the Nazis were preparing to seize power; every day there were attacks on the Jews; an Italian reporter has been mistaken for a Jew and severely beaten. This was all bad news, but absorbed by my infatuation for Trude, I attached no importance to anything else; I wanted only to stay in Berlin as long as possible and see Trude every day.

After lunch, I went to look at a room for rent in a residential district. It was on the fourth floor of an old, gloomy building with a Wilhelmine façade. The door was opened by a tall and slender boy with cropped blond hair, restraining a big Pomeranian on a leash. He showed me the room, big and dark, with many grim and massive pieces of furniture. I told him it suited me, and he immediately gave me the keys of the apartment, saying I could move in whenever I wanted. So I went to the hotel, collected the suitcase I still hadn't unpacked, and returned to the apartment, where I immediately telephoned Trude, inviting her to come and see my new lodging: I was impatient to be alone with her, to make love. Once again she seemed surprised and embarrassed, but still agreed to come and visit me in my furnished room. I waited anxiously. I wondered if Trude would like the old and lugubrious apartment. I was determined, if she didn't like it, to change rooms again. She arrived very late and wasn't alone: she had brought her brother along. She was all dressed in city clothes, in a style new to me, since I had known her in beach dress, in Sorrento; the beautiful and melancholy face, sensual and sleepy, was the same as ever, and yet already I lost all illusions: the brother's presence, somehow insulting, as if she had been afraid I would rape her, gave me an almost immediate premonition that my German adventure was over before it had begun. In fact, she wouldn't even come into the living room; she said quickly that she couldn't see me, that the whole Sorrento thing was finished now. Her brother looked at me from behind his sister's back and in the end asked me, correct and stiff, if I planned to stay long in Berlin. I answered that I would remain a few days, then leave again. She kept looking at me with an expression of unsatisfied desire and asked finally if I would be in Rome in August: she might come to Italy during the summer. I replied that I had no idea; I realized that, with this question, she apparently wanted to continue her exasperating game of inconclusive meetings.

After a few more words they went off, and I also left the house. I didn't know what I was doing, I was more sad and bewildered than angry. There was a great crowd of people who seemed to be heading all in the same direction, many Nazis among them, amid a great din of excited voices. I let myself be drawn along by this multitude; I didn't know where to go, but they, it seemed, did know. All of a sudden in the crowd I saw a tall, slim, blonde woman, wrapped in a white raincoat, walking alone — not, it seemed, letting herself be dragged by the crowd like me, but proceeding in her own direction at once specific and purposeless, as if to display herself, the walk common to prostitutes. I began following her mechanically; the white raincoat appeared and disappeared in the night; there was in the woman a determination not to share in the general enthusiasm (because it was, in fact, an enthusiastic crowd), a stubborn and independent attitude that fascinated me.

And so, following that white raincoat, I arrived in a big square crammed with people; the crowd was shouting cadenced slogans and applauding; suddenly on the third floor of a building, a window opened and Hitler appeared, in a brown shirt, his arm extended in the Nazi salute. The crowd applauded, then silence fell, and Hitler spoke in a voice immediately furious and hoarse, as if he had already been speaking for a long time, until the power of his lungs was exhausted. He spoke briefly then repeated the Nazi salute and vanished. The crowd stood there and applauded and shouted slogans for a long time, then began to empty the square. I realized that the white raincoat was still there, not far from me: the woman, heedless of Hitler and politics, was waiting for me. I went over and spoke to her; she was willing and took my hand, drawing me hurriedly towards a taxi rank. I looked at her as the taxi gained speed. As often happens in these cases, when I saw her closer, she seemed to me less pretty and interesting than from a distance. After so much display, she seemed especially anxious to act professionally, conceding nothing to pleasantness, not even the conventional sort. Coldly she sat beside me in the taxi, turning her head toward the window; coldly in the elevator of my building she stood facing the door; coldly, once we were in the room, she undressed, arranging her clothes on a chair with great care; coldly, at last, we made love, as she turned her head aside as if not to see me, and I busied myself on top of her with the clear determination to get it over as fast as possible. She dressed again with that pathetic care for her clothes, and then I accompanied her to the vestibule and saw the white raincoat for the last time, as it disappeared into the elevator.

The next day I left for Rome. This time I took a sleeping car because it was no longer necessary to save money in order to stay longer in Berlin. It was raining furiously over all of Germany. I resumed reading Leopardi; at that time he was my favorite writer, and reading his poems, I somehow consoled myself for my disappointment with Trude. It had been, as I said, a momentary infatuation but with an unconscious substratum perhaps connected with the Germany of that time and Hitler's rise to power.

Where did you spend your vacation?

I used to spend the summer at Forte dei Marmi or on Capri.

Whom did you go with?

I went alone.

And whom did you know there?

At Forte dei Marmi everybody, all the writers from Florence, who contributed to the magazine *Solaria* and were, without exception, anti-Fascists. But as I said before, they were also hermetics and therefore reluctant to discuss politics. We met at the café in the afternoon and at night. In the morning everybody went to the beach. To visit the different groups you had only to walk up and down along the beach or the sea road. I remember those summers at Forte dei Marmi as a constant coming and going, very wearisome and oddly sterile.

What were they like, Montale and Landolfi and the other So-laria writers you met at Forte?

The thing that most characterized them was lack of communication. At the Giubbe Rosse café in Florence or at the Forte café sometimes there were as many as twenty or thirty literary people who didn't speak or confined themselves to joking remarks. I remember that Montale constantly hummed scales, because he had studied voice; and Landolfi, though he remained silent, nervously wiggled the tip of his foot. Italian literature was characterized by the presence of men of genius, among them Montale, Landolfi, Delfini, Penna, Saba, and so on. But all of them were encased in a hermetic impenetrability, and at the same time, perhaps as a reaction to Fascist grandiloquence, they tended to underline the mediocre or even squalid characteristics of daily life. A bit like the American minimalists today. But it's also true that I saw them rarely because I lived in Rome and at that time the real capital of Italian literature was Florence.

Was it very different from the world of Bloomsbury?

Naturally! In Bloomsbury you felt the decline of imperial England; there, you felt the mediocrity of the Tuscan or Emilian provinces. It's like saying Eliot and Montale. Both great poets and in a way similar, both having the same theme, basically: the end of Western society. But Eliot looks at this end from a much vaster background than Montale does. Naturally I am talking about content. Their poetry, on the other hand, cannot be compared.

But how was your cosmopolitan attitude judged?

Many thought I was too social. In fact, I remember a caricature that appeared, drawn by Bartoli, with the future of various writers. I was portrayed as an old playboy in full evening dress. It was a petty bourgeois ambiance that imagined the world in its own likeness.

What did you talk about?

We didn't talk about anything. That's the funny thing. Even today writers never talk about anything.

During those years did you see Malaparte often?

Yes, of course.

But he didn't mix with the Giubbe Rosse and Forte café group?

Obviously he did. But he preferred people with power. He could meet a general, say, and walk up and down with him on a railroad station platform with his arm around the general's waist. He knew everybody, bankers, generals, heads of industry, Fascists, anti-Fascists. He called everybody *tu*. He possessed a phenomenal social nonchalance.

He was older than you?

By ten years. There was an abyss between me, who hadn't been in the first war, and those of the preceding generation, who had. An abyss, because I belonged to the modern world and they belonged still to the nineteenth century.

He belonged to the generation of Céline?

Yes, the same generation, or rather Malaparte was just a bit younger, because he had been a volunteer in the Argonne when he was only sixteen. But Céline if anything resembled more Eliot than Malaparte. His work reflects the crisis of the French Empire as Eliot's the crisis of the British Empire. Céline with fury and Eliot with funereal elegiac spirit. Malaparte, on the other hand, was truly a Fascist, because at heart he was an optimist like all Fascists, who believed they had made a revolution and didn't realize that instead they were continuing the nationalist tendency of the Risorgimento. Malaparte had been educated, true, at the Cicognini, a famous boarding school in Prato, like D'Annunzio. But he was also a provincial; naively, he said to me once, "When I enter a grand hotel, my heart leaps with joy." I remember that at Forte dei Marmi, in the thirties, I was Malaparte's guest at Villa Hildebrand. Malaparte was there under house arrest because of a political *querelle* with Italo Balbo. The arrest was a joke, when you compare it with the confinement of the Rossellis and other anti-Fascists. Malaparte saw his friends, his women, strolled along the beach in a bathing suit, holding his Lipari greyhound on a leash. That arrest lasted three years, from 1934, when we went to Paris together, until 1937. In the summer of 1937 I was living in Malaparte's house. One day I went out on the promenade and saw he was expecting someone. I asked him, "What are you doing?" "I'm waiting for somebody," he said to me. "Who are you waiting for?" "The richest woman in Italy." At that moment a Fiat arrived driven by Virginia Agnelli.

During those years you also saw something of the Pecci Blunt family?

Yes, I spent a whole summer at their villa, Marlia.

What year?

In 1934. There were many Roman nobles. There were also some French fascists.

French?

French fascist intellectuals. There was a well-known Catholic professor who was also a shameless fawner. In the vestibule of Marlia, a splendid villa in Empire style, he would sometimes leave his diary open on the table, having written in it "Prié pour Mimi." Mimi was our hostess. Mimi Pecci had married a very rich American who had been made a papal count. Mimi, for that matter, was the niece of Pope Pecci, Leo XIII.

What did the Forte dei Marmi intellectuals think of Malaparte?

They felt a suspicious liking for him. They considered him a brilliant journalist, something of a man of letters, between Papini and D'Annunzio, but not a true writer.

In 1935 you finished Le ambizioni sbagliate. *Why did you decide to give it to Mondadori?*

Because I had a contract dating back to the time of *Gli indifferenti.*

Whom did you deal with at Mondadori?

The director at that time, Rusca. Who didn't like the new Italian fiction. Still he duly published the novel, which came out in fact in the spring of 1935. Between 1929, the year of the publication of *Gli indifferenti,* and 1935 I had become openly anti-Fascist. Everybody knew it, and especially the Minculpop (the Ministry of Popular Culture) knew it. So at the moment I received the galleys, I learned that the book had been blocked by the censor. I went to see the censor, who was a vice-prefect by the name of Stroppolatini. Our dialogue went more or less like this. He said, "Your book contains some risqué parts." I replied, "Look" — I called him by the Fascist *voi* — it is an absolutely chaste book." "And besides, it's written in Manzonian style." "What does that have to do with censorship?" "Finally, it is said that you are a bit gray" (he meant to say not a proper Fascist, not completely black). I asked, "Is my book going to come out or not? I could be a new Dostoyevsky!" "How do I know you're Dostoyevsky?"

In addition to the publication of Le ambizioni sbagliate, *what else happened in the years just before 1935?*

I had two love affairs, both with foreign women, one Dutch and the other Swiss. The Dutch woman was the wife of a friend of mine. I'll tell the story of my relationship with her because it failed in a meaningful way, because of a conflict between love and friendship in which friendship won out. One evening I was having supper with that friend of mine; for a long time I had felt a strong attraction for his wife. At a certain moment he left the room, and then, acting on an irresistible impulse, I kissed her. Now, the problem I set myself the next day was not a matter of morality but of pride: if I become the lover of the wife of my friend, later I can only feel inferior to him. You might say that I set myself this problem because I wasn't in love. That's not true. At least, I believed I was. But a criterion of "relationship" prevailed: I didn't feel like altering my relationship as a friend for a lover's relationship. So I decided to tell the whole thing to my friend, and I did. He didn't consider it very important and in any case he wasn't grateful to me. As for his wife, since she was an intelligent and sensitive person, she continued to be my friend, but a little later she took a lover. I was hurt by this predictable conclusion; I would have liked her to remain faithful to her husband; after all, I had sacrificed my love to that fidelity. I remember that finally I came to think it futile to mix matters of morality with matters of love. On this subject there are some verses by Baudelaire in his poem "Femmes damnées":

> Maudit soit à jamais le rêveur inutile
> qui voulut le premier dans sa stupidité,
> s'éprenant d'un problème insoluble et stérile
> aux choses de l'amour mêler l'honnêté.

Every now and then I ran into that friend's wife, always beautiful and desirable, and I thought of Baudelaire's quatrain.

What happened with the Swiss woman?

She was a young and pretty painter by the name of Lelò. She was rather gifted, she belonged to a good family from Lausanne, and besides her passion for painting she had a passion, frequent among the Swiss, for outdoor life and nature. She had come to Rome after spending a year in London. She was accompanied by a young man named Paul, a native of Mauritius. They had been lovers and I had taken Paul's place; nevertheless, he and I were friends, and we went everywhere together, Paul, Lelò, and I. Paul's story foreshadowed, in 1933, certain elements of the student protest of 1968. He had a fellowship in London, he spent all the money with Lelò, then he committed a minimal but symbolic transgression: he broke a telephone and pocketed the coins. In other words, as the saying goes, he burned his bridges behind him. Madly in love with Lelò and convinced that he could never go home again to Mauritius, he roamed around with a pistol in his pocket and kept saying he was going to kill himself. He and Lelò lived in an attic at the top of an ancient building in Via di Panico, behind Piazza Navona. I had the key to the attic; one day

I went there. I found the pistol in a drawer. I extracted the clip and threw it out of the window onto the roof tiles of the building. A week later Lelò told me that Paul wanted her to go with him to Positano, where he was planning to spend the winter. I told her to go ahead, and so they set off for Naples. Once they were on the little boat for Positano, Paul checked the pistol and realized it was unloaded, and said at once, "Moravia did this." But he didn't reveal, nor had I noticed, that there was a bullet in the barrel. Lelò came back to Rome. One gloomy winter day, Paul set off from Positano for Naples on foot in the driving rain. In Naples he took a room in a little hotel and there, at night, he committed suicide, shooting himself in the temple with the single bullet that had remained in the pistol. The motive of the suicide, or at least the exterior motive, so to speak, was his double existential failure, as Lelò's lover and as English student. But I believe in graphology, and I took a letter of Paul's, written three years before his death, to a good graphologist, who read it and said to me at once that the writer of the letter would kill himself. Lelò and I were greatly affected by this suicide. I actually developed insomnia and for a year was unable to sleep, inexplicably, because after all Paul had been nothing to me. I spent the winter with Lelò. Then she discovered she was pregnant and we agreed on an abortion.

Why?

Because she didn't want to have a child and neither did I. Perhaps we didn't love each other enough to marry. In any case we were very young; I was twenty-five and she was twenty-four or twenty-three. For that matter, after the affairs with France and Silvia, I was no longer so anxious to get married. Finally there was my economic situation: I was virtually penniless. If I left my family's house I would have no money, and I had no job. So we went to Switzerland, from one place to another: Lugano, Davos, Geneva. We met with refusal everywhere. Until, outside Geneva, we found a *sage-femme* who performed Lelò's abortion. But our love, if it had ever existed, was over. So I left for America, and she for Tahiti with a man I myself had introduced to her. Lelò worshiped the myth of Gauguin and of life in the heart of nature. They stayed in Tahiti two years. They lived in a hut and their only companions were some fishermen of the island. Tahiti was not good for Lelò, and when she came back she had greatly changed from the girl she had been. She was worn, aged, both because of the Tahiti climate and because of her drinking. Though we no longer loved each other, we made love a last time, but it was a disappointment; not even the accord of our bodies existed anymore. Oddly, she reproached me for Paul's death, which in reality was due neither to her hardness nor to my presence, but only to himself and his morbid attraction to death.

At about that time *Le ambizioni sbagliate* came out, and a circular from the ministry forbade the newspapers to talk about it. Furthermore, Mussolini invaded Ethiopia and all of Italy was seized by a belated provincial colonialism. Then, in despair, I left on the *Rex* for the United States, where I had been invited by Giuseppe Prezzolini, director of the Casa Italiana at Columbia University. I set off after sanctions were imposed on Italy by the League of Nations. I traveled in tourist class in a cabin for four that, in the absence of travelers, I had all to myself. In the dining room I shared a table with an old Sicilian peasant woman, terrified by the voyage, and the two nieces of a priest in the province of Salerno. To suggest the atmosphere of cultural and social inferiority that reigned in tourist class, I will recall that, having said I knew someone at the Waldorf Astoria in New York, one of the girls interjected seriously, "You could only know a bellboy." Two further mortifying features: on landing I was asked if in my suitcases I had any salami, apparently banned in the United States; then, like everyone else for that matter, I was made to sign a declaration and be fingerprinted.

4

ALAIN ELKANN: *What effect did arriving in New York have on you?*

ALBERTO MORAVIA: The effect of being an unexpected person, because Prezzolini took great care not to come and meet me. All the same, I was awestruck by the sublime skyscrapers of New York. Ships docked in an area just below Wall Street. It was early morning; the sun was rising behind the skyscraper towers, and in the deserted avenues you could see clouds of steam coming out of the manholes. Everything seemed to me strange, grandiose, and beautiful. Then I took a taxi, gave the address, Amsterdam Avenue, and crossed New York. I arrived at the Casa Italiana of Columbia University and found only a janitor, who showed me my room, a bare little room with metal furniture. I looked outside and saw an ordinary street. I was hungry, I didn't know what to do, I went downstairs. I said, "Something will happen." I was completely ignorant of how things work in America. I saw a drugstore with books displayed in the window beside the menu of the day. I went it and ordered two eggs and bacon. Then I went back to the Casa Italiana, opened my suitcase, and put my things away. I had brought two changes of clothing: a brown tweed jacket with gray trousers, and a blue serge suit. I started smoking, while I waited for Prezzolini, who finally arrived and greeted me coldly.

You already knew him?
No, I didn't know him.

What was he like?
Prezzolini was Tuscan, tall, thin, spare, with an ancient Tuscan's face. Haughty by nature but then mortified by life, he represented a mixture of intellectual stiffness and existential humiliation. He was one of the most austere men I have ever known. His idea of himself was this, "I am the last heir of a magnificent race, the Tuscans. After me there will be nothing but bastards." Coldly cordial, seriously austere, practically a Quaker.

He intimidated you?
I wasn't the least intimidated. If anything, I regarded him with curiosity. Actually, Prezzolini suffered at having become a Fascist — because he *was* a Fascist. Practically, he said this, "Fascism is what it is, but it's the best thing possible for Italy." He lived in a small apartment with nothing attractive about it. I had one room; he had three because he lived with his wife: that was the only difference. Prezzolini introduced me to some professors and then dropped me, literally, going on with his life as if I didn't exist. I used to go and eat at John Jay Hall, the Columbia University refectory, which had only two or three specialties: chicken à la king, curried chicken, and hamburgers. In fact, when I returned from America I was anemic; I hadn't been eating enough. Furthermore, I wasn't used to that frightful cold; the winter was arctic. When I went to catch the bus at Riverside Drive my knees froze, and I would curse America. I went to Macy's; I bought a leather jacket, Indian mocassins, and wide-wale corduroy trousers: a hippie getup, way ahead of its time. At the Casa Italiana I was considerably inconvenienced because I didn't have a telephone

in my room. I wasn't an early riser then, as I am now. I got up around nine. Once somebody telephoned me at eight. I slipped on a robe and went downstairs in the elevator. Prezzolini got in, "What do you think you're doing?" "I'm going downstairs to answer the telephone." "Go back to your room at once!" That was Prezzolini. I went upstairs and didn't answer the phone.

As for social life, it was the exact opposite of England. In London I had behind me the great success of *Gli indifferenti* and I knew how to make use of Berenson's letters of introduction in the social world. In New York, on the contrary, I had behind me the failure of *Le ambizioni sbagliate* and my relationship with Lelò, as well as the Ethiopian war; I was depressed and in doubt, and I decided not to use the forty-four letters that, once again, Berenson had written for me. I had lost all self-confidence. I wanted to reflect on my life, my writing, and moreover I realized that life in America was too far beyond my means. I sent only one letter, to sound out the situation, and I was immediately invited to a very formal supper in a house on the East River. A rich, elegant young couple lived there. The invitation comprised supper and then for each guest a ticket to a performance of Ibsen's *Ghosts*. The dinner proceeded normally; at a certain point the hostess asked me, "Do you believe in God?" I replied, "No, not at all." She asked why not. Caught unprepared, I replied, "It's a word, not a real fact." She said, "If the name exists, then so does the thing." I replied, "That's not true! For example, the name of the unicorn exists, but the unicorn doesn't exist." Afterward, there were the usual ceremonies: the women left the room, the men remained seated, to smoke and drink in the English fashion. Finally, we joined the women; we all had our tickets for the theater; we left the house and went to see *Ghosts*. Afterward we went to a nightclub and stayed up until three. One way or another, I spent a hundred dollars, which was too much for me. Many years later, in Rome, the phone rang and it was a woman's voice. She said, "Is this Moravia?" I said, yes. "I would like to see you." "Come over. Who are you?" "Mrs. such-and-such. You remember, in New York?" When she arrived, I recognized the hostess of that dinner.

She said to me, "After your explanation of God, I left my husband, I took a lover, and now I'm happy."

But, to get back to America, I started meeting ordinary people, in bars. I would stand there and drink something and talk. Now and then I went to a brothel. But only a few times and always to the same woman, who had a bit of a crush on me.

What was the brothel like?

An ordinary apartment. You had to say "Henry sent me." Then they admitted you to a living room, and a little later two or three women came in, completely normal and absolutely respectable looking. You chose one, and the normality continued also in the bedroom and even in the lovemaking. Another memory: Prezzolini, irritated by my frequent lateness, since I didn't own a watch, gave me a dollar watch, a very nice steel timepiece: it was the first watch of my life. Another thing: at the Casa Italiana I saw something of a professor of Greek, who was a racist and anti-Semite. He was Tuscan, like Prezzolini: a first-rate Greek scholar. He subscribed to the ideas of Hitler.

Didn't this bother you?

I wanted to see what he would say. You have to understand one thing: the basic quality of the novelist is schizophrenia. The ability to put yourself in another's place and erase yourself. So I listened to the Nazi professor expounding the ideas of Gobineau about the Aryan race. The odd thing is that he knew perfectly well that I was half Jewish. It was a situation typical of those years: you could be friends with people who could then become your enemies, even your betrayers, even your murderers. In fact, when I returned to Italy and happened to run into the racist professor at Forte dei Marmi, he pretended not to recognize me. After the war, I said to Prezzolini that the professor was a scoundrel. Prezzolini snickered, tried to excuse him by saying that everyone is entitled to his own ideas. I replied that ideas had nothing to do with this: if he was my friend in New York, he should have been my friend also in Italy.

Did Prezzolini ask you to do anything at the Casa Italiana?

Yes, he had me give three lectures: one at Columbia, one at Smith College, and one at Vassar. All three times I talked about the Italian novel: Manzoni, Nievo, Verga, Fogazzaro, and D'Annunzio. I remember it was very difficult for me to procure the books. I found some odd, dog-eared volumes at Brentano's; Prezzolini lent me the others.

How did these lectures go?

At Columbia there were only students, of both sexes; at Smith and Vassar there were only girls. At Vassar I actually flirted a bit with a rich heiress. Her boyfriend was ill, and she asked me to be her escort to the prom. I bought her the ritual corsage, orchids. I filed past the professors with her on my arm; I was in the photograph that was then published on the society page of the New York Times. With this girl I then spent a weekend at the country house of her family, then I never saw her again. By the way, I also spoke about Italian literature in a downtown Italian-American social hall. I remember one man shouting, "Traitor! Why don't you mention Marinetti and the Futurists?" I replied that I was talking about the novel and the Futurists hadn't written any novels. The man shouted back, "What about Mafanka il futurista?"

Did New York seem to you very different from Europe?

I had my real shock in London, not in America.

But it did seem to you very different from Europe?

The skyscrapers were different, yes. It was different, of course, but less than England.

What about everyday life?

I was an individual who came from a country of peasants, with peasant customs, peasant culture, and there I found myself in an industrial civilization: this was the real, great difference. Furthermore, there was the difference in size. In Italy, despite Fascist magniloquence, everything seemed little to me; in America everything seemed big. That is why, before my trip, I dreamed of America! Achieving that experience had become a genuine obsession with me. More or less everybody had that same obsession in those days — Pavese and Vittorini, for example — but I'm the only one who went to the United States. I owe to them the discovery of the Third World, which was later to become so important in my life.

Why?

At a certain point during my New York stay I became fed up. It was always so cold, a polar cold. And then I decided to go to Mexico. Instead of consulting a travel agency, I did something nobody does: I packed my suitcase, took a taxi, and went straight to Pennsylvania Station. I reached the window and said, "I'd like a ticket for Mexico City." The clerk looked at me, wide-eyed, and asked, "Why don't you go to an agency?" "Because I don't have time!" Unhappy, he gave me a ticket one meter long, with all the coupons for the intermediary stations. I paid and set off. The journey, if I recall correctly, lasted five or six days. I crossed half the United States, from north to south.

What was the route?

We went, I think, via Saint Louis. When the train stopped in a station, I would get out, walk up and down, buy cigarettes, chewing gum. Most of all, I wanted warmth. At a certain point I woke up; the train had stopped at the Mexican border station, Laredo. It was hot, with a dusty, sultry sun, and I saw a boy with a huge hat, a straw sombrero, energetically playing the guitar and singing a song in Spanish. I thought, "The south at last!" and I felt a thrill of joy. And at that moment I realized another thing: previously I had been in Germany, England, and France. All northern, civilized countries. I realized that what I liked, on the contrary, was the Third World. Ever since then what I have always most enjoyed is heading south. Because I was a man accustomed to the industrial civilization and the Third World fascinated me and allowed me better to understand who I was and where I came from.

Why?

Because, comparing my culture with the culture of the Third World, I realized more and more that I was first of all a European, a Westerner. And this allowed me to know better my limitations and my deficiencies, which were, in fact, those of the Western civilization with which, ever since, I have often been in conflict.

In going to Mexico were you perhaps hoping to meet Trotsky?

No, I didn't want to meet anyone. If anything, my model was Lawrence. I had read *Mornings in Mexico* and *The Plumed Serpent*.

Mexico then was a literary idea?

It was an avowed escape from the United States. Literature had an importance in my life only when I wanted to be a Dostoyevsky character. Mexico did then partly inspire *La mascherata*, but that was after the fact. Then and there, I went to Mexico because of a question of metropolitan life: New York was too cold.

What impression did Mexico City have on you? Today it's one of the biggest cities in the world. What was it like then?

Then it was a city of five hundred thousand inhabitants. I remember that I telephoned the embassy, introducing myself as the correspondent of the *Gazzetta del popolo* of Turin. I was very politely received by the ambassador, who, among other things, said to me, "Never take a taxi when there are two men seated in front; they'll do you in." Mexico had emerged from a frightful civil war in 1920. In Mexico City I had an attack of that disease that in English is called "homesickness."

You felt unhappy?

Yes, but not so much because I missed Italy. My suffering was caused more by my incapacity to appreciate the country where I was. An invincible repulsion, a violent desire to leave. I have had this illness twice: once in Mexico City and once in Washington. In

Mexico this is what happened: I couldn't stand on my feet and I was horrified by the country and its inhabitants. I went to an American doctor, who said, "You have homesickness. Take these medicines." I bought the medicines, but I didn't take them. It was a whole pile of jars, and just looking at them, I got over the homesickness. In Washington, which I visited many years later, homesickness assumed a more characteristic form: I looked out the window of my hotel and began to cry, just like that, for no reason. Then I looked at myself in the mirror. I had a yellow stripe across my chest: it was an attack of jaundice. I wept hot tears, and inside myself I couldn't understand why I was crying; I considered myself ridiculous.

While you were in Mexico didn't you say to yourself, "Now I must go back to New York"?

No. In fact, in the end, I adjusted and even enjoyed myself. I followed a party of American girls to Taxco. They had rented a villa; I stayed in the hotel. I saw them every day, we went for walks, we took part in a fiesta, with the peasants who slept in the church, fireworks, and the *toro de fuego*. Then, suddenly, they all fell ill with dysentery, they left, and I was alone. All told, I was in Mexico a month and a half. But I could have stayed on; I had in a way become a vagabond.

Didn't you have a commitment to the Casa Italiana?

Yes, but I was only a guest; I was my own master. One day, in Taxco, I read in the paper, "LOS ALEMANOS ENTRARON EN RENANIA" I thought, "This is it. The war will break out." I hastened my departure: I was anti-Fascist, I concerned myself to some extent with politics, I sympathized with the Communists. I went back to Mexico City, packed, caught the train. On the train I found myself in a compartment with a middle-aged German woman who looked like Göring in skirts. You remember Göring? The woman was tall and buxom, with a face like Göring's, only haggard, and a big hat shading enormous eyes ringed with bister. She must have been fifty, perhaps even older. She began by asking me, "What do you do? Where do you come from?" "I'm traveling." "What for?" "Pleasure." "What country are you from?"

I said, "Guess!" Then she began to say: England, France, Spain . . . she couldn't guess. I said, "I'm Italian." "Ah! I should have guessed!" This German woman owned a ranch in Mexico and was going to New York. We began to chat, then slowly we walked through the train to the last car where, as in the Chaplin film, there was a little balcony. The train swayed through a barren, dusty landscape, thick with cactus, and we made love, standing up, amid the jolts of the train. As I said, she was well into middle age. I embraced her, and I would feel her flaccid, sagging flesh shifting oddly on her skeleton. But I liked her, and her visible emotion flattered me. We went to New York. I telephoned her, I don't know why, I had never had any dealings with a woman that age, and I invited her out to a restaurant. She was very pleased because for a long time nobody had invited her like this. I danced with her, she had difficulty breathing, once again she was overcome with emotion. We made love a second time. Again I had the impression that her flesh was made of rags and these rags wound around her skeleton. I was twenty-seven, she must have been sixty. I stayed in New York a few more days and then I left. On the ship I found a great bouquet of flowers, which she had sent. This was the end of my journey in America. Prezzolini, as always ascetic and hostile to any sentimentality, didn't accompany me to the pier; he confined himself to saying, "We'll see each other in Italy." During the voyage I thought about the adventure with the German woman and once again I realized that love was something very, very strange.

Strange, in what sense?
It's omnivorous.

What do you remember of your arrival in Italy?
A great joy at the first appearance of the Bay of Naples. Then, unfortunately, the same old Italy of those days.

Aside from your illness and writing, you lived rather the life of a playboy then.

No, I felt and was, if anything, an outsider. Just as I am now, for that matter. The very same.

Have you never had a sense of uneasiness about being an outsider like this?

No, absolutely not. In reality, I was and am a man of letters: my homeland was and is literature. I traveled with my head enfolded in a cloud of literature. I lived the adventures of the modern world and at the same time I read the classics. I have done this also recently: I traveled up the Zaire River and was reading Henry James and Fitzgerald.

And your contemporaries? Didn't Vittorini and Pavese travel?

No, they never traveled. They experienced not travels but the myths of travel, the myth of America, for example. I didn't want to have any myths. That's why I went to America.

Italian culture is usually made up of professors, people who are very cultivated but also bourgeois. You represent a very special case, particularly in that phase of your life.

Of course.

But did you then adjust? Did you become like the others?

No, I didn't adjust. My life has constantly been a series of adventures. Even what happened to me with Fascism was, basically, an adventure: among the many writers I'm the only one who lived in the mountains with my wife, in a hut, between refugees and Germans. While I was living up there, I was watching myself live, as in Mexico.

In any case, before then you lived like a slightly degenerate English aristocrat, outside the family, an artist.

Yes, in a way my model in life was Lawrence, who traveled always and wrote in the most disparate places. But you have to remember that in those years I was very restless because I couldn't bear Fascism and therefore couldn't bear staying in Italy. For this reason, too, when I returned from America, I left again almost at once for China.

During this period did you have friends?

Yes, I've always had many friends. First Caffi, then Carlo Levi, then Pannunzio. Pannunzio was a young man from Lucca, half Abruzzese and half Tuscan, who concerned himself with literature. He didn't like to write; he was a very lazy man. He preferred founding literary reviews and editing them. He began with *Caratteri*, then *Oggi*, and then *Il mondo*. I forgot to tell you that before leaving for the United States I stopped over in Naples one day. I went into a palazzo filled with books, with shadowy passages and corridors. In the midst of a great pile of books I found Senator Croce, who said to me, "Oriani also wrote a novel of a man who wants and doesn't want and stops wanting, like *Gli indifferenti*. Oriani was a great writer." But he didn't talk about my work at all. I consider Oriani nothing, absolutely. The Fascists had resuscitated him.

What was Benedetto Croce like?

Very likable, very Neapolitan in the best sense of the word, that is, both human and philosophical. In short, a grand bourgeois of the south, with a vast European culture. They said of him that he was a bomb loaded with common sense, and perhaps he was. In any case, at that time there was a Benedetto Croce cult, especially in the world of Pannunzio and *Il mondo*. In my opinion, his best books are the ones on Naples. And there is also a beautiful book entitled *The Baroque Era in Italy*. Very beautiful, very amusing. His books on Italy and on Europe before Fascism are simply contradictory: if everything was going so well, why did Fascism and Communism come then? Everything was going magnificently, Europe and Italy were a paradise of freedom and culture, and all of a sudden all those catastrophes. Why?

What happened during your voyage back from America?

Something very important for me happened. One day I went to see a movie in the theater on the *Rex*. While I was watching the movie, I felt a woman's hand stroking my arm. The film ended, the woman took me by the hand and led me to her cabin, and we made love immediately.

Who was she?

Helen. An English girl, daughter of a lord, blonde with huge blue eyes, a wide red mouth. She died last year in California. Her father was a country gentleman, a passionate hunter and horseman, very ignorant, but sensible. At twenty, she knew nothing at all. She married a chemist or something of the sort who for two years, instead of making love, every evening before going to bed made her act out always the same sequence: a lily in her hand, a long cotton nightgown down to her ankles, then sleep. Finally her father, noticing that his daughter seemed a bit strange, questioned her and discovered she was still a virgin. She then made up for lost time with many lovers. I used the scene of the lily and the nightgown in my play *L'angelo dell'informazione*. When we arrived in Italy, we arranged to meet in Positano. I remember it was the beginning of summer. First I stopped in Rome, where I went to the doctor; he examined me and told me I was absolutely anemic and prescribed a cure. Then to recover my health I went to Positano.

Did your parents, your sisters, ask you a lot of questions about your stay in America?

Yes, but as usual I spoke very little. I couldn't tell my family about my travel experiences because they were a part of my private life, and I lived that life outside the family.

5

*A*LAIN ELKANN: *What about Fascism?*

ALBERTO MORAVIA: Fascism continued undaunted. In Germany Nazism was born. I'd like to make a parenthesis here. I remember a trip I made in 1932. I left with the idea of going to Poland. On the train I met a famous Florentine snob, related to all the noble families of Florence. He asked me, "Where are you going?" I said, "To Poland." He answered, "But there's nobody in Poland." He was a real snob! He said, "Come with me to Czechoslovakia, to meet the Prince and Princess Thurn und Taxis. I turned around and we went to see the Thurn und Taxises. The princess was very old; it was said she had made love with D'Annunzio. Anyway she had a book of D'Annunzio's with this inscription, "To the most beautiful princess of the blue Danube, D'Annunzio." The castle was magnificent, filled with stuffed African animals shot by the prince, also elderly, a great hunter and dowser. I also visited Prague, the old city on the hill, the square where Jan Hus was burned. I remember the Jewish cemetery: it made a deep impression on, me, very beautiful, overgrown, full of black, twisted trees. And then I went to Kammersee, near Salzburg. There was a castle there that belonged to the family of the composer Mendelssohn-Bartholdy. There was a group of English friends, writers, actors, politicians in an atmosphere that today we call prewar: civil, a bit decadent, refined. As for me, I stayed in a pensione in the neighboring village. Every morning, on the jetty at the lake, there were swastikas. The whole town was full of swastikas. You see, these swastikas were the true discovery of that journey.

What effect did those swastikas have on you?

They had the effect of telling me Nazism was coming.

Yes, but what did you think about it?

It didn't concern me much. I thought mostly of literature. Naturally I couldn't remain ignorant of what was happening in Europe. But you have to bear in mind one thing: Nazism had no precedents; literature did. It was impossible, in other words, to foresee the catastrophe that was approaching.

You had already met some leading Fascists then?

Yes, Galeazzo Ciano, when he was minister of the Minculpop.

What sort of person was Ciano?

He was plump, medium height. Pompous and courteous. He imitated Mussolini a bit, with his jutting jaw. But unlike his father-in-law, he had nothing proletarian about him; he was a bourgeois from a Livorno family, transplanted to the smart Parioli district. He had, however, one Tuscan quality: a singular, unfeigned realism, which came close to cynicism. It is quite evident in his diaries.

Let's get back to the English lady you had met on the ship and were to meet again in Positano.

I could think about nothing else. So I went to Positano, which then was a deserted beach with a village where they didn't even have electricity. The only other foreigners were a Prussian lady who had escaped from Germany because her daughters were half Jewish. She wasn't Jewish, but her husband was. Nobody else. I took long walks with my English friend in the mountains behind Positano. She collected plants, flowers, and explained to me what they were; she knew even the Latin names. She was a passionate botanist. I perhaps wasn't truly in love with her, but in a way, I had fallen into a trap between sensuality and the novelty of a psychology that was unfamiliar to me.

And you continued not writing?

No, I wrote. I wrote some stories that then came out in 1937, with the title *L'imbroglio*. In Positano I wrote "La tempesta," "L'architetto," "La provinciale." My English friend meanwhile hunted for little bits of coral among the rocks on the totally deserted beach. If you go to Positano now, crowded as it always is, you are amazed and can't believe that the place was then so genuine, so untouristic. That is why I said I was happy to come back to Italy, because Italy at the time of Fascism was incredibly beautiful. Italy then was still as it had been in the nineteenth century. Poverty had saved it in the same way that wealth is now destroying it.

Was your friend your age or older than you?

She was thirty-six. I was twenty-seven. At a certain point, God knows why, I became jealous. Perhaps because she would leave me alone when I was writing and would go off with a group of Germans. I made some scenes. Then she said to me, "It's not possible for us to stay together anymore; you're too jealous. It's best for us to break up." She was right. I no longer knew what I was doing. As I said, I wasn't in love but all the same I had lost my head. In short, she went off, and for a few days I was desperate in a way I'd never been before. Maybe only France had caused such an upheaval in my life. I tried to understand, however, why all this had happened. I remember that I went to talk with the old German woman, but she could only give me advice dictated by common sense, and instead I wanted Helen, who was no longer there and whose absence

I found intolerable. At a certain moment I went off to Capri. I rented a room, I started leading the usual Capri life. And all of a sudden my English friend announced her arrival. I wrote a story about that one day I spent with her. It's called "L'amante infelice," and apart from another story, called "La casa è sacra," it's the only story of mine in which I narrate something exactly as it happened, neither more nor less. A story that, you could say, was found ready-made in everyday life. You just have to transcribe it.

Normally you don't transcribe from everyday life?

No. I invent, as I've said before, characters and situations, setting out from a generic personal experience.

What happened that day on Capri?

We spent a magnificent day. We went out in a boat to swim at the Grotta Verde. Then we ate at the Piccola Marina: a perfect day. We took a carriage and went up to my room. She fell asleep. But I tried to make love, and then an inexplicable and absurd drama exploded, something that makes me feel ashamed still. She rejected me crossly, and — as if seized by a temporary homicidal insanity — I grabbed her by the neck and tried to strangle her. She began to cough, I let go at once, and she ran out of the room, reached the pharmacy, and there she fainted. Then she went to spend the night at the house of a woman friend of mine I had introduced to her, a young and very ingenuous woman. Undressing at the mirror, the English woman told what I had done to her. Overcome with fear, my friend wet herself. These are comic details, but in their contrast they serve to give depth to a reality that wasn't the least bit comic. The next day I sent her a great bouquet of flowers, but at that point I had tried to kill her and it was really over. In 1955 I went to Washington and read aloud some passages from *Agostino*, you know, those readings they give in America. I heard a voice, her voice, saying, "Do you recognize me?" "Yes," I said, "naturally." It was her. A number of years had gone by. I was unspeakably moved. Tears came to my eyes. Then I saw her again, that same year, in San Francisco, where she lived. We had supper together, then I never saw her again. Last year when I went to Positano, the daughter of the Prussian lady told me she was dead.

When did you go to China?

In Rome I was bored, the Englishwoman had vanished from my life, I had stopped writing stories, and so I decided to set off for China. I want to Amicucci, the editor of the *Gazzetta del popolo*, and I said to him, "I want to go to China." "What are you going to China for?" "It interests me. And anyway I want to travel." "If you like, I can give you a ticket, and then I'll pay you for your articles."

Then you left for China?

I made some preparations. Practically speaking, I had two white dinner jackets made and I bought a pair of evening shoes. I knew very little about China; what mattered most to me was to leave, to get away. Then when I was in China, I bought many English and French books about the country.

What about your parents?

By then my parents had realized that they had a son who was never going to stay home! As I told you, my mother always encouraged me to travel and to broaden my experience because she was ambitious for me. Then I booked passage on the *Conte Rosso*, first class. The *Conte Rosso* is one of the most beautiful ships I've ever seen in my life: there were twin liners, the *Conte Rosso* and the *Conte Verde*, that plied between Trieste and Shanghai. They were ships built in England, without paintings of Italian landscapes, without Renaissance decorations like the other Italian ocean liners. Everything was functional, metallic, mechanical, with pipes everywhere, painted and polished, even in the dining room. The ship was a genuine industrial object, in short, it was complete, perfect. On the ship there was a Prince Sanseverino, owner of a work by Michelangelo. He said he would have sold it gladly to buy himself a private plane. I asked, "Why are you going to China?" "We're going to Shanghai. There are wonderful nightclubs there!" I remember also a Teodoli. He resembled the king of Italy, an accurate copy. When we arrived at Port Said, he declared to me, "Young man, whoever holds Port Said holds the key to the Mediterranean."

Did they know you were a writer?

Perhaps, but they couldn't have cared less.

Had you read Maugham?

No, I had read Conrad.

Maugham made voyages of that kind on ocean liners and wrote about them in his books.

I traveled to escape from Italy.

Did you like Port Said?

It was still oriental. There was a souk that seemed fabled to me. It was the first time I had seen a souk. Then we went into the Sinai; I made an excursion on camelback. Finally we set off again for Aden.

Did you meet Freya Stark?

No, I met her only a few years ago, in Asolo.

What was Aden like?

I've seen Aden many times since then, most recently under a totalitarian communist regime, with a Soviet military base. In the old days it was a British colony: a colonial city built inside the crater of a spent volcano. I bought a pith helmet, English, from the famous shop of Simon Arzt. The English went around wearing khaki shorts and shirt, a crop under their arm, and boots. On board ship, among the other travelers, there was a young and fairly handsome Swiss, very rich, who had a mania about brothels. Every time we got off the ship, he rushed to the red light district. I followed him out of curiosity. For example, in Bombay we visited the Kamatipura quarter. There were wooden cages with wooden bars, and inside some women were shut up like animals at the zoo. Prostitutes. The customer entered the cage, at the back there was a curtain they could draw, and they made love behind the curtain. That time, in Bombay, the Swiss and I hired a car, drove out of the city, among the plantations. We arrived at a great bungalow, very beautiful. We went inside; there was a big salon, mirrored and deserted, not a soul about. Then, peering more closely, we could see what looked like a number of bundles on the floor. At a certain point, on a V-shaped staircase a European woman appeared, blond, wearing a cloak of red silk, with a collar of white monkey fur, and high heels à la Louis XV: a truly fantastic apparition in that place! She clapped her hands and the bundles stood up: they were the prostitutes and the blond woman was the madam, a Parisienne. My Swiss chose a beautiful prostitute and went off with her. I looked for the one who least appealed to me, so I was sure I wouldn't have the slightest temptation: I found a girl from Goa, at least thirty centimeters taller than I, with enormous breasts, hard as bronze, and pubic hair as stiff as iron filings: she was all metallic, black, shiny. A face like a primitive mask, with enormous rolling white eyes and a puffy mouth. I followed her. There was a burned, sickly garden, then a kind of circular exedra with many bedrooms, each room assigned to a prostitute. I made it clear at once to the Goan that I wasn't going to make love but would pay her all the same. I just waited for the Swiss in that melancholy Indian garden.

After Bombay we went to Ceylon, to Singapore, to Malaya, then to Manila. But my initiation to Asia and the Orient came, somewhat like the case of the protagonist of Conrad's *Youth*, on the day I arrived in Bombay, seeing the Indian crowd all dressed in white and smelling for the first time that odor, new for me, of dust, spices, and decay. Finally we arrived at Shanghai. All the Italians rushed to the nightclubs. That was why they had come. I stayed in Shanghai long enough to visit the city; there was nothing special to see, except the people, whom I would encounter anyway in other cities. I stayed in a hotel called the Katai, where there was the longest bar in the world: fifty meters. The bartender would take a glass and slide it to the customer, even at a distance of ten meters. Shanghai was a city invented by the

British: ugly, modern, muddy, an industrial city, but with that relentless Asiatic industrialism: every morning, I was told, in the streets they found dozens of bodies, people who had died of starvation.

But before reaching Shanghai we went by Canton, where I saw the China that today no longer exists: thousands of sampans, boats, in the Pearl River, and a part of the population living on them. Bustle, trafficking, music, and so on, with gangways to skip from one boat to the next. Today the river is empty, that amphibian population is gone. As for Hong Kong, it was in miniature what it is on a big scale today: a bunch of very white skyscrapers against a very green hill. While we were in Hong Kong, I asked my Italian traveling companions, "Are you going to Peking?" "Of course not!" they replied, "We're staying here, with the most beautiful nightclubs in the world, with Siberian taxi girls and mirrored floors." I left them to their entertainments and accepted an invitation to Suchow from the head of the local telephone company. Like all the rich Chinese, he lived inside a great compound, which comprised a number of pavilions all connected with one another by hermetic little courtyards. In each pavilion there was a member of the family. In China, at least at that time, the family was not composed, as ours are, of husband, wife, and children; but sisters-in-law, brothers-in-law, and other relatives were also part of it, and if a gentleman arrived, no telling from where, and says, "I am Mr. Li, and I am your relation," then they would put him up. So I went to eat at this man's house. We sat, just the two of us, on some chairs with marble seats. We were served forty-four dishes, which, after us, were passed around in the various pavilions of the house. I remember especially one dish that impressed me: a pyramid of cubes of ham, half red and half white, half lean meat, in other words, and half fat, arranged symmetrically, so that a red cube never touched another red cube, or a white cube another white one. At the end rice was served. But in China at that time if you ate the rice that they served at the end, it meant you hadn't been given sufficient food and you offended the host.

After lunch we went into a yard filled with peaches and walked for a long time among the trees, and my host finally gave me a flower. I roamed some more in this city that is called the Venice of China because of its many canals. I visited a famous pagoda. I was followed everywhere by boys who touched their nose and laughed; my nose impressed them because it was so big. The next day I went back to Shanghai and took the Shanghai Express for Peking, the same train Marlene Dietrich took in the famous film. I crossed all of China. On every side you could see hovels with many mounds around them: the graves of ancestors. Everything was always the same: a house with the rice paddy beside it, a water buffalo in the water, and then the graves, and all around, the vast plain, crisscrossed by invisible canals on which the sails of invisible boats glided by. I arrived in Peking. The train passed the Great Wall. The contrast impressed me as a metaphor of the Chinese world: the locomotive, symbol of industrialism, and the wall, symbol of the imperial past.

Did you meet anyone on the train?

No, nobody. In Peking I went straight to the Hôtel de Pekin, the best in the city, where I settled in. The Hôtel de Pekin is a very beautiful art nouveau hotel, which still exists, only now it has been enlarged with two wings in modern style. Once I was settled there, I began my Peking life. The city then was a wonder; now it's nothing! Then it was as it had been for centuries, a tangle of picturesque lanes, like the Venetian *calli*. Now it's as if in Rome only the Colosseum and Saint Peter's had remained, and nothing else. All the rest has been swept away, to make room for enormous desolate streets, flanked by semi-skyscrapers of the American kind. This is today's Beijing. They are crazy: they have destroyed the ancient face of the city. China was older than Italy: now it's all new. New and ugly. I remember how you wandered among walls all a pearl-gray color, a bit like the gray of Paris, and the roofs of the pavilions were visible above them, with glass tiles of splendid colors: these roofs had upturned tips, like hats with a brim pulled down over the eyes. They were mysterious, fascinating.

What were the people in the streets like?

They were the Chinese still partly traditional, with the clothes and manners of the past: vanished now. It's pointless to describe it. The Chinese have done that in countless drawings and statuettes over the centuries, all realistic and precise. When it comes to the picturesque, I remember in Shanghai for example a great warehouse store, with many big rooms bare and squalid, in some of which goods were sold; in others actors and acrobats performed. And in the corridors the prostitutes were lined up along the walls, side by side, each accompanied by her elderly procuress. The Chinese called prostitutes "salted meat." There was an inconceivable number of them, giving a sensation of corruption and poverty.

In Peking, too, was there much prostitution?

Less than in Shanghai. Peking was more Asiatic and had no industries. The appearance of Peking was unforgettable: the streets were unpaved, they were like the beds of dried-up streams. Sunk between two high banks and filled with refuse, flanked by sheds and telegraph poles. You could see big chow dogs, camels, Mongols with fur busbies: it was all like the days of Marco Polo. I went to a fair; everything was on sale. Amid music and shouting, there was a tooth puller who pulled the poor people's teeth and had a table on which, to encourage the customers, he kept an enormous cardboard tooth. To tell you the truth, in Peking I enjoyed myself very much: everything for me was new, strange, a fairy tale.

How long did you stay?

I stayed a month.

How did you get around? With rickshaws?

Yes. They were available, and I was a bit afraid because among the many diseases in Peking then there was also the plague. These rickshaw men, after helping me to climb in, covered my legs with their cloak of quilted cotton. Now, I knew quite well that the plague was spread by fleas. As soon as the men started running like horses, I would think, "Now a flea will jump on me from that cloak and I'll catch the plague." In any event I quickly adjusted to Peking life, which for me meant the life of the foreigners who lived in that city. For example, one day I was strolling below the city of the legations, because the legations were gathered all together in a special quarter surrounded by a wall that now no longer exists. There was a riding ring, to allow the foreigners to go riding. All of a sudden I heard someone calling, "Moravia! Moravia!" I turned and it was a beautiful English girl I had met in Cortona, at Morra's. She was in Peking with her father, who had a diplomatic post. This gives you an idea of how cosmopolitan that city was then. I remember also that I went to Jade Street, and in a bookshop I bought the complete poems of T. S. Eliot, which I then read as I walked in the gardens of the Winter Palace. At a certain moment I decided to visit the interior of the country. I wanted to reach Inner Mongolia. So I went to the Italian Embassy and asked, "Do you have a trustworthy person to act as courier?" "We have an electrician." So this electrician came with me; his name was Ma and he said he knew Italian.

Why did you want to go to Mongolia?

The myth of Genghis Khan, literary reasons. I went there after talking with Monsignor Zanini, who was the bishop in charge of the missionaries. He told me that the Chinese were by nature Christians. But in the outer office a capuchin popped up, skeptical about the faith of the Chinese. He said to me, "Don't believe Monsignor Zanini. Often the Chinese, for reasons of convenience, are capable of having three religions: for example, Islam, Buddhism, Taoism. And then there are the 'rice Christians,' who become Christians in order to receive rice."

Anyway, one fine morning I went to the station with Mr. Ma, my electrician-interpreter, to catch the Chahrar Express, which would take me into the region north of Peking, the Jehol, and then, perhaps, into Inner Mongolia. But I discovered that the great Chahrar Express was a string of freight cars, sealed like the ones that took the Jews to Poland. I was dressed as if for a stroll on Via Veneto, in a little blue topcoat, tweed jacket, flannel trousers. The cold was frightful! A biting wind was blowing, like a wave of razors. The so-called Western Hills were green as when the *bora* is blowing in Trieste and blue turns green. I got into one of the many freight cars. I sat down, the sides were closed, and in the darkness the journey began. There was a stove in the center of the car, with the pipe sticking through the roof. All around it, on a bench, the passengers were seated; they were either peasants or soldiers. The latter slept, leaning on their rifles, with the bayonets fixed. In the complete darkness, with the glowing coals rolling even between our feet, all of its cars swaying, this train stopped at every station. I would get out and try to walk, but a terrible cold would strike me, and I would get back into the car. At a certain moment I went back through the train to look for Ma, my electrician guide; I found him eating pumpkin seeds, engaged in an animated conversation with the other travelers. In reality he spoke no Italian and wanted to take the free trip perhaps to go and visit some relatives.

In any event, I eventually reached Kalgan, which now has some other name. I recently read a travel book about China with photographs of that same period and I discovered that Kalgan was considered a rare and unusual place, even justifying a little street plan with an itinerary indicated on it. This will give you an idea of the singularity of the place where I ended up. I arrived in Kalgan. I got off the train. Ma also got off. We climbed into two rickshaws, I with my suitcase, he with his. To make you understand what a city of the Chinese interior was, I'll tell you this one thing: the mud was half a meter deep. There were deep furrows made by the rickshaw wheels and so you had to be very careful not to stray from them. But the rickshaw man set off along a track with great gusto, missed the curve, and I ended in the mud with the suitcases. I stood up, totally mud-stained, and then we continued to the Hotel of the Three Qualities, as it was called. I went up to a shabby, dirty room, as always in China then, with old furniture from Siberia that had somehow fetched up there. English mahogany furniture and many cockroaches in the corners that, as soon as I turned on the light, scurried off in every direction. There was a Chinese bed, with the blanket sewn to the sheet, stains of crushed bedbugs, and as pillow, a hard cylinder stuffed with straw. Then I waited.

I was waiting for chicken with rice, but instead at a certain point the door opened and a dozen women came in. The proprietor thought I wanted a prostitute. Peasant girls, all young, the oldest must have been twenty-two, the youngest no more than ten, in black pajamas, bangs on her forehead: a child. After some reflection, I said, "I'll take the child," not because I'm a pervert but because I wanted her to keep me company. This child had a guitar with a single string, so I said to the innkeeper, "I don't want to make love, I want to eat, but I'll keep the girl here so she can play and sing while I'm eating." And so it went. She sat beside me on the bed and began singing in a tortured voice, very shrill, strumming the guitar violently. Meanwhile I ate the chicken and rice. This was my evening at the Hotel of the Three Qualities. The next morning I went out, with a splendid sun in a sky swept clean by the icy wind, and I discovered something that, arriving at night, I hadn't noticed: the city was blond.

What do you mean? Blond how?

Because it was all built of clay, mixed with straw, and the straw glistened in the sun. Behind one of these blond houses, I saw a Chinese answering a call of nature, and I was struck by the color of his bottom: pink. I still remember it! Twisting and turning, I climbed a hill, and at the top there was a great bronze bell, its clapper wrapped in rags. From up there I could see the infinite desert, in waves, like the sea, with a little caravan of dromedaries going off among the dunes. I don't know why, but I took the clapper and struck the bell. Immediately, some guards appeared. They wanted to arrest me, the bell was used to warn of the arrival of bandits. In the end I went back to the hotel and sought information; as a result of this search I learned that the railroad ended just a short distance after Kalgan and therefore there was nothing

I could do but return to Peking. I returned to Peking. During the return journey, I made a detour. I went into a city to visit a bishop, in a mission. On that occasion the bishop questioned me in Latin, "Filius meus, latine loqueris?" I then found out some odd things: for example the cities barred their gates at eight in the evening, red gates with gold studs. If someone arrived late, he was hauled up in a kind of basket. It was still the Middle Ages. Furthermore, the bishop acted as the bandits' cashier and in return the bandits left the people of the area alone. You see what China was like?

What was the political situation of China then?

There were the so-called war lords, the generals who warred among themselves. While I was in Peking, there was a terrible uproar. Chiang Kai-shek went to see a marshal, who was called Chiang Sue Liang. The latter seized his visitor and held him hostage: he wanted Chiang Kai-shek to fight against the Japanese, who had occupied Manchuria.

China made more of an impression on you than Mexico and the United States?

China seemed to me the end of the earth, if you went from West to East. After China there was nothing to do except cross the Pacific and find the West again. Many years later, when I went back there with Dacia Maraini, I had the same impression. China is the antipodes, the opposite, the other.

How long did you stay there altogether?

About two months. I was gone four months, including the trip out and back.

Tell me something: you always say that you're bored —

Yes, very much.

Were you bored also when you were traveling?

No, I wasn't bored at all. I was bored in Rome. For that matter, travel still distracts me today, it relaxes and enriches me. Here the question of time arises: traveling is a project projected into the future, and this means that as long as the journey lasts, time exists, it is really time. If, on the contrary, you stand still, time also stands still. I decided to come back by sea, via Canton. I took a ship of the Dollar Line. All the ships of that line were named after presidents, Lincoln and so on. It was a 100 percent American line. When I was on board, some sailors came out from the engine room, the stokers all covered with tattoos; they looked like green lizards. I remember one fireman; his body was completely tattooed with dragons and snakes. The waiters were students, also American, of course.

Halfway between Shanghai and Canton we caught the tail end of a typhoon. It's an awesome sight. The sea becomes all black, the sky black, with a black elephant's trunk that moves along the horizon and seems to want to pump up all the water it passes. From Canton I had to go to Hong Kong, in order to return to Italy. I went to the consul, who received me very well, offered me a good dinner, and said to me, "You're Italian. Do you love Italy?" "Of course. Obviously." "Then you must do me a favor: you must take a package through the customs at the border guarded by the English and deliver it to the Italian consul in Hong Kong." I took this package, stuck it in the pocket of my raincoat, and easily passed through customs. Once I was in my hotel, naturally, I promptly unwrapped the package. It contained charts of the sea beds at Hainan, which is a large island not far from Hong Kong. Apparently, Mussolini wanted to seize that island and make it a colony. On the chart there were the sea beds, which went from pale blue to dark blue, according to the depth.

Did you take it to the consul?

Yes. The consul thanked me, explained to me what it was, and it all ended there. Meanwhile, however, I had acted again as a spy: first it had been for the anti-Fascists, through my cousin, and now for the Fascists, through the Canton consul. All this seemed very literary to me, and therefore it amused me.

How was Hong Kong?

Not as big as it is now, white on a blue bay against green hills. Beautiful and light-hearted. From Hong Kong I went to Macao, and in the port I ran into a boy who said to me, "You want to make love with my sister?" I replied, "All right." Then we took a rickshaw and went to the old city of Macao. There was a big room and at a table the whole family was sitting down to supper: father, mother, and children. At the end of the room there was a curtain, and behind the curtain there was a bed where the daughter was waiting. I made love with her behind this curtain, which was transparent, to make matters worse. Then I came out, paid, and left.

And then?

I went back to Hong Kong and took the ship home. During the voyage I rather inconclusively pursued an Australian girl, who didn't let me see even the tip of her nose. I courted her for twenty-five days without results. Apart from that, there were some beautiful ports of call. I saw a bit of Malaya, I saw the orangutans, we got off at Colombo and I saw elephants. I saw also the elegant inhabitants of Ceylon: erect and slim, with their hair in a bun, and a cloth wrapped around their legs. Seen from behind, the men looked like women. We went past Port Said again, and I finally landed at Bari.

Did you feel some sadness at returning to Italy?

Yes, rather a lot, that time. Going from Bari to Rome, I happened to be on a train where all the other travelers were local Fascist officials from Puglia, heading for Rome to attend some convention or other. Throughout the whole journey, the conversation was focused on this subject: in the *Domenica del corriere*, Dr. Amal — who was a woman — held out hope to those suffering from arteriosclerosis. The boredom! In Rome I began writing the articles on China. My only consolation was when they asked me, "Where've you been? Haven't seen you for a while," I could answer, "I've been in Peking." I must say that the trip to China was an important experience.

What did it teach you?

Nothing, finally. But it gave me that sensation of youthful adventure that, as I said, Conrad described so well in *Youth*, when he says that the protagonist, coming out on deck, realized he was in the Orient from the dark hands of the Indian stevedores, as they gripped the railing of the ship to pull themselves aboard.

PART II

6

*A*LAIN ELKANN: *What about your writing?*
ALBERTO MORAVIA: On my return from China I began working hard. I finished the short stories of *L'imbroglio* and sent them to Mondadori, according to our contract.

Say something about L'imbroglio.

It consisted of five stories, written in a very dense, thick prose, almost magmatic. After a long wait, a letter arrived from Mondadori, more or less in this vein, "Dear Moravia, sorry, but we can't publish your book, because we have to publish the diaries of Marshal Badoglio." This letter indicated two things, one public, one private: the first was the now-completed conquest of Ethiopia by the Italian army under Marshal Badoglio; the second was that *Le ambizioni sbagliate* had been boycotted by the government and by now I was a well-known anti-Fascist. I took the book to Bompiani. He hesitated, asked the opinion of Paola Masino, who was the companion of Bontempelli, and she said, "Why, Moravia must be published." And Bompiani published me. Between then

and now Bompiani has published about fifty books of mine, a lot
to be sure, but not too many after all, considering how young I
was when I began.

How did that book go? How was it received?

Fairly well, neither splendid nor miserable. But before I could regain my initial position I had to wait until the winter of 1943,
when I was in the mountains with Elsa, and *Agostino* came out in
Rome. *Agostino* was the starting point of all my later work and the
conclusion of the long travail after *Gli indifferenti*. I received the
Corriere lombardo prize. Until *Agostino* I didn't count at all; everybody said, "He's the author of *Gli indifferenti*, he'll never write
any other books." They considered me a one-book author. On the
contrary, I was to write forty-nine more.

What effect did this have on you?

It had the effect of my being completely on the sidelines, an
outsider.

Did it make you suffer?

Absolutely not. I've never suffered at being excluded from something social. Existence always remains and nobody can take that
from you. I thought, "One life is as good as another."

Can you explain what sort of book L'imbroglio *is?*

The stories are long and fairly complex, almost like little novels.
Thirty, forty, fifty pages each. The writing in those stories is
somehow the transposition of my person onto paper. I mean they
are stories in which, besides my voice, I am also physically
present.

Can you try to explain? What is the writer? The novelist?

I'll answer with a slogan: the poet is concerned with himself, the
novelist is concerned with others. Two truisms. Another truism is
that poems are short and novels are long. Final truism: poems
cannot be translated, novels can be. This implies how writing is

fundamental in poetry, less important in the novel. I would say this: the writing of the novel can range from a maximum of personal language to a maximum of impersonality, but it must always be objective and communicative. The language of poetry, on the contrary, is very personal; it records all the shifts of the person's character, like a seismograph, and it is not necessarily communicative. Why, after all, is poetry often avant-garde, while the novel rarely is? Because the poet is not competing with reality. What do I mean? This: the poet's reality is himself, there is no other reality. This explains why every poet is in the avant-garde with respect to the poet that preceded him. For example, Baudelaire is avant-garde compared to Victor Hugo, but Rimbaud is avant-garde with respect to Baudelaire, and Mallarmé with respect to Rimbaud. In the case of novels, on the other hand, if you take a novelist like Tolstoy and you take me, the difference as far as reality is concerned in minimal; for Tolstoy a tree is a tree, as it is also for me. Thus Tolstoy can be translated, as I can be translated. Poetry cannot be translated; all those who translate poetry deceive themselves and are in error. Poetry can be recreated, true: a poet who translates another poet is in reality writing a new poem. In short, the writing of the novelist cannot help but take into account an objective reality that limits it and is reflected in it, whereas the poet can ignore it. Furthermore, the novel is based less on its writing than on ghosts or structures that are not so much "written" as "presented" in the form of what Joyce calls "epiphanies," apparitions. What, then, is the ghostly texture? It is situations and characters. Before he is "written," the character "appears," like a ghost, in fact. As for the situation, it is the relationship among the various ghosts.

In the thirties how did you address your literary language?

The Italian novelist's classics come from abroad, with the exception of Manzoni, and this is because the Italian novel doesn't exist. Naturally, in addition to Manzoni I admired Goldoni, I admired Boccaccio: all three had described Italian society, and the description of society is finally the aim of the novel. Further, I thought that Manzoni had created modern Italian narrative prose. As I have said, I consider Manzoni a mediocre novelist and a great writer. Manzoni's prose is beautiful: it is modern prose. I admired Goldoni for the grace and richness of his dialogue; and finally I admired Boccaccio for the magic of his narration, at once inventive and precise. Probably you wonder why I consider Manzoni a great writer but not a great novelist. You see, there is a difference between novelist and writer, and in fact you are born a novelist and you become a writer. I mean, you are born a story-teller, with the vocation of narrating, and then, through talent and innate sense of art, you become a writer. In any case, after *Gli indifferenti*, and with the sole exception of *Le ambizioni sbagliate*, I have always written in the same way. Did you find much difference between *L'imbroglio* and *Il viaggio a Roma*?

No, but what sort of work produces this prose of yours? How does it come to you?

First of all through uniting reason and action. Both things are very rational. That is, my prose is that of a novel in which something must always happen. Action is a rational thing in itself: when you act, even when you are in the wrong, you have to believe you are doing the right thing. And to do means to move your own body according to the laws proper to it. Let's say you take the wrong road; still, even mistaken, you will proceed along that road with your body — rationally, in other words. Action is consequential, rational.

Yes, but I'd like you to explain something else first. How do you work out your page? Your writing, apparently so direct and simple, seems the product of genuine labor.

My ambition is to be at the same time complicated and clear. Most writers, to achieve clarity, simplify. I, on the contrary, would like to retain all the complications, the contradictions of reality, and at the same time display them with clarity and precision.

Is Italian a difficult language for self-expression?
Very.

More difficult than English or French?

Yes, because it didn't have the great revolution of the Enlightenment. The language has remained more or less as it was in the Renaissance: literary, humanistic, still influenced by Latin. So in Italy there can be contemporary and equally valid writers who write like Leon Battista Alberti or perhaps Leopardi and writers who write like Svevo. It is as if in France there were novelists who write like Rabelais and in England, like Chaucer.

Do you consult dictionaries?

No. Or rarely. I try to do what Stendhal did with French prose: that is, I give the page the rhythm of the action. In other terms, in a novel the characters must always act. When they think, it must be as if they were acting; they must think, that is, in a pressing manner. If they act, they take some steps, don't they? From here to there, from there to there; they move an arm. If they think, they must do the same, one thought after another, *enchaînant.*

But it's your way of writing that tends toward this result.

My writing is the seismograph of my temperament. In my opinion, "voice" and "style" are the same thing. Now the voice, through infinite nuances, expresses character, moods, thought, and so on. In fact, the first thing I do, on beginning a novel, is "set" the narrating voice. The style, that is.

But how do you work at your writing? How do you enrich it? How do you construct it?

I have a literary culture, I know the Italian classics; when I speak, I try to be expressive and precise. I repeat: my ideal is to retain all the complications of reality, keeping them, whole, in the depiction, and with the greatest possible clarity. Metaphor: a clock that, instead of a steel case, has a case of glass so that you can see all the mechanisms in movement. This is my ideal. Stendhal said: you should write the prose of the civil code; it's a *boutade,* meaning he didn't want frills.

You have a tendency to hide Moravia the artist, and you present yourself always as an intellectual.

That's true. The artist always attributes great importance to his own thought. And often he is amazed that others don't recognize that importance.

You have stated often that you write mountains of paper until you have found the music of the novel, the voice.

Yes, as I said, I have to set the voice. The style is simply the written transposition of the voice.

I'd like you to explain how your narrative process works. I'd like to remove your mask. You always say you're a rational man, but when you tell about your life, it seems that the only thing that interests you is individual relationships, primarily love.

At last you've got it! Every artist is foremost a man of a sensitivity at once original and excessive. Art is born from the excess of an unusual, rare sensitivity. To make art means to create a new world of sensitivity. In fact, I keep saying: the artist is superficial, sensuous, he moves on the surface of things, like God at the moment of creation. Now I'll come to the point: I have an abnormal sensitivity, like all artists. This abnormal sensitivity would have overwhelmed me, driven me mad, in other words, if I hadn't had the ability to express it. The expression of sensitivity is extremely complex, because it isn't guided by reason, that faculty I love so much, because I don't possess much of it; but I have intuitive willpower. In fact, at heart I am not a rationalist; I am a person who suffers anguish, irreality, a sense of void. Or rather, it isn't exactly suffering: it would be more correct to say that there is never a moment when I don't feel within myself an attraction toward the extremes of imbalance.

Is there a great childish naïveté in your life?

All artists are like that.

But you have a tendency to hide this, almost as if you were ashamed of it.

A tendency to hide it because I have had to be a social man from the beginning. I was curious; my curiosity has impelled me to approach others. I could have cut myself off; instead I faced the obligations of social living first with crude and conscious schizophrenic pretense and then gradually with some sincerity.

At this point I'd like you to try to explain how your artistic process happens.

I can tell you in two words. It doesn't proceed via the head; it occurs through successive illuminations. The artist is always assisted by a demon, and it is this demon that illuminates him. In short, everything I've written that is any good I received through illumination. It comes to me rather easily. I am illuminated. "I am illuminated by immensity," as Ungaretti's poem says. I am illuminated by the thing I am writing. Without illuminations, no writing, no books. Now, what is illumination? It's what Joyce called epiphany. Joyce was fond of this word "epiphany"; I prefer "illumination," which is Rimbaud's favorite term. What is illumination? I'll come to a perhaps even more interesting point, which is entirely mine, because no one else would say it. Illumination is this: a rational operation of dizzying speed. If you have a fan at home, and you turn it on, at a certain point you won't see the blades anymore, you'll see something like a blur. Now, illumination in reality is a fantastic acceleration of rationality. And this is so true that the critics, when they examine something really beautiful, have to dismantle and analyze piece by piece the dazzling and rational mechanism of illumination. If this weren't so, it wouldn't be possible to criticize a work of art.

This speed — do you have to release it immediately in writing?

Oh, yes. But I release it through the filter of my literary and cultural ability.

They say that you don't keep diaries and never answer letters. Why not? Do you want to concentrate everything solely on your writing?

Yes. Otherwise, I prefer to telephone. I have a genuine repugnance toward writing letters. I'm uneasy about revealing privacy. Perhaps there is a privacy hidden in my novels, but it is unrecognizable.

You say that in Eco's books there's no understanding who Eco is. In Moravia's books can it be understood who is Moravia?

Yes, it can. But it is always a question of writing. I probably pay more attention to connotation than communication; Eco favors communication, which necessarily is not connotative.

What do you mean by connotation?

I mean more subjective expression.

The really great effort of your life was not writing but the mastering of yourself after the illness, in the sense of making yourself take a place in society. Am I right?

It wasn't just the mastering of myself, but also the recovery of health, which is the same thing. The recovery, I mean, of moral health. Because I had a psychosomatic illness; tuberculosis is a psychosomatic illness.

Have you ever wanted to be psychoanalyzed?

No. If anything, I would say that I write books and my books are dreams, but I possess the key to them. *Gli indifferenti*, for example, isn't the story of my family, it's a kind of dream that reflects the intolerability of family life as I had experienced it. The basic experience of the novelist is always autobiographical; the writer doesn't talk about things he doesn't know. For example, in the case of *La ciociara*, I talk about the war because I experienced the war. On the other hand, characters and situations are invented. Perhaps the exception is Proust, who, though he started from an autobiographical base, didn't invent characters but transformed them radically, identifying himself with them.

Were you afraid while you were writing Gli indifferenti?

I wasn't afraid, I was ashamed. Yes, ashamed, since in my mind, in my spirit, there are taboos of every sort; I had to overcome my taboos. I had to overcome some repugnances I can't explain.

Did you leave them on the paper or did you cut them?

I cut them. For example, to describe Leo, who lays his hands on Carla, I had to overcome a certain repugnance, which is evident in the fact that Carla says, "No, not that," and there's no indication what "that" is. I conquered it in the sense that I have always overcome modesty of a social order, and modesty about sex is social. In any case I try to be very precise, not to sink into what can be called pornography, even in the psychological sense.

Did you have a Victorian sort of education?

No, I had no education at all. That's the truth: my education didn't exist. I made my own. These examples of modesty show how I was creating my education.

7

ALAIN ELKANN: *Going back to 1937, we were saying that was when you published* L'imbroglio *and when you met Elsa Morante.*

ALBERTO MORAVIA: Yes, I met Elsa Morante then. We had supper together with some friends, and as I was saying good night to her, she slipped the keys of her house into my hand. In 1937 my Rosselli cousins were assassinated. I remember how that year and the following years I suffered with spasmophilia, which is a form of nervous colitis. I was filled with air, I didn't eat, I became very thin. In reality, everything was going badly for me. For one thing, I wasn't writing anything that satisfied me; for another, the fact I was anti-Fascist didn't make things any easier; and finally, I had no money. I should emphasize that I felt the Rosselli crime very deeply, and in fact, years later I wrote a novel, *Il conformista*, in which the story is adumbrated, but reversed — seen, that is, from the point of view of the man who participated in their killing. In other words, I wrote the novel not "for" the Rossellis but "on" the Rossellis. And this because I thought it should be a tragedy, though with a historical background, and not a hagiography, an improving book.

Did you go on seeing Malaparte?

As I said, I'd known him since the days of Novecento. In 1934 we went to Paris together. He took me here and there, to meet his friends. I remember I called on Mauriac, who had lost his voice. Referring to Malaparte, Mauriac said to me, in a whisper, "Votre ami Malaparte, son visage manque de lumière." Malaparte was very fond of talking about himself; he never let anyone else talk. In the French salons they were beside themselves with rage! He talked and showed off and was a bit too clever, but in his way he was also ingenuous.

Ingenuous how?

He was ingenuous probably because he believed he was Malaparte. A bit like Hugo, of whom a critic said, "Victor Hugo was someone who believed he was Victor Hugo."

Where did you and Malaparte live?

We stayed at the Hôtel Pont Royal.

What was Malaparte like physically?

Malaparte was tall, very well built, with a small head. The sarcastic used to say that his head was only an extra vertebra that had grown on his neck. He had black eyes, black brows. Beneath these big eyes and thick black brows there was a tiny little nose and then a rather large mouth. With teeth like a rasp, slanting inward, shark's teeth.

Did he speak with a Tuscan accent?

I'll say! Very much so. Malaparte was a great egoist, but not in a vulgar sense. He was a narcissist, he made a cult of his person. Therefore during his whole life Malaparte sacrificed everything to himself, all the things that he had, that he did, that existed in his life. Writing, for example, politics, women, and so on, served only as part of a pedestal for himself. Malaparte, in other words, was a character, a role that he played. For example, when he was in political confinement on the island of Lipari, the articles he wrote were typical of him. They came out in the *Corriere*, signed Candide. These articles were entitled, "A Woman Like Me," "Dogs Like Me," "A House Like Me." You understand? "Me" came before anything else.

Was he a writer or not?

He was a literary man, not a poet, absolutely not. He was a literary man and a journalist.

Was he a Fascist when you met him?

He was actually one of the founders of the party in Tuscany. A Fascist, and how! Later it was said that he had always been an anti-Fascist, and it could even be true. At the front he was with the English. You could say he was an unconscious anti-Fascist, like all the Italians who publically were Fascists.

Did Elsa already know him?

Elsa met him in 1937.

What did she think of him?

Like me, she thought he was a journalist, a literary man, but not a poet. But she found him fairly fascinating, and at the same time ingenuous. When he was dying, she was very upset and began to write a novel that was to have been entitled *Senza i conforti della religione*. Elsa, in her way, was rather fond him, but so was I, except for his terrible vanity. And, as I explained, I can't be the friend of a writer who isn't a good writer. Books like *La pelle* and *Kaputt* are dreadful.

At that time you also knew the Principessa di Bassiano, editor of Commerce?

Yes, I had met the princess in the thirties, when I went to Paris and I found Caffi there, who was tutor to the Bassiano children. Caffi said to me, "I want to introduce you to the princess." I went to Versailles, where she had a beautiful house, where all the most important writers of the time visited, Valéry and Larbaud, Léon-Paul Fargue, Jean Giono. In fact, for a moment she thought of publishing *Gli indifferenti*, which was still unpublished, but then instead she chose Giono's *Colline*.

Did you meet Cocteau at that time?

No, much later.

Where?

In his studio. He was very kind. An extremely kind person, exquisitely refined and elegant.

Let's get back to 1937. That year, as you say, was sadly important. Tell me about the death of the Rossellis.

I was in Florence not long before they were murdered, and I saw Nello. He said to me, "I'm going to Paris." I said, "What for? Are you going to visit Carlo?" "Yes." "They've given you a passport?" "Yes." I said to him, "Look, it's not a good idea for you to go. If they've given you a passport, it means they'll spy on you. They'll follow you everywhere." Follow him! They assassinated him! The Rossellis were killed by the *cagoulards*. They were an extreme Fascist group, and they needed arms. The negotiations for the murder were conducted by the SIM, which was the Fascist Cheka. The *cagoulards* said, "We want arms, and in return we'll kill Carlo Rosselli." And that's what happened.

In your home what effect did the Rossellis' murder have?

A great effect, but without any talk. My mother kept silent because, most of all, she was afraid for me. My father kept silent because that's how he was: taciturn and uncommunicative. He wrote his sister a letter, but he didn't show it to me. For my part, I was silent because I was traumatized, and traumas are traumas precisely because they can't be released in words. This silence, for that matter, was also the silence of the terror that reigned then in Europe because of the totalitarian regimes. None of my friends or my acquaintances talked with me about the Rosselli murder. My friends thought the same way I did and perhaps it seemed to them superfluous to talk about it; my acquaintances were afraid. Terror begins with silence, which serves the double purpose of disassociating you from those who have been struck and, on the other hand, from the regime that has struck them.

When you met Elsa how old was she?

She was born in 1912. We met in 1937. Figure it out: she was twenty-five. She lived alone and was literally dying of hunger. And also of loneliness. She told me that one day, to hear a human voice, she dialed the telephone number that gives the correct time. To subsist she tried to earn a living by writing theses for lazy students. She was extremely literary; at twelve she had won a contest sponsored by the *Corriere dei Piccoli* with a little novel, *Caterina della Trecciolina*, which she illustrated herself: it was very charming, very well told. It was published and she was given a prize.

What was Elsa like then?

She had had white hair since adolescence, a big mushroom of hair above a round face. She was very near-sighted; she had beautiful eyes with the dreamy gaze of the near-sighted. She had a little nose, and a big, willful mouth. A rather childish face.

What sort of family was she from?

Very poor lower middle class. The father a humble clerk, the mother a schoolteacher. Her mother was Jewish but the children were Catholics, and Elsa was also a believer, though not a practicing Catholic.

What was her cultural background?

Very Italian, humanist, scholastic. But her great vitality had driven her beyond national borders. She knew the classics of foreign literature fairly well. As to the relation between her culture, whatever it was, and her life, I would add that Elsa was totally focused on a creatural concept of existence and to hell with social life. She considered herself, as it were, an angel fallen from heaven into the practical hell of daily living. But an angel armed with a pen.

When you met her she lived in Via del Corso?

She lived in Via del Corso with an older man whose name I don't recall, then she had another lover, younger, and then me.

Did you fall in love with Elsa immediately?

I was never *in* love with Elsa. I loved her, yes, but I never managed to lose my head: I never fell, in other words. She always knew this, and it was perhaps also the chief reason for the difficulties of our life together. I wasn't in love, but I was fascinated by an extreme, heart-rending, passionate quality in her character. It was as if every day of her life were the last, just before her death. So, in an atmosphere of impassioned aggressiveness on her part and defensive affection on mine, we lived together for twenty-five years. You may ask: Why defensive? I will answer with a contradiction: Because Elsa tried to annihilate me and, at the same time, through excess passion, she annihilated herself.

You saw each other every day?

Not at the beginning. Then gradually, yes. I would pick her up in the evening, we would go out to supper together; she would tell me of her life. The life of lovers is not made up of culture, it's made up of reciprocal information about themselves. Elsa's life had been poor in events, but she enriched it, I believe, with what you might consider benevolent lies, benevolent toward herself. Private myths.

Give me an example of one of these lies, a private myth.

Not long after our first meeting, Elsa told me that she had had an English lover, the son of a lord, a certain T., a Byronic type, like the Byron who took as his mistress in Venice the daughter of a gondolier, a cynic, slothful, no-good who spoke Roman dialect, lived without doing anything, ate breakfast in bed reading the *Times*. This T. was "also" homosexual and had an Italian male lover, slimy and squalid. During a party, when T. was drunk, he was confronted by the Italian lover, who sank to his knees before T., holding out a pistol to him and crying, "Kill me! Kill me!" T. then took the pistol and killed him. Naturally, he was arrested and sentenced. But the war between Italy and England arrived, and then, at the last minute, T. was exchanged for an Italian who had been jailed by the English. T. was released and returned to England a free man. Elsa hinted that she had had relations also with the victim and that this had given her for the rest of her life a taste for three-way relationships, namely, with a lover who was also homosexual and had a male lover. Naturally, I believed Elsa, and in fact the scene of the apparent death of the homosexual in *Il conformista* comes from that lie of hers. Because it was a lie, actually. Forty years later, Elsa revealed to me, casually, that while it was true she had had an English lover who in turn had an Italian lover, the whole story of the killing was invented.

Did you introduce Elsa to your family?

No, indeed. I introduced Elsa to my mother only when we were married.

But you went on living with your family?

Yes. The incidental reason why I married Elsa is that I couldn't bear going to her house every evening to collect her. It was a freezing winter, and after taking her back, I went home chilled to the marrow. The cold of those nights expressed my discomfort.

What sort of life did the two of you live?

The life of artists in Rome. If you read the *Memoirs* of Benvenuto Cellini, you'll know: he led the same life I did. In the evening he went with his mistress to a trattoria to eat with their friends. That was a Roman habit. He had a mistress whose name was Pantasilea. I had a mistress whose name was Elsa Morante. The difference was that Pantasilea was probably a model from Ciociaria and Elsa was a writer of genius. We went to the trattoria and we would meet painters like Capogrossi, Scialoja, Guttuso, and so on. We met literary people like Pannunzio, Brancati, De Feo, and others. We were a recognized couple. All Rome knew us. The Morante-Moravia couple. In fact, when we separated, someone said, "Pity. Morante-Moravia had such a good sound." We were poor. I remember that every now and then I would give Elsa a suit of mine and Elsa would transform it into a *tailleur*. A tan chalk-stripe, for example. For some reason, my father paid for my clothes. No matter what I had made. But he gave me only five hundred lire a month, which even then was very little.

Was Elsa elegant?

In her way, yes. I remember she had a black dress, very close-fitting, and a beautiful fur of blue fox, from which her face emerged, fresh, round, childish, with that enormous mushroom of white hair.

At night did you sleep at her place?

Never. We never slept together.

But you made love every evening?

No, not at all. To tell you the truth, I never felt a violent desire for her. I was fascinated by her personality, yes, so original, so strong.

But you liked making love with her?

Yes, I liked it because she loved me and this attracted me. In love-making, Elsa was an absolutely normal woman. But this normality included a very strong modesty, almost hostile to the transports of physical love. In sum, she was very passionate but not very sensual, if by sensuality you mean allowing your body complete freedom.

But she was very much in love with you?

Let's not talk about that. When I met Elsa in 1937, she was a woman of an almost saccharine sweetness, the deceptive sweetness that comes with being in love. But this sweetness vanished, though she went on loving me, you could say, until death.

You met her, you said, in 1937?

Yes, in '37. Somehow my relationship with Elsa was from the very beginning connected with political situations: 1937 was the year Hitler came to Rome, then in the years that followed there was the Rome-Berlin axis, the racial laws in Italy, the fall of Mussolini, the Badoglio period, my escape into the mountains at the front, the Allied victory, and so on. Thinking back, I realize that Elsa was really the woman with whom I shared the most political and most public period of my life. So my whole memory of Elsa is shadowed by the tragic events of those years. Perhaps this is another reason why our relationship was so dramatic.

You realized immediately that Elsa had genius?

No, I wouldn't say that. If anything, I realized that she was a genuine writer. She hadn't yet written *Menzogna e sortilegio*, but she wrote short stories. She was much influenced by Kafka. Later she repudiated Kafka and fell in love with Stendhal. Kafka perhaps seemed "heavy" to her. She would have liked to be "light," like Stendhal, like Rimbaud, like Mozart, her three tutelary deities.

Was she very ambitious?

Ambitious is putting it mildly. Writing was her life.

But was she also domestic, did she look after the house?

Pretty much, like all people born poor. But not by vocation. At a certain point, she tired of it and wouldn't bother about it anymore. I remember it annoyed her if I watched her in the evening while she was writing out the menus for the next day's meals. In the end, she didn't concern herself with the house at all. She wasn't untidy, no, just completely disaffected.

Did you talk much about politics?

Not at all. We agreed from the beginning that Fascism was a horror, and that was that.

Did you continue going to salons?

After meeting Elsa I visited them less and less, and after our marriage I stopped altogether. I spent my time with artists.

What did you think about the rise of racism, the anti-Semitic laws?

We thought that the laws were horrible, as very many Italians did, for that matter.

Did you feel somehow affected by them, or not?

No. Also because the atmosphere was not anti-Semitic. They were a nuisance, but not our chief concern. We were like many others, simply anti-Fascists.

How did your mother react to the racist laws, which must have concerned her too, after all, since she was married to a Jew?

She never mentioned the matter also because she understood nothing. Then she would say, "Something must be done." But she said it as she might have said, "We must pay our taxes." She had great common sense and therefore didn't let herself be too upset. You have no idea what Italian common sense is! Italy is a country that is very hard to budge. My mother wasn't afraid of anything, but she urged caution. In the end she had me and my sisters change our name, and we became Piccinini, the surname of my maternal grandmother.

Didn't you become indignant on reading anti-Semitic articles?

I didn't read them, but they annoyed me — and not only the articles about race, but also those against France, a country to which I was greatly attached, and against England, which I admired. The articles about race were part of a huge network of disagreeable things. Elsa and I belonged to a little group of intellectuals who spent their time speaking ill of Fascism all day long. But I was the one who said least, because the subject bored me, especially when I had to listen to jokes. I considered Fascism something very

boring but unfortunately also very serious that couldn't be resolved with witticisms.

At a certain moment in 1938 you went to Greece. Why?

Because I was neurotic. In 1937 I was really in a bad way. My
cousins had been assassinated, I had a kidney stone, I had no
money, and I wasn't at all sure I wanted to continue my affair with
Elsa. Furthermore, I felt the war coming, and I thought vaguely of
not returning to Italy. But once I was in Greece I realized that if
you want to hide you have to choose a big country like Italy and
not a little country like Greece. In Athens I stayed at the King
George Hotel. I had a beautiful room. I didn't write a line. I spent
hours in cafés, I walked, I read books on Greece. In other words, I
was waiting for the war, which duly arrived.

8

*A*LAIN ELKANN: *Were you afraid of the war?*

ALBERTO MORAVIA: No. I was fairly clearheaded. I thought at first that the Germans would win, but I certainly didn't imagine the horror that their occupation of Europe would prove to be. Generally speaking, nobody foresaw anything then. Everyone was waiting, as if paralyzed, dazed, as if confronted by an enormous serpent that is about to strike. I remember, on this score, that a year later, the evening before the war broke out, I was having supper with Bobi Bazlen and Landolfi, and Bazlen said, "Do you smell the odor of war?" And Landolfi replied that he couldn't smell anything. The next morning war broke out.

Why didn't you consider going to Paris and then to America, like Nicola Chiaromonte and Paolo Milano?

Paolo Milano was Jewish and Nicola Chiaromonte was pathologically intolerant of Fascism. I was neither the one nor the other; I had a kind of masochistic curiosity to see what would happen in

Europe. The same curiosity that later, in 1943, kept me from fleeing Rome before the return of the Germans.

But at that moment wasn't it clear that Fascism would collapse?

That wasn't clear at all. Everyone thought it would go on and on. Even the anti-Fascists thought so. In reality, regimes like Fascism fall only through action from outside. In Spain it lasted until Franco died. Now, there's something I want to tell you. I remember I was truly in despair. I was an intellectual and I could see no cause for hope in Italy or abroad. In Italy there was Fascism. England and France were two imperialist countries that had helped Italian and Spanish Fascism. In Russia there was Stalin, whom I always hated. America seemed to me infinitely far away. Perhaps it was this same despair that kept me from emigrating. In Athens I knew only one person, the brother of Anfuso, who was Ciano's secretary at the foreign ministry. He was there as press officer; in other words, he did practically nothing and thought only about women, who for him were a kind of benign obsession. In the morning I read, scribbled a bit, not much, then I went to the Averoff restaurant and met other Italians. There was a tableful of quite simple people, Greeks and compatriots.

Was Indro Montanelli there?

Montanelli came for a few days. Our sincere friendship dates back to that time. He was anti-Fascist the way he is perhaps anti-Christian Democrat today: you hold your nose and put up with it. Then, leaving Averoff's, I would walk back through this beautiful-ugly city of Athens and sit in the café with a book or a newspaper, and so the afternoon went by. Sometimes I went to the museum, or else I would go for drives with Anfuso. I remember one day Anfuso informed me that at Piraeus he knew a procuress and she had promised to introduce him to a beautiful girl from Smyrna, who had just arrived in Athens. I went along, to keep him company. We reached a little art nouveau villa, the procuress led us into the living room, and in a little while, on a kind of platform, she had the Smyrna girl enter. We were dumbfounded: before us there was a giantess, enormous and very young, a genuine Fellini character, her face covered with pimples, an enormous mass of hair down her back. Then I had another adventure, of a quite different kind, the opposite, in fact.

What adventure was that?

One day I was walking along the Queen Amelia Avenue and I saw a very beautiful woman walking ahead of me. She must have been English; she had a mass of red hair. I spoke to her; she stopped. We sat down together on a bench. She knew who I was, she had read *Gli indifferenti.* We talked for a long time, and I was rather attracted. She looked hard at me; she also seemed interested in me. Then all of a sudden she threw her arms around my neck, bursting into tears. She said she couldn't help it, she had to tell me: her husband, whom she loved passionately, had been dead for a month! So the giantess from Smyrna and the inconsolable Englishwoman were my only two female encounters during my stay in Greece.

Did you talk about the war with Anfuso?

Yes, but with opposite feelings. Despite a veiled skepticism, he was a Fascist. I, on the contrary, ardently hoped that Fascism would fall. We did agree on the basic idea that all this would not last.

But in 1939 did you know Hitler was doing terrible things, or not?

Yes, in 1939 everybody knew. I knew also about the Russian concentration camps. I went often to Paris and received all possible information: I bought books, I met Russian and German exiles. I remember that in 1940 Alberto Mondadori, returning from Poland, told me, "Horrible things are happening." "What?" The Germans had invited him to witness a massacre of Jews, like a performance. He didn't accept, naturally, but he went around Milan telling about it. At this point there's an observation I'd like to make. You constantly ask me questions about the racial laws and the concentration camps; now I must say these were horrible things, true, but they were part of a very horrible general picture, they were only brush strokes of horror among many other horrors. We were somehow accustomed to living with horror. Being in Greece and having nothing to do, I devoted much time to reflecting on the history of Greece and of Rome; I remember, for example, that in Athens I bought and read the history of the Roman Empire by Rostovtzeff. I made comparisons: Rome was a bit like the United States, and Greece was a bit like Europe. That is, Europe was a very refined continent, decadent and, in those years of fascism, completely steeped in death. The United States was a young, vital country, alien to Europe, as Rome was to Greece, and therefore destined to dominate in the end: in Marxist terms I saw the United States as the final synthesis of the European antitheses.

When did you come back to Italy?

In April 1938. I went to Capri with Elsa Morante. There we heard Mussolini's declaration that Italy would remain neutral. The mayor of Anacapri, getting into the bus that went from the lower square up to Anacapri, said to those present, "Magnum gaudium nuntio vobis, neutrales sumus!" In reality, like that mayor, the Italians, after saying far and wide that they were all ready for the war, didn't want it at all.

And then?

I was in Capri when I received a letter from my father, in which he wrote that we were ruined. I had asked him to buy me the works of Montesquieu. He sent them to me, adding, "We are ruined, we have no more money, soon we will be beggars." It wasn't entirely true, but he was arteriosclerotic and irrational by then. I didn't care one way or the other. I thought that poverty might be an interesting experience. In reality, I've been protected all my life by my indifference.

This letter from your father saying the family was ruined —
wasn't it something of an encouragement to get to work?

No, absolutely not. My father didn't want me to work, because he knew I could only be a writer. On this score, I remember a dialogue between a poet friend of mine and an industrialist, discussing the job of the writer. The poet was asking to marry the industrialist's daughter. The man asked, "What do you do?" "I'm a writer, a poet." "Yes, I understand, of course, but what do you do?" "Writer, poet." "Come now, what do you actually do?"

My father, on the contrary, never talked to me like that. He was a man who, in his way, was involved with art: he was an architect and an amateur painter. He was aware of the values of art, in other words. My mother, on the contrary, as I told you, would have liked me to have a more socially important profession, like the foreign service. She was a bourgeoise; for the bourgeoisie, at that time anyway, art didn't count, it wasn't a profession.

Did your parents know you were with Elsa?

They knew more or less, but they didn't care at all. My mother saw her on the day of our wedding. Elsa quarreled with her and they never saw each other again. My father was already ill and he never met Elsa.

With your brother, what did you talk about?

We never talked about anything. Once we made a trip to Holland.

When?

In 1934, before I went to America. I went to Holland with him and a schoolmate of his. I was older than they, but still a boy myself; we joked, went to eat in quaint restaurants, remarked on the different cuisine in France: things like that.

Did you bully your brother?

Not at all. I've never bullied anyone.

Besides being the older brother, you were also famous.

Please! He respected me greatly, he respected me for having succeeded, but not in the sense of being famous, like today. Today I'm a celebrated person; then I was simply someone who had had

a success. I had arrived, while he, on the contrary, was just beginning his life and hoped to succeed, like me, in his own field, as an
engineer. Perhaps he considered me more experienced, yes. One
day he said to me, on the subject of Fascism, "I don't believe in it
anymore."

And what did you tell him?

That he should act according to his conscience. To be honest, I
considered him still immature. And in fact he was, like all those
brought up under a dictatorship.

Did you have many friends?

One at a time. Not friends exactly: more like accomplices. In those
days my close friend was Pannunzio. I saw him every evening. We
talked about literature and politics. He had a car and picked me
up at home. We were inseparable. In the end we started a magazine, or rather, two magazines: first *Caratteri*, then *Oggi*.

Did Pannunzio come to your house?

No, it was a bourgeois house furnished in the taste of my mother
and father, and we didn't feel at ease there. For the same reason I
didn't go to his house. We met in a café, at the movies, in his car.
My sisters, on the contrary, received their friends in our home.
They gave parties, hired musicians and waiters, danced all night.

Did you go to those parties?

Sometimes. I would put on my blue suit and stand there, glum. I
didn't know any of their friends, nor, to tell the truth, did I want to
know them. I was what's called an intellectual and they were
bourgeois. I felt this as an enormous, unbridgeable difference.

**To get back to the beginning of the war: you were chiefly on
Capri?**

Yes, I stayed there perhaps half the year. Apparently because it was
less expensive than Rome, but in reality, strange to say, the marvelous natural beauty of the island, during the war years, acted as a

counterbalance, a kind of eternity, inhuman if you like, which counteracted the social horrors of the war and Fascism. I felt very close to something that would never change, nature, and the enemy of something that could only change: Fascism and the war.

And Elsa?

Elsa, to the extent that it was possible, was not unhappy, I imagine. She had great plans. Probably she had already begun writing *Menzogna e sortilegio*. Our real difficulty was money.

What did you write in those years?

I wrote a volume entitled *Racconti surrealisti e satirici* and I wrote *La mascherata*.

Is La mascherata *a novel?*

Yes. It's a novel that I wrote in a month and published in 1940. I had an enormous creative drive. *La mascherata* is important in understanding what was going through my mind in that period. It's a novel that takes place in an imaginary Latin American country, which in reality is Mexico. In this country there is a dictator whose name is Tereso. A dictator who is basically Mussolini. But he is an army officer. He has lost an arm. Tereso, since he is popular, wants to rid himself of the followers who have helped him become dictator, in particular, the chief of police. But the chief of police, having learned that Tereso wants to eliminate him, organizes a fake assassination attempt, to show Tereso that his chief of police is still indispensable and must stay where he is. The idea came to me from the burning of the Reichstag, provoked by the Nazis to enable them to bring off a coup d'état. In this novel there is a skeptical and desperate character whose name is Sebastiano and who was me. I used him to illustrate my hopeless situation, with no way out. A situation of total, bitter disappointment, because I no longer believed in anti-Fascism or Fascism or communism or capitalism. I was in a period of absolute unbelief. I had seen France capitulate to Italy in the Ethiopian crisis. Fascism was triumphant everywhere. I hated not only Fascism but also those unable to resist it. I hated also the masses, who rushed to join fascisms and Stalinism. Sebastiano, who incarnated this generalized disgust, proclaimed his repugnance toward the masses and their ideologies and declared that life was all a game. Sebastiano in other words was, as I imagined him, a Stendhalian character, adventurous and unbelieving.

Unless I'm mistaken the book was confiscated and withdrawn shortly after publication.

Yes. Then I mustered my courage and went to Ciano.

Why Ciano?

He had been minister of the Minculpop, I knew him, I used to see him at Countess Pecci Blunt's cocktail parties. I went because I was a bit in despair after the confiscation but, strange to say, a limited despair. What happened to me — and still happens to me — was this: anyone else in my position would have been outraged, but I took refuge in indifference. After having hated indifference at the time of *Gli indifferenti*, now, in a different situation, it was useful for me. Ciano received me at the Foreign Ministry. I entered his office at the very moment that a very beautiful woman was leaving it.

What was Ciano's office like?

It was a large salon in Palazzo Chigi.

Ciano was foreign minister?

Yes.

How was he dressed?

In civilian clothes. I never saw him in uniform.

With black shirt?

No. In elegant, civilian clothes, a suit tailored by Caraceni, who was the fashionable tailor then among all rich Italians. Anyway, in his Caraceni suit he received me, "Good morning, Moravia, what do you have to say to me?"

He addressed you in the "voi" form?
It was obligatory.

Did he give you the Fascist salute?
No. He was wiping his mouth with a handkerchief, which he then examined several times to see if it bore any traces of the lipstick of the woman who had been there before me. I said to him, "The fact is, Your Excellency, that difficulties have been made for me for some time, and now they've confiscated a novel. Now you understand I'm not a critic of Fascism: I'm a witness. I don't criticize. If anything, I depict." Things of that sort, which didn't deceive him or me. He listened. Then he said, "All right, give me your book. I'll read it on my trip." And without thinking, I asked him, "Where are you going?" "To see Hitler." I left and that was the last I heard. The book remained confiscated. I wonder if he really did read it, between meetings with Hitler.

Did you ever see Ciano again?
No.

It was only after La mascherata *had been in circulation for a while that it was confiscated. Were there any reviews?*
Nothing. Not a line. In fact, all of a sudden I received an order from the ministry not to publish anything. They told all the newspapers not to commission me to write. Until then I had written under the name Pseudo. Then I started writing film scripts with the director Castellani. I wrote three or four, I think.

Did cinema interest you?
I've always liked films. As a boy I would see even two movies a day. It's my favorite art, after literature and painting. Cinema and painting have a great influence in my fiction because I live very much through my eyes.

How did you find writing scripts?

Fine. But it had two annoying aspects. First of all, it wrecked your life. You would sit for hours and hours with the other writers, smoking, drinking coffee, now and then telling obscene or anti-Fascist jokes. A constant tug-of-war. Even now many do it, but the process has changed somewhat, it's become more rational. And second, I always had the sensation that I was giving something precious, for money, to someone who would exploit it for his own ends. I've defined the scriptwriter as a kind of governess. He raises the children, then he's dismissed, and the child remains with its mother. The scriptwriter, that is, gives himself totally to the script, but the director's name is on the movie.

Why do you say that the movies inspired you considerably in your work?

Cinema solved many problems of realism. I'll explain. Take, for example, Balzac's *Père Goriot*: it begins with the description of a family boardinghouse, where Goriot lives. Balzac takes seventy pages to describe the boardinghouse. A movie shows it to you in one sequence: the house, the people coming and going, the table with the boarders, and so on. It's a lesson in realism; it resolves immediately the reality as background. So we have returned a bit to classical literature, which doesn't describe interiors or landscapes. Take a novel like *Manon Lescaut*: there are no landscapes, America is just named and that's it. Realism was destroyed by cinema, completely destroyed. Realism à la Tolstoy, who wrote pages and pages about the marvelous Russian forests, with streams, foliage, cows, and so on, is no longer possible. There is a return to classicism. A return to the abstract and synthetic depiction of things.

Something that fits your character very well.

Indeed it does! Movies offer one explanation of why *Gli indifferenti* is the way it is. On the one hand, there was the idea of tragedy, the theater, and on the other there was cinema, Aristotelian unity of time and place rediscovered in photography, which is always, inevitably in the present.

You hadn't yet written for the theater?

No, I hadn't yet written for the theater; I thought about it all the time, but I hadn't written plays, I wrote novels. Anyway, as I said, I worked with Castellani. I worked also with the producer Guarini. Guarini was a man with big, languid black eyes. He was the lover of Isa Miranda, a star of the Fascist period. I remember this film because it coincided with the declaration of war in 1940. Mussolini's speech was delivered while I, in a room off Via Veneto, was occupied with the script of *Senza cielo*: that was the title of the film. Instead of calling it "without heaven," I called it "senza culo" (without ass), because I was so angry at having to do it. I remember that it took place in a fictitious Brazil; *Senza cielo* was the forest, without sky, and for it I had invented a locality called Desperacion. I was really desperate! We kept the radio on and at a certain moment we heard the voice of Mussolini saying, "I told His Majesty to draw his sword, and he has drawn it!" At that moment the typist burst into tears and hid under the sofa. I looked out at the door; Via Veneto was completely deserted, because everybody was in Piazza Venezia. I could see only a squat little man, walking along among the tables outside Rosati's; he was holding the hands of twin little girls with crooked legs. That was how the war began for me.

Where was Elsa?

Elsa was at home. She was writing *Menzogna e sortilegio.* She was obsessed with *Menzogna e sortilegio.* Imagine, a book of eight hundred pages conceived with the imaginative capacity of genius, after having spent only three days in Sicily, which is where part of the novel takes place! In any case, immediately after the declaration of war, we went to Anacapri, where everything was the same as before and the war was represented only by four enormous, useless cannons that were meant to prevent the British Home Fleet from entering the Bay of Naples.

What were you reading in those years?

In that period I remember reading Céline for the first time, and I remember I made a kind of critical reflection on his *Voyage au bout de la nuit.* I had recently read the poems of T. S. Eliot, who was then one of my favorite poets. I thought that Eliot's universal catastrophic view was like the chauvinist catastrophic view of Céline: they were provoked by the individual catastrophes of English and French civilization in the great war of 1914.

Had you read the American writers? Had you read Hemingway, Dos Passos, Fitzgerald?

Yes, I had read them. In fact, during that period I was interested especially in American writers. I translated the first story of Hemingway published in Italy, "The Killers," translated as "I sicari" for *L'italiano,* a magazine of Longanesi. I had read Faulkner's *Sanctuary* in 1931, a month after it appeared. I knew Hemingway, Faulkner, Dos Passos, Fitzgerald, Steinbeck, Saroyan: the so-called Lost Generation, in other words.

But were you much influenced by American culture, the way Pavese and Vittorini were?

The odd thing is that, though I knew and loved the Americans, I was particularly influenced by the Russians and the French.

Were you a friend of Pavese and Vittorini?

I didn't know Pavese then; I met him after the war. I barely knew Vittorini. They were neorealists; I was a realist of the existentialist kind, which is something very different. If you like, I can explain to you what neorealism was in fiction.

What was it?

All our neorealism derives from a single novel, Hemingway's *A Farewell to Arms.* It is an autobiographical, almost journalistic account raised to the lyrical level. This is my definition. Italian neorealistic cinema did more or less the same thing: no studios, no plots, no characters, people taken off the streets instead of actors. I wasn't at all like that! I was and still am a constructed, intellectual writer of the Franco-Russian school and, without having been aware of it, one of the first existentialist writers.

Like Camus and Sartre?

Yes, but less intellectualistic. Look, the French have said this, I'm not just being vain. I was one of the precursors of European existentialism. Now, the existentialist novel comes from Dostoyevsky, who had in fact been my master.

Did you know Sartre and Camus?

I met them after the war. In any case, *Gli indifferenti* came out ten years before *La Nausée* and *L'Étranger.* But it was only because I hadn't gone to school, while Sartre and Camus had. I loathe the idea of being the first in anything.

Did Joyce's Ulysses **make a great impression on you?**

Very great. I read it in 1926. I bought it in Florence in a bookshop in Via Tornabuoni. A thick volume of almost a thousand pages with a pale blue cover. It was the edition of 1925.

Did you use Ulysses **as an instrument in your own work?**

No, but I liked it very much.

Did it seem to you a revolutionary work of literature?

Yes, a bit. Also with *Gli indifferenti* I had aimed at one day, or rather only two days: unity of time. But I didn't like the analytical style, either of Joyce or of Proust, who was the other Pillar of Hercules of the literature of that time. They were two great analysts, who had expanded the confines of realism as no one before them had done.

But you like Proust very much?

Proust perhaps more than Joyce. Joyce followed the road opened by Flaubert with *Bouvard et Pécuchet.* He's a comic writer, who created an immense character named Bloom. The whole book is in a comic, or rather epic-comic key. Proust, on the contrary, belongs to the great French realistic tradition. He depicts French society, as before him, over the centuries, Molière, Stendhal, Balzac, Flaubert, Zola had depicted it. Molière wrote theater, but the world is the same as Proust's. The comedy of *Les Précieuses ridicules* and of *Le Bourgeois gentilhomme* is the same as the salon of Madame Verdurin. Identical. Nothing has changed. France's strength lies in this society, which had continued to be the same since the days of Louis XIV or even earlier. After Proust perhaps the pattern was shattered.

In Italy the first critic to take an interest in Proust was Giacomo Debenedetti — isn't that right?

Yes. But perhaps not entirely. Still, he concerned himself with Proust in a more original and fundamental fashion than the others. He was a part of that phenomenon of identification with Proust that is found not only in France but also in England.

Did you know Debenedetti?

Yes, fairly well. At the time of his essays on Proust Debenedetti was living in Turin. Every time I went to Paris, since I went by train, I would stop overnight in Turin and I would call on Debenedetti, whom I liked a lot, a man with the fascination of a literary person, an aesthete.

To go back to scriptwriting, what Italian writers have also written screenplays?

Soldati, Pasolini, Parise, Flaiano, Berto, Cerami.

Were you a friend of Soldati's from childhood?

Our friendship began at the beach, at Viareggio, where we were both spending a summer vacation. My mother was always telling me that the Soldati boy had saved a child his age from drowning in the Po and had received a medal for civilian valor. After that summer I didn't see him again for at least ten years. Then one day around 1929, Morra di Lavriano said to me, "I want to introduce you to someone, a very likable young man." I went to the meeting, and from a distance I saw a man of fifty with a black beard in Assyro-Babylonian style, very serious. I said, remembering his age, "It must be someone else; it can't be Soldati." Then, the next day, I saw him without the beard, just with a mustache. A wonder! Another four days went by and I met him again: no moustache. He was clean-shaven. This chameleonlike ability to shift from one psychological color to another is typical of Soldati. With Soldati, immediately after my marriage to Elsa, I made a film drawn from a novel, *La trappola*, by Delfino Cinelli. The other scriptwriter was Bonfantini, a literary critic who had written an essay on Baudelaire and said constantly "my Baudelaire," as if the French poet were his property. Bonfantini was serious about being Piedmontese, with the virtues and defects of the Piedmontese. Soldati, on the contrary, acted the Piedmontese, exaggerating those virtues and defects into caricature. That's Soldati: now you see him, now you don't. He's sincere and he's play-acting.

How many screenplays did you write?

My first film was *La trappola* of Cinelli, for fifteen thousand lire, which even at that time was very little. Then I did two films with Castellani: one called *Il colpo di pistola* and the other *Zazà*. No, wait, that's not all: then I did *Senza cielo* for Guarini, I told you about that, remember? And later, as Fascism fell, I was writing *La freccia nel fianco* from a story by Luciano Zuccoli. After the war I wrote *Il cielo sulla palude* for Augusto Genina and *La romana* for Zampa. I tried again to do a film with Castellani, but it didn't work out and I gave up movies. Since then I haven't written any more films.

Did you ever work with Visconti?

I was always on excellent terms with Visconti; I liked him a lot. I met him in 1939, when I was called to work on *Ossessione*, a story stolen from *The Postman Always Rings Twice*. I worked with Ingrao and Alicata. Beside the swimming pool of Visconti's villa,

Jean Marais lay stretched out, naked. Visconti was young and very handsome. He suggested a figure in some great Renaissance portrait. *Ossessione* was enormously important in Italian cinema because it marked the beginning of neorealism. The actors were Massimo Girotti and Clara Calamai. Though I collaborated on that film, only one word of mine has remained, "Cretino!" Calamai says this word to her husband. I had become a friend of Visconti's through Guttuso, whom I saw often at that time.

What was Visconti like?

He was courtly, in a double sense: he was polite and he had to have a court. Those who surrounded him had to devote themselves to him as courtiers in the past devoted themselves to the lord of the moment. This always happens with directors, to some extent. With Visconti it was accentuated by the fact that he was very generous, very hospitable, and in some ways, a master of both art and life.

What other directors did you know?

I knew Lattuada. When Fascism fell, I was working on *La freccia nel fianco* with Lattuada. We both fled and the film was never made.

Did you know Rossellini?

Yes, I knew Rossellini and also De Sica. I knew everybody and everybody knew me. You must realize that I'm a part of the Italian cinema because, first of all, I've written about two thousand articles of film criticism and also because at least twenty films have been based on my novels.

I'd like you to tell me something about your first steps in that world. Explain what the directors were like.

First of all, Italian cinema was very poor, there was no capital. It was perhaps poverty as much as any aesthetic considerations that caused Roberto Rossellini to begin shooting *Open City* in the streets, without professional actors. So necessity, as well as a reaction to the so-called white-telephones cinema of Fascism, brought about the birth of neorealism. At that same time I wrote, as I said, the script of a film by Augusto Genina, *Il cielo sulla palude,* which told the story of the recently canonized Saint Maria Goretti.

You were married at about that time, weren't you?

In 1941, on the Monday of the Angel, the day after Easter. I decided to get married because I didn't want to live apart from Elsa any longer. We were married by Father Tacchi-Venturi, a Jesuit who had drawn up the concordat between the Vatican and Mussolini. We were married in a chapel dedicated to the Madonna. Father Tacchi-Venturi at first would have preferred another chapel, where the remains of Saint Ignatius Loyola are preserved. Father Tacchi-Venturi disapproved of Elsa's decision, because he wanted Elsa to become a good typist. You know how he used to hear her confession? He would close the door of the church, which was immense, and confess her aloud, in any old pew. It was a fairly Dostoyevskian scene. Our witnesses were Longanesi, Pannunzio, Morra, and Capogrossi. Elsa was wearing a new suit and had a purse with a stain, which she modestly hid by holding it against her skirt. I didn't have the money to buy a ring; I bought simply the ritual bouquet of lilies of the valley.

What about your family?

My family, at my wish, didn't come to the ceremony, but when it was over, my mother, as I said, gave a dinner at home. Those were the days of Stalingrad, and during the ceremony, behind my back, our witnesses talked only about the battle of Stalingrad, which was still in progress. Meanwhile, Father Tacchi-Venturi preached an exhausting sermon, saying that we should live united, that the husband should care for the wife, and so on. Actually, I remember my wedding as something not exactly happy, oppressed as I was by the war, lack of money, my family, and not least, the great and proper importance that Elsa attached to the ceremony.

Marriage wasn't important to you?

No. First of all because I wasn't a believer like Elsa, and besides, I'm by nature refractory to the symbolism of ceremonies. I loved Elsa, and this seemed to me enough for us to live together.

How did the dinner go at your mother's?

It was unreal and in the end downright catastrophic. My mother wanted to give Elsa some bits of domestic wisdom. Elsa answered her rudely and never saw her again after that. Elsa always used to say that there are people who have a soul and others who don't have one. My mother, according to her, didn't have a soul; whereas, in my opinion, she had a soul exactly like everybody else. Elsa's character was unworthy of her intelligence. She should have understood that my mother was simply a bourgeois lady and let it go at that.

Why didn't your family give you the money to buy a ring?

I never asked for anything, I didn't want anything. I was independent, and it wouldn't have been decent for me to ask for money. So, instead of asking to occupy a big apartment in a house we owned in Via Sgambati, I asked simply for the use of a little two-room attic. This unassuming request was to have, a few years later, a devastating delayed consequence. The pied-à-terre obviously wasn't sufficient, but Elsa at a certain point lost her temper in an excessive and cruel way, actually jeopardizing our life together. After the war I had to sell in great haste the whole house, whose apartments moreover were all rented at prewar rents; it constituted my share of my father's estate. I then bought the apartment in Via dell'Oca where Elsa and I lived until the end of our marriage and where Elsa went on living by herself until her death. But the apartment in Via Sgambati, though it was very small, had a magnificent view over the trees of the Borghese Gardens and the Borghese Museum. In that apartment we lived a kind of students' life. We ate two meals a day in trattorias; both of us slept and worked in one room.

After your marriage did you go on a wedding journey?

Wedding journey!? All I had was a fifteen-thousand-lire contract for that film with Mario Soldati I mentioned. Instead of a wedding trip, we went to Siena and stayed in a beautiful villa transformed into a hotel, the Villa Scacciapensieri.

Were the two of you worried about lack of money?

Neither of us was. Elsa because she had always been poor, and I because I faced poverty as a new experience. And so our life was dealt with day by day. I lived for ten years almost without money. There is a legend current in Italy that I've always been well-off. It's not true: until the publication of *La romana* I was without possessions, absolutely, and after the war I came to know poverty in the real sense of the word. This was the situation; otherwise the *Racconti romani* and *La ciociara* would be incomprehensible, because they are descriptions of poor people, of poverty. I'm not a writer who writes only about the middle classes; I have known the working class intimately. I want this to be quite clear. I'm annoyed with Italian writers and critics who say I'm only a rich, prosperous bourgeois. Besides being false, this idea prevents an understanding of a part of my work that is totally concerned with the poor.

From Siena where did you go?

To Anacapri.

What sort of life did you live there?

This is how we lived: I got up around seven, I started working on *Agostino*. Elsa was writing *Menzogna e sortilegio*. Then at nine we would walk down to the Piccola marina, where we would stay till midafternoon, then we would climb back up to Anacapri, often in the rain, sometimes quarreling. Always on foot, everywhere on foot. We were two extraordinary walkers, partly through lack of money. We spent time with painters, foreigners, local poor people. We went to the taverns, drank the Capri wine, had great arguments about artistic problems, and in spite of the war, we almost never mentioned politics.

Were you there also in winter?

Yes, we spent half the year on Capri. We rented two big rooms at Anacapri in the villa of Cavalier Mazzarella, the former Liberal mayor of Anacapri. It was a stupendous place, very beautiful, one of the most beautiful memories of my life. Anacapri was a genuine village, very likable, with hospitable, simple people, who had remained just as they had been before the 1914 war. They never locked the doors of their houses because nobody would think of stealing. We ate sandwiches on the beach, or we ate in a trattoria, Maria's, at the Piccola marina, four tables under an arbor. We ate eggplant, octopus, things like that. Then around four we would go back up to Anacapri, where we would have tea. I'd buy the newspapers in town, writing paper, cigarettes. The tobacconist, who knew me by then, would throw several packs of cigarettes on the counter so I could squeeze them and pick the softest. At five we would take a walk in the interior of the island. The war was on, and in Anacapri there were only some Swedish families, so boring that we preferred to be alone. We went to see the cannons that were supposed to defend the Bay of Naples. By a strange coincidence, my uncle Gualtiero De Marsanich came to command this group of cannons. They were enormous, and to understand the attitude of the inhabitants of Capri toward the war, in that year of the *drôle de guerre*, this is what happened: on Sunday, all dressed in their best clothes, they went to look at the cannons. The cannoneers would open the breech of the cannon, and the Anacapresi would stick their head into the cannon and say, "I can see the sky!" But my uncle warned me there was an ammunition dump quite near my house, with some enormous shells. I said to my uncle, "What happens if they bomb us here?" "We'll all blow up." They never fired a shot. Elsa walked around with a Siamese cat on a leash and I had an owl on my shoulder.

Where did you get it?

Some children had caught it and were carrying it around, because its wing had been shattered by a bullet.

Why did you walk around with the owl?

No reason, just to be a bit original. I walked around with an owl, I was called, in dialect, "o' librista" — "the book man" — everybody knew me and considered me an inhabitant of the island.

Had your brother already died?

My brother died in 1941. He was the best mine layer of the Pavia division. He was an engineer and he made mines. A friend of his, also a mine layer, asked him to come see if his minefield was all right. My brother went for an inspection, his friend stepped on a mine, it exploded, and they both died. It was a very sad thing.

Do you remember the funeral?

What funeral? He was buried there. Outside Tobruk there's his grave still. The soldiers put a cross on it and made a wreath with a lot of opened sardine cans, sticking one inside the other. There lies my brother, Gastone Pincherle.

Did this make a great impression on you? Do you remember where you were when you received the news?

At home. Poor boy, I felt sorry for him. It was a wretched fate for such a generous person. He sacrificed a home leave in Italy as a favor to a married comrade, and so he lost his life. He was a normal boy who would have become an engineer. Mussolini's war cost me a brother and my family's patrimony. What's more, Fascism persecuted me as a writer and an intellectual as long as it lasted. I never think of these things, but they have their significance.

While you were on Capri, where were your mother and your sisters?

In Rome.

Did they stay in Rome the whole time?

Yes. My father died in 1942. In a hospital, where my mother had had the foresight to send him. She put him in the hospital, concealed the fact that he was Jewish, then, when he was dying, she made him convert. As a widow my mother went on living in the house in Via Donizetti, but it was all falling apart, abandoned. In fact, immediately after the war she left that house and went to live in an apartment in Parioli, near Via Archimede.

Who was on Capri during the war?

In summer there were the Fascists and the Germans. Edda Ciano with her entourage and many Nazi officers. In winter there was nobody.

Did the Germans bother you?

No, they were very polite. They considered us Italians in good faith, loyal and reliable allies, and they didn't realize that almost all of us were against them and against the war.

What did you and Elsa talk about?

Very little. She complained of my silences. She always said, "Either you babble too much or you're too silent."

Did she talk to you about the book she was writing?

No, absolutely never.

You never talked about it?

I talked about what I was doing, but she didn't. Elsa was very secretive; I'm not. I'm not secretive for a very simple reason: I hate secrets. My public persona has no secrets. What I believe in is complexity, which is in itself secret. I have a second persona, call it private, and that is, in fact, complex. An artist always has something hidden. And the novelist is often schizophrenic.

Did you ever talk to her about Agostino?

No. Many years afterward I remember that for the first time I had Elsa read a manuscript of mine; it was *La noia*. She said, half alarmed, half surprised, "Why, this is a love story."

9

*A*LAIN ELKANN: *Is it really true that you wrote* Agostino *in a month, in August, and that's why you gave the book that title?*

ALBERTO MORAVIA: Yes, it's true. I wrote it with great inspiration, illuminated by a great expressive felicity. We might talk some more about it, because it's fundamental in my work. That book is the hinge that connects *Gli indifferenti* with my later books. *Agostino* is about the relationship between a boy and his mother, at the seaside, during a holiday. Agostino loves his mother and at the same time he joins a group of working-class boys who make up the court of a kindly homosexual. In those summer days at a little bathing resort, which is Viareggio, Agostino discovers two things that, at least today, are basic in life: sex and class distinctions. Sex is what basically determines his relationship with his mother, seen first as the sacred and inaccessible genetrix, then as an ordinary woman. Class distinctions are what separate him from his proletarian playmates. It is the story of a childhood vacation, but it is also the story of Agostino's encounter with modern culture, and its premise is the work of two great unmaskers, Marx and Freud. Obviously I just wanted to tell a story, but it is also obvious that every story, carried to its extreme consequence, can only reveal its secret rapport with the culture of its time. Shakespeare also wrote stories, but in the end it was discovered that these stories involved a humanistic, Renaissance view of the world, between Montaigne and Plutarch.

When you are inspired, do you write more rapidly?

Some books I wrote rapidly, because my head was working rapidly. But there was no haste in the narration. I'll explain with a metaphor. In the first case, inspiration is the skein already wound up, which unwinds quickly and easily. In the second, you must first untangle all the strands and arrange them to make the skein. Felicity consists of having the skein all neatly wound up in your head, I believe. You pull and pull, and it all unwinds easily, never stopping.

That's what happened with Agostino?

Yes. But take, say, *Le ambizioni sbagliate.* It was an enormous tangle of threads. So first I had to untangle them and then make the skein and play it out. Also *La vita interiore* was a bit like that. All things considered, however, *La vita interiore* is much more felicitous than *Le ambizioni sbagliate.*

When you were writing Agostino, *did you realize it was an important book?*

No, it seemed to me a well-made story.

Nothing more?

No, the story of a boy's holiday with his mother.

But when the book was finished, you realized it was important, didn't you?

I was pleased, but you must understand that I have always been very modest in my personal opinions of my books. My books never satisfy me completely. I've always had the impression that I could improve them, make them better. But it's equally true that you never know when revision has to stop. This reminds me of that film Clouzot made about Picasso. You see Picasso painting a bull. Gradually the bull becomes more and more beautiful, but Picasso wants to perfect it and then, just as gradually, he ruins it. We know where Picasso should have stopped, but he didn't know. This happens also with me. Probably the secret of successful writing consists in letting go of it in time, imperfect. That imperfection then is revealed later as the maximum of possible perfection.

When was Agostino *published?*

In 1944, right in the midst of the Nazi occupation. My sister Elena corrected the proofs.

Why in 1944, if you wrote it in 1942?

Because Fascist censorship wouldn't grant permission for its publication. What was anti-Fascist about *Agostino?* Absolutely nothing. But the censors are functionaries, and functionaries must justify their function even if they have nothing on which to exercise it. In any case, with *Agostino* that's how things stood, so I went to the ministry, and in the censor's office there was an admiral, a nice man, for that matter. He began by saying, "You're not well liked. You have a very bad reputation abroad." At that moment a clerk came in and told the admiral he was wanted elsewhere. The censor went out; my dossier was on his desk. I opened it and discovered that the "abroad" the admiral mentioned consisted of a poetaster cultural attaché in Brazil, who informed the ministry that some cheap newspaper in that country had published a news item saying I was hostile to the Fascist regime. I've told you this story, one of many, to show you how the functionaries operate in a dictatorship. With fear and a zeal fed by fear. It's the law of tyrannies. The inferior is afraid of the superior, and from one superior to the next you arrive at the dictator, who, precisely because he's a tyrant, is afraid of everybody. So *Agostino* came out in 1944, published by Documento, a firm run by a friend of mine named Federico Valli. An edition of five hundred copies with three drawings by Guttuso. It was published while Elsa and I were in the mountains. Guttuso's illustrations, by the way, are a story in themselves. On the eve of the fall of Fascism I decided I wanted an illustration by Bartolini, who was a good engraver and a good painter. I began telephoning Bartolini. No answer: I was told the painter was not at home. Then finally on the phone I heard a voice that sounded, as they say, like nothing human, and the voice said, "Stay away from me, you dirty anti-Fascist scoundrel! If you don't leave me alone, I'll shoot you!" In other words, Bartolini was afraid of being compromised! After the war I was with Pannunzio in his office at *Il mondo*, I remember, and Pannunzio said to me, "Bartolini's on the phone." And I said, "Tell him, please, that I'll kick him in the ass!"

What were people saying in those war years? Did they sense that Fascism was coming to an end?

Everybody thought that Fascism could, and should, collapse, but since the outcome of the war was uncertain almost to the end, its fall wasn't a certainty; depending on the person, it was a hope or a fear. The anti-Fascists, of course, hoped; but those who feared weren't only the Fascists but also a part of the population who had got used to Fascism and were afraid of change. In any case, everyone was waiting. When something serious is about to happen, you don't predict anything, you're fascinated by the imminent event and that's that. There were also the stupid, who were the majority, in fact. For example, I remember Ardengo Soffici, who was a painter and a writer of considerable talent. We went to Via Veneto for an aperitif. "Leave it to him. Leave it to Mussolini! Everything will work out, just wait and see! He'll take care of everything!" And this was an intellectual, a man who had lived in Paris, had known Modigliani and Picasso. "Leave it to him, Moravia, keep out of it. Let Mussolini handle everything!"

In 1942 did you still think the Axis could win the war?

No. There had already been Stalingrad. To understand the Italians, you have to bear in mind that they are an extremely jolly people. There was no gloom: they ate and drank, they had every-thing they wanted, also because there was a very well-organized black market. Until 1943 we went to a restaurant called Ci Penso Io (Leave It to Me). I remember that in the dish there was a big potato and, under it, a steak. To give you a graph of what was hap-pening: in 1939 many hoped that Italy wouldn't take part in the war at all. In 1941 they hoped that Italy would win. In 1942 that Germany would win. In 1943 that we could get out of the war without too much damage, and in 1944 that the Allies would win.

But did you and Elsa also think these things?

No, that's what other people thought. The papers talked about the victory of the Germans or about the strategic withdrawal of the Italians in Greece and Africa. In reality, Italy had entered the war completely unprepared. This lack of preparation then had been somehow justified by the hope that the war would end at once with the victory of the Germans, and hence also of the Italians, their belated allies.

Were you in Rome when the Fascist regime fell, in July 1943?

Certainly I was in Rome. I remember that the whole city was full of people who went around shouting, "They've arrested Mus-solini!," "We have freedom!," and things of that sort; then they dragged through the streets some plaster busts of Mussolini and other symbols of Fascism. Some climbed up on ladders with ham-mers and chipped away the Fascist symbols that were carved more or less everywhere. The city was in a state of upheaval, everybody was overjoyed, but immediately afterward a nightmare period began, which in our national history is called the Badoglio pe-riod, from July 25, the date of Mussolini's fall, to September 8, the day of the return of the Fascists. I remember that on July 25 I left the house and put a pistol in my pocket, my brother's Glisenti, which had been sent back to us after his death. It was an auto-matic revolver. I saw at once that it wasn't at all necessary. Every-body was delighted, they danced, they sang, there was an enormous explosion of joy. A freezing reaction followed when

Badoglio, named prime minister, announced, "The war continues." That is how the Badoglio period began and our anxieties resumed; the war continued. The Germans were in Rome and there were more of them all the time. There was a feeling that something was about to happen. One day I went to see Malaparte.

Where?

In Rome, at his house. Malaparte welcomed me with great cordiality and said, "Come with me, come to Capri!" I said, "Why should I go to Capri?" "Because here, my friend, in a little while it's *kaputt!* The Badoglio government is secretly negotiating a peace settlement with the Allies. I'm clearing out, my friend, and going to Capri. Come with me!" Then I said something that determined that I would then spend a year in the mountains and that Elsa and I would write two novels, *La ciociara* and *La storia.* You see how everything matters in life, even a single sentence. I said, "No, I want to stay here and see what happens." Why did I say that? I've never known. I realized there was genuine danger. I could have gone to Capri, to Malaparte's house. I would have spent a magnificent year of bathing and sunshine, and instead I said no, I'm staying here. Why? I repeat: I don't know. Perhaps because I never really trusted Malaparte, no matter what he said, even if he was telling the truth. I went home; Malaparte vanished.

A few days later came the predictable catastrophe. One morning I looked out and saw a whole Italian division, tanks and troop trucks, moving along Via Pinciana. The Germans were occupying the city. The king had run off. Badoglio had run off. The division reached the suburbs, then retreated. I went downstairs, again with the pistol in my pocket. I reached Via Veneto. I ran into Soldati, I remember, under the Porta Pinciana. He shouted, tragicomic even at a moment like that, "We have to run away, there's nothing left but communism!" I went home and stayed there two or three days. Meanwhile, the Germans had occupied the whole city, but you didn't see much of them. You saw plenty of Fascists, in groups, in their black shirts, waving little pennants with the slogan "Viva la morte!" I didn't do anything; I was waiting. This is another thing that strikes me: my irresponsibility. I wanted to watch, and I watched. Everybody was fleeing, and I stayed. A few days later I was walking through Piazza di Spagna and I met a Hungarian journalist I knew, a likable man, the head of the foreign press club, and he said to me, "What are you doing here?" "What should I be doing? I'm here. I'm a Roman; this is where I live." He said, "But you're on the list of people to be arrested." "Ah! really?"

I went home. I said to Elsa, "We have to flee." She said, "Where are we going?" "We're going to the husband of my Swedish translator: nobody suspects him." He was a Swedish businessman, importer of engines for motorboats, and we went to him. He was two meters tall, blond, laconic, and he said, "All right, stay here." So we moved in with them. With me I had a bag with some cans of sardines. In my pocket I had fifty thousand lire, just drawn out of the bank: it was all I possessed. For two days we stayed in the Swede's house. Then I said to Elsa, "We can't stay here: this is a good man, but he's not a relative or a friend or anything. We have to move on." Then we went to Carlo Ludovico Bragaglia, the brother of Anton Giulio Bragaglia. Carlo Ludovico Bragaglia was a movie director, a friend of Elsa's, a good and likable man; he welcomed us warmly, and for another two days we stayed with him.

Meanwhile, there were stories circulating of arrests and searches. The Fascists were taking their vengeance. I began to think of seeking refuge in some embassy. We went to see a Belgian countess I had known for some time, whom I believed a fast friend of mine. We waited in a drawing room; the countess sent word that she couldn't, she simply couldn't. So we left. Then I sent Elsa to Father Tacchi-Venturi; at the church of the Gesù, I knew, there were vast cellars. I said to her, "Go to him and tell him to let us hide there until the English get here." As we could have foreseen, he said no. He was very hostile to me and in favor of the Fascists. In fact, in the cellar of the church, after the Allies' arrival, he hid a Fascist, and a consumptive one at that, who died a short time later.

What to do? We decided to take the train for Naples: we were told it was still running. We found a suitcase; in it we put our toilet articles and what we would need for the summer. Yes, because this is how we thought: the English will arrive in ten days, it's summer, so it's pointless to take heavy things. Elsa had a flowered cretonne dress and I had a light sharkskin suit. We went to the station; it was all full of Blackshirts there to welcome some German big shot. I almost had the impression they were there for us. I said, "Now they'll grab us." Instead, we bought tickets for Naples; the ticket agent gave us a slightly funny look but said nothing. We got onto the train. The train moved almost at once. Clank, clank, clank. Then it began to pick up speed. It was a very beautiful September day, particularly warm and serene; we were fine. I said to Elsa, with my usual irresponsibility, "We'll go to Naples, we'll swim, we'll visit Malaparte on Capri . . ." At a certain point the train stopped at a completely deserted station. A railwayman came and said, "You have to get off." "Why do we have to get off?" "Because there aren't any more tracks." What a surprise! "And why aren't there any more tracks?" "Bombed, obviously!" That was how everything was in Italy.

We got off and found ourselves in the station parking lot, with the sun beating down, hot but beautiful, the Italian summer sun. The countryside was filled with the rasp of cicadas. An atmosphere of extreme peace, nothing to suggest the war. We set off along a dusty road between hedges of blackberries. We reached Fondi. There was nobody in sight, everything was closed, barred, the inhabitants had fled. We wandered around Fondi in vain, and finally I said to Elsa, "There's nobody here in the city, but I'm sure the peasants have all stayed where they are, because they have to take care of the fields and the livestock, they don't run away!" In fact, I was right, the countryside was full of people. We went along one path, then another; in the end we reached a farmhouse. We went inside. I told the peasant we were evacuees. I was already using this neologism, a beginning of awareness after so much heedlessness. I explained, "I'm a schoolteacher from the outskirts of Rome, could you put us up for a couple of days until the English get here?" They were very kind; they gave us a fairly big room, with a frightfully dirty bed. I remember there were night tables with chamberpots yellow with urine; a sharp, ancient stink. Wasps and hornets everywhere, a cloud of flies. But they were good people.

One day went by, a second, a third, and the English didn't arrive, but on the other hand the Germans began rounding people up. Then I said to Elsa, "We can't stay here any longer." So one fine morning, I in my gray double-breasted suit, Elsa in her flowered cretonne, we loaded the suitcase on a donkey and began to climb. At the end of the valley there were two mountains, and between these mountains a gorge and a path that zigzagged upward. We climbed and climbed, and finally we arrived at a little house. Nearby we saw a peasant who was working his field. His name was Davide Marrocco; he was young, but he had one walleye, and this had saved him from the draft. The other men of the area had been sent to Russia, where they all died. So I had happened onto a community all of women. Still thinking that the Allies were about to arrive, I said, "Give me a room until the English get here." These were mountain peasants, very poor, absolutely without anything. They tilled the slopes with a system of terraces and steps. If you go to those areas you'll see that the mountains are divided into terraces that in dialect are called *macere*. These *macere*, seen up close, are patches of arable land, sustained by little walls of stone, homemade: the women bring the stones in baskets, and the men lay them. On these *macere* they grow everything: wheat, flax, corn, potatoes, tomatoes, and so on. Not only what they need for food, but also for their clothes, because with the flax and the wool they weave their own cloth. It was a *ciociaro* community, or rather, since the men were absent, *ciociara*.* There is an old and I believe obscene song that says, "When the *ciociara* takes a husband, who gets the *ciocie* and who the string?" I should point out that once the *ciocie* were made with leather and today with old automobile tires.

---

*The peasants of this mountainous area, instead of shoes, traditionally wear *ciocie*, a kind of slipper with long laces that crisscross the leg and are tied at the calf. The region is called Ciociaria, and the original title of Moravia's *Two Women* is *La ciociara*, "the woman from Ciociaria."

The place where we lived can still be seen: it's exactly as it was. A little room, huddled against the wall of the *macera*, a wall of live rock, that is, with a little roof of sheet metal. Inside, you could barely turn around. There was a big bed, made of two iron supports and three planks, and on the planks a sack filled with cornshucks, which creaked and shifted every time I moved. On this cornshuck mattress there were two sheets, one beneath and one above, of rough handwoven linen. There were no blankets. Davide gave me his *ferraiolo*. A *ferraiolo* is a round cloak, like the ones that enfold the characters in Verdi's *Ernani*. But the room was so small and we were so close when we slept that I never suffered the cold. There was no flooring, just packed earth. When it rained the water came in and I stood with my feet in the water. For nine months I sat on the bed; we didn't have a chair. The dwelling was narrow, but long: besides the bed it contained a loom for weaving cloth. At this loom a young peasant girl was constantly seated, making a deafening racket. Believe me, the noise of a wooden loom is really deafening.

And what did you and Elsa do?

We didn't do anything, we had no ink, no pen. We had only two books, *The Brothers Karamazov* and the Bible. Lacking toilet paper, we used the pages of Dostoyevsky. We read the Bible now and then, but less than you might imagine. In reality, we waited for the Allies, and the waiting wore us down with the conflicting news — good, bad, and, above all, false.

Did these peasants know who you were?

I told them I was an evacuee schoolmaster, as I'd told the others.

What was your life like?

We met once a day around five in the afternoon in a hut that served exclusively for eating. We ate only one meal a day. In the morning I limited myself to eating carobs or a piece of bread. We sat around the fire where the pot was hung; in it some beans were boiling. There were no chairs, only logs. The head of the family, who was Davide, took the loaf and, holding it against his chest, cut off many slices and filled a terracotta tureen. Over those many layered slices he poured the contents of the bowl of beans, and then we waited. After a while the bread steeped in the beans formed a kind of tepid mush, and each of us served himself with a tin spoon. Then Davide produced a bottle from among the rocks of the wall of the hut and gave each of us a glass of acid wine, the home product. But what I remember most about these afternoon meals at Sant'Agata was the smoke. The hut was built in this way: a circular dry wall of stones with a little low door and a sloping roof of straw that almost touched the ground. There were no windows, and the smoke from the brazier could hardly escape through the straw of the roof. This smoke, besides smoking the sausages hanging from the ceiling, made all of us cry: the peasant, the women, Elsa and me, the two dogs and the cat.

And the rest of the time what did you do?

I told you: nothing. We looked at the landscape, we studied it, to see if there was anything new. Every now and then they bombed the houses in Fondi, every now and then they blew up the dams of the lakes down in the valley. A couple of times we witnessed dogfights in the sky, between Germans and English. I'm summing up, because I've told these things better and in greater detail in my novel *La ciociara*. The only thing I'd like to say that I didn't say in *La ciociara* is that this waiting for the Allied troops, this living always in the open, immersed in nature, this solitude formed around me an atmosphere at once desperate and filled with hope, something I've never found again since. True, I had experienced it in another extreme moment of my life, during the sanatorium years. There, too, I waited for something in a condition of suffering. And this something I was waiting for was basically the same thing, then and later. The end of a condition, unhealthy and painful, and the return to normality.

What did Elsa do? What did she think? What did she say?

Elsa behaved with great courage and great serenity throughout the stay at Sant'Agata: in those difficult conditions she revealed qualities that didn't appear often in the routine of daily life. She was a person who, so to speak, lived in the exceptional and not in the normal. And in war the exception is the rule.

From the way you talk it sounds as if the Sant'Agata period was one of the happiest in your life, or am I wrong?

Now I sometimes say, joking, that war after all is only a long picnic. In any case I was fairly aware that it was an adventure and I lived in it with that element of contemplation that accompanies us in adventures. This doesn't mean that I didn't consider it a very dangerous adventure. I remember that as soon as I arrived at Sant'Agata, having heard the Germans were making roundups, I said to Elsa in absolute seriousness, "Rather than end up in Germany I'd throw myself off that cliff." Elsa agreed with me, but further, she was in great torment because she had left behind, in Carlo Ludovico Bragaglia's house in Rome, the manuscript of *Menzogna e sortilegio.*

Did the Germans make many roundups?

In the nearby valleys they did, to collect young men and send them to be laborers in Germany. Then, in those early days, two boys from Fondi and I decided to spend the day at the top of the mountain. We left the house at five in the morning, when it was still dark, and we climbed up some stony, very toilsome paths to the top of the mountain, where there was a meadow of very green, emerald grass, among the rocks. We took something to eat with us and we stayed there the whole day, in the sun. There we were safe, because the Germans in their raids never came more than halfway up the slope. At sunset we went crashing down again to the valley, slipping on the stones. It had taken us three hours to climb up, and in half an hour we were back at the house. These climbs, too, tinged with fear and some sense of adventure, when I recall them now, make me realize that I then had a fundamental experience. The kind that, in the philosophy that was in fashion just after the war, was called existential.

How were your relations with the peasants?

Neighborly. I paid rent and I tried to make myself useful. Davide asked me to give lessons to his son Bruno. I thought he wanted me to teach the boy Italian, but on the contrary, he asked me only to explain arithmetic to him: the son had to learn how to do sums, this was what mattered most. One day I had the unusual idea of reading the gospel to them. I chose the story of the resurrection of Lazarus, but I quickly realized they weren't understanding anything. That is, they didn't appreciate the symbolic and religious character of the tale. The women talked among themselves, the children whined. Davide, with his knife, was whittling the tip of a stick. After that day I laid the gospels aside.

How did you spend the day? Were you very cold? How did you wash?

I told you: we weren't cold because the place was so small that we warmed each other. As for washing, this was the system: Every day early in the morning I would go to the well and drop the bucket to the bottom. The water was frozen. The bucket broke the ice and filled. Elsa threw that icy water over herself once a day; I did it once a week. We were relatively clean. Then, all of a sudden, when two months had gone by and the Allies hadn't arrived, there was the problem of heavy clothing for the winter. At this point I want to recount an episode that will show you how brave Elsa was and how she was also very generous. By now we were well into October, we were in summer clothes, it was beginning to turn cold. I had bought a pair of shoes from some Italian deserters, real army boots. But my summer suit was no protection. Then at a certain moment Elsa decided to go to Rome, collect our winter clothes, and return to Sant'Agata. To understand Elsa's courage on that occasion you must bear in mind on the one hand the discomfort we suffered in the mountains and, on the other, that she had come only to be with me: she wasn't wanted by the police, she could easily have stayed in Rome instead of living in that horrible discomfort. In any case, she went down to the valley, went to the station, and took the train. By then she was so used to the rustic life that in Rome she went around the streets and on the tram with the staff she used in the mountains, which I had made for her from the branch of a tree. People looked at her and murmured these words, which she later repeated to me, "Poor thing, she's pretty but she's mad." She went home, packed a suitcase with winter things, and came back to Fondi. A German soldier helped her carry the case. She came back reassured about the fate of the manuscript of *Menzogna e sortilegio*, but about Rome and the situation of Rome she said nothing. All she cared about was me and the manuscript.

Up at Sant'Agata did you really feel the war or did it simply mean being evacuees?

We felt the war, all right! First of all because of the scarcity of anything to eat — food became scarcer all the time — and then because of the Allied air raids. As a rule they would bomb Fondi and then, up at Sant'Agata, there were scenes of desperation, because the evacuees thought, rightly, that their homes were being destroyed. A couple of really dangerous things happened to me, and even today I think it is almost a miracle that I wasn't killed. The first time was on a straight road that cut across the entire Fondi plain. Elsa and I were walking in the middle of the road and an English Spitfire aimed at us, determined to kill us. It dived at us, emptying its machine guns, and we saved ourselves by jumping into a ditch. From the ditch we could see the strip of dust from the bullets, following the path of the plane. Which, however, was not content with that first attack. It flew to the end of the valley, then returned, still bent on killing us, and we saved our lives a second time, again throwing ourselves into the ditch.

The other occasion was when we were going down the slope toward Fondi: Elsa and I and a black marketeer named Tommasino and a child named Raniero. We were looking for the German soldiers, to trade eggs for bread. All of a sudden I heard the familiar din of a squadron of American Flying Fortresses. I looked up and saw them right over our heads. I wasn't afraid, because we were far from Fondi and they only bombed Fondi. On the contrary, my blood ran cold, seeing a long red ribbon coming out of the plane that was leading the flight. I knew that the red ribbon was a signal to release the bombs. Almost immediately the bombs fell in the pass where we were. Now the miracle was this: There was a very loud explosion and I saw all around me a number of steel fragments skipping in the dust. Just one of those fragments would have sufficed to cause me a wound the size of a fist. It still seems to me impossible that I should have remained unharmed, a miracle, casual though it was. The flying fortresses went off, their roar died away, silence. I looked around and saw that luckily we were all there. Elsa and Raniero were higher up than I, they had been less exposed. Only Tommasino the black marketeer was missing; but I could hear him whimpering some-where. I discovered that he had hidden behind a rock. I shouted at him, "Tommasino, come on out. There's no danger now." Fi-nally, still groaning, he appeared, but he refused to go down to Fondi with us. He climbed back up to the cave where he had left his family. He collected his family and his belongings and took them to an even higher cave. There he spent several days trem-bling, his teeth chattering, as he moaned. Finally he died, obvi-ously of fear. Thinking back to that episode, I'd like to say now that in those days I realized many things about the Italian people.

What?

I realized that Italy, under Fascism, was divided into two parts, one part that dominated, people with education, and one that was subject, the ignorant, those people who had only bureaucratic dealings with the state, a power relationship: tobacconists, sol-diers, police, district doctors, tax collectors. They went on living as in the days of the grand dukes of Tuscany, the Bourbons of Naples, the kingdom of Piedmont. The great revolution was to some extent effected by Fascism, with the massification of poli-tics; then, immediately afterward, by the modern Italy of the Christian Democrats and the Communists. But the Italy of those old days had virtues that today are lost: people were ingenuous, not at all greedy about money, helpful, often Christian in the literal meaning of the word. Then, in my difficulties, I found everywhere people who were very kind; I rarely encountered rogues, criminals. Now criminality is frightful. Perhaps this was so because people were poor then and had no hope of becoming rich.

Poverty for you has a special fascination, doesn't it?

Yes, that's true. In this sense I'm a Christian. In the postwar period I actually made a personal myth of it: not only was I poor, but I was pleased to be poor. As a boy, I had a moment of prosperity when I lived in grand hotels at my father's expense, but then there was a period of poverty, when it seemed that in poverty there was also a great elegance.

Perhaps it was an infatuation: you made a virtue of necessity?

No, it was a deep feeling! You know the Neapolitan proverb? It goes, "Three are the powerful: the pope, the king, and the man who has nothing." Being poor is a form of power. In fact, what is called existentialism was the idea that man exists and that existence is an indestructible strength.

Yes, but you are also willful?

Willful, yes.

Spoiled?

No, I'm not spoiled. I'm a person capable of bearing the worst hardships. Poverty, however, does not mean being absolutely without anything at all. It means only having nothing superfluous. It's a form of rationality, that's what it is. You know what Stendhal said? That one should have only the necessary. Because if you have too much money you have to worry about managing it, and if you have too little, you have to earn more. My "necessary" is somewhat limited; a bedroom with a table and a chair, paper, a typewriter. Today, since I have trouble walking, also an automobile.

While you were in the mountains, were you impatient to know how it would end?

Yes, I was impatient; in fact, at the time of the unsuccessful landing at Anzio, I sent someone to Terracina, the nearest city, to ask for news. He was a grave digger and, for this reason, was the only one to have a horse. He went on his horse to Terracina, gathered information, also from a lawyer, then came back and told me the following story: "The landing failed because one of the admirals was German and nobody knew it. Since he was in love with the daughter of an English admiral and she wouldn't have him, he avenged himself by making the landing fail." In short, the same story as the defeat at Roncevalles and of Ganelon of Mayence. The illiterate are outside of history, and at the same time, for them the universal explanation is in the French phrase "cherchez la femme." It's the commonplace that in Italy is expressed with the saying "one hair of the c—— has more strength than a hundred pair of oxen," but like all commonplaces it refers in fact to something too common to be ignored.

What was the winter like?

It poured rain, and we spent all day in our hut with the door open to get a bit of air. At Christmas a Scot and an Australian, escaping, came by Sant'Agata. They were part of a unit that had landed near Anzio, then the ship hadn't come to collect them; they never knew why. The Sant'Agata evacuees were terrified, because they knew that having any contact with the Allies was very dangerous and the German police didn't joke. I let them into the house, and since it was Christmas I bought a chicken and some wine and we had supper together. We drank the health of the Allies, and the next day the two left. The following morning two German soldiers immediately arrived, irritated at having had to make all that climb, and searched the huts. Perhaps there had been an informer. On that occasion Elsa proved very quick. She pretended we were sleeping, and when they knocked on the door, she peered out, shouting, "Can't we at least get some sleep around here? What do you want?" The Germans mistook this just indignation for innocence. After the war an Australian called on me, the head of the Australian Red Cross: he was the father of one of our two guests. He came to thank me, with emotion, for what I had done for his son, and he told me that the son and his companion, shortly after leaving Sant'Agata, had been taken prisoner by the Germans.

How did the stay at Sant'Agata end?

It ended when the American seventh army broke through the line after terrible bombing and shelling. On that occasion I realized that it was easier to avoid planes than cannons. Airplanes fly over and go on their way; cannons remain where they are, and they seem to surround you. The day of the advance I was admiring the luminous trajectory of the shells through the sky, then suddenly a shell burst not far away. Then a second one, still closer. I didn't know where to look for refuge. It was as if the cannon were deliberately seeking us out. In the end Elsa and I crawled into a tiny cave, full of chickens and their excrement. The sign that the advance had succeeded was the arrival up there of five German artillerymen who were escaping and wanted to surrender to me because in battle it often happened that those who surrendered were killed all the same. Those five Germans were in very bad shape, tattered and grimy. They handed me their rifles, then they threw themselves into the straw in the yard and immediately fell asleep. I sent down to the valley for some American soldiers I could hand the Germans over to, and after a few hours they arrived: two little Italian-Americans, short, dark, broad-shouldered, who duly took the five tall, blond Vikings in charge. The next day we said good-bye to everybody and went down to the valley. We took also our cat, named Filippuccio, but once we were in the valley, he ran away and was never seen again. That night I had the last war adventure that could have had a fatal outcome. To sleep, Elsa and I had lain down on the floor of an abandoned hovel along the road. Around two in the morning there was suddenly a blinding green light in our room. By then I knew enough about war to realize that flares were being fired by the Germans so they could see the countryside better and strike the Americans. I grabbed Elsa's arm and dragged her out of the house. We spent the night in an open field. The next day I went back to see the house, I found a heap of ruins, and learned that seventy Americans had been killed. That afternoon I went to the American checkpoint and found a jeep with two officers ready to take me to Naples. Apparently the two soldiers with whom we had celebrated Christmas had informed them of our presence at Sant'Agata. But an American sergeant didn't want to let me go. When I complained, he addressed me in this fashion, "Do you want a slap in the face?"

What effect did Naples have on you?

Incredible, because it was full of soldiers, full of whores, full of blacks. Malaparte described that Naples in *La pelle*, but in journalistic, actually sensationalistic terms. But reality is never journalistic: for me Naples was freedom regained, something like the bandage falling away from a healed wound. I remember that, getting out in Naples, I saw the whole city under an enormous quantity of silver balloons: they were a defense against the German planes, but they looked like a fantastic, festive decoration, a Christmas tree. As I said, the city was full of beggars, whores (the so-called *segnorine*), and people who were living by their wits. At the entrance to the city a sign said BEWARE OF PICKPOCKETS. But all of this was accompanied by a boundless joy. Or maybe the joy was all mine, after a year at Sant'Agata.

Had Naples become an Anglo-American city?

No, but it was full of British and Americans, as in various past periods it had been full of French, Spanish, English. The American GIs sat close together in lines, like birds on telegraph wires, on the steps of the churches, staring straight ahead.

Did you feel a liking for them?

Yes, it was the first time foreigners really got to know Italy — British, Americans, and also French — because the occupation was literally spreading into the most remote hamlets of the Appenines. In other words, the occupation was a great experience in both directions: the Italians understood the foreigners, and the foreigners understood the Italians. Italy emerged from the invasion completely renewed. You must remember: from the time of Belisarius, of the Byzantine Empire and the wars between Goths and Byzantines — in other words, this was the first time that a war of such dimensions had been fought in Italy.

Whom did you see in Naples?

English officers and also Italian intellectuals. Especially politicians, the anti-Fascists. I called on Croce, who was staying in a hotel in Sorrento. I said to him, "Look, things are going very badly here, we're poor, hardships, and so on." I was a pessimist; I saw Italy in ruins, totally destroyed. Croce wrote in his diary, "Yesterday the writer Moravia came, to pour onto my bosom the force of his despair." Truly a Croceian sentence!

What did you and Elsa do in Naples?

We waited to go back to Rome.

How long did you stay there?

A month. We were very poor; we had nothing. The English fed us and gave us a place to sleep, but nothing more. We didn't even have the money to buy newspapers. We went back to Rome in a jeep. Rome was all up in the air, in the sense that there was the confusion that precedes revolutions.

Where did you go when you arrived?

We went to my house in Via Sgambati. I was told that the ss had come five times. Then I went to my mother. I found her in our old house, completely intact, but at the same time somehow dreadfully drained. The dog Aloha that Virginia Agnelli had given me was dead; also the Angora cat was dead; the whole house seemed dead. Naturally, my mother didn't seem dead in the least. For her it was just a situation like so many others, to be faced with her usual common sense.

You've always had dogs. Why?

That's not true. For the twenty-five years I lived with Elsa I had only cats, almost always three at a time. Before and after Elsa, on the contrary, I also had dogs. I think it all depended on Elsa. With virtually no distinctions I love all animals, not only cats and dogs. At this point I will say why I love animals. Well, I feel myself an animal, too, at least 95 percent. This feeling inspires in me an obscure and affectionate attraction to all animals. As increasingly, every day, I discover a sensibility so similar to my own, I believe that I am also an animal. Even — or especially — when I write.

Where were your sisters then?

My sisters were with my mother. They were also more or less unchanged. Perhaps in the midst of disasters women resist better than men. I remember in any case that in that period I didn't work, I hustled. That is, I wrote some pieces for radio, meaningless in my opinion, I scribbled for newspapers, I looked for script jobs but didn't find any. I earned twelve thousand lire a month: it was very little even then. Here I want to express an idea that is very important for me. My drama, until the escape into the mountains, was that of being an antibourgeois bourgeois. A child of the bourgeoisie who hated the bourgeoisie, not because it was Fascist, but because it was bourgeois, and I felt that, despite my anti-Fascism, I bore that seed within me. I freed myself of this bondage the same year in which Italy was freed of Fascism. From this point of view, Italy's liberation from Fascism was mirrored in the liberation of my spirit from that element of the bourgeoisie that it contained. This was the effect of my life of suffering and waiting at Sant'Agata, an entirely unconscious effect that, however, later proved decisive.

I must add that the period in the mountains was the time of my greatest intimacy with Elsa. After that our relationship slowly cooled, also for a specific and curious reason that I have already mentioned: in life Elsa preferred the exceptional, impassioned moments, the sublime in other words, and she was, on the contrary, strangely awkward in dealing with daily routine. At Sant' Agata she had found herself in her element: danger, devotion, sacrifice, contempt for life. In Rome, on the other hand, daily life made her lose patience and become difficult, intolerant, and even cruel. In any case, normal life began again, though still as it had been before the war, marked by poverty.

When you resumed your normal life what did you live on?

I lived by writing articles.

For what paper?

First I wrote for *Libera stampa*, then I contributed to the *Corriere della sera* and a whole chain of newspapers: *Messaggero, Nazione, Resto del carlino*, and so on. Later I returned to the *Corriere della sera*. I also wrote a script, *Il cielo sulla palude*, for Genina. I was almost penniless. I had only one suit; it had belonged to my brother killed in the war, the jacket turned, with the breast pocket on the right. In the evening I often went to a British officers' mess and we would talk. There were also Communists, a bit of everything. The English made the Communists talk because they wanted to understand which way the wind was blowing. We got along pretty well together. I saw a lot of Guttuso, Carlo Levi, and in general the left-wing intellectuals, but I didn't feel like joining Communism or producing Socialist realism, which seemed to me mere propaganda and *pompier* to boot.

About your contributions to the Corriere della sera: *what did it mean to you to write for a daily paper?*

It meant being able to travel. I'll explain: I have written for the *Corriere della sera*, as I just told you, from 1946, when the editor was Emanuel, till today, when the editor is Ugo Stille. The paper has underwritten my traveling; otherwise, as you know, I couldn't have made those journeys. Then this financial security also became a stimulus, an inner incitement to find places and countries to visit, to discover. And it also fosters writing, in the way of narrating, or even just reporting, because when confronted with the new you must necessarily assume a new attitude.

What happened then with Agostino?

Agostino received the first postwar literary prize: the prize awarded by the *Corriere lombardo*. I didn't have enough money to go to Milan, and I had the prize sent to me. They were offended because I didn't go in person. *Agostino* was my first literary success after *Gli indifferenti* seventeen years earlier. Until *Agostino* all the literary experiments with surrealism, Dostoyevsky, Stendhal, and so on, had served only to unleash my imagination. As for my father's estate, he left two houses at the beginning of Via Sgambati: one went to my sisters, the other to me. Then there was an apartment house in Via Paisiello, which he left to my mother along with the little villa in Via Donizetti, where she lived. This was all the property: three houses and a little villa. Shortly after the war I sold the Via Sgambati house for twenty-one million lire, with which I bought an apartment in Via dell'Oca, where Elsa and I went to live, and a tiny apartment in Via Archimede as a studio for Elsa, and, also for Elsa, a beaver coat. After that I didn't have a cent left in the bank. The change of address gave me the appearance of a well-to-do man, which in reality I wasn't: houses are like clothes, they serve your so-called image. I remember that in those days, shortly after my settling in the Via dell'Oca apartment, the wife of a well-known industrialist came to see me. Entering the apartment, she said, "Why, you have a real house, with two bathrooms and all modern conveniences!" A remark that revealed the picture that capitalists had then of intellectuals: tramps.

10

*A*LAIN ELKANN: *When did you write* La romana?
ALBERTO MORAVIA: In 1947.

And the Racconti romani?
The *Racconti romani* were written between 1950 and 1960.

What happened to you in the years after the war?
A great boredom. My feelings for Elsa were cooling. Basically my whole life can be considered as divided into so many periods, each of them dominated by a woman. Until then Elsa had dominated; now she longer dominated, but at the same time, there was no other woman.

Did you see Togliatti and the Communists?
Not in the least! Just once I went to see Togliatti at the Ministry of Justice.

What was Togliatti like?

As I said, I saw him at the Ministry of Justice. He was short of stature, with that keen, alert, bespectacled face, the face that certain religious men have when they are also intellectuals. Like the Jesuits, for example. I asked him, "Do you have a lot to do?" He answered, "Nothing, as you can see." We talked about politics and he, to my amazement, uttered what you might call a technical eulogy of the Fascists and the Common Man movement, "They are the only bourgeois politicians capable of handling the masses." At that time, as it happened, I saw a number of Communists, not because they were Communists but because they were artists, writers, intellectuals. Guttuso had a habit of always dragging some left-wing personality along with him. When we lived in Via dell'Oca we often went out in the evening to eat at La Campana. We would take a table and some others always turned up. Writers, politicians, painters, journalists, and so on.

Was Pavese also among them?

No, I saw Pavese a few times at the offices of the publisher Einaudi, or he came to our house, because he was a friend of Elsa's.

What was Pavese like?

Pavese was tall and thin, a broomstick with a crew cut. He was touchy, taciturn, snickering. I barely knew him, as I said, but he was great friends with Elsa.

When did Elsa finish Menzogna e sortilegio?

She finished it after the war and won the Viareggio Prize, shared with Palazzeschi.

Did Elsa's book have a success?

It was a great critical success. The culture industry didn't exist then. One article appeared; it said, "This is a fine book." Period.

It was generally considered a fine book?

Yes, absolutely. There was a long article by Pancrazi in the *Corriere della sera.* I remember one sentence of it read more or less like this, "With her weak womanly strength, Elsa Morante shifts an enormous weight of narrative." True, *Menzogna e sortilegio* is a novel of enormous complexity and richness. Eight hundred closely printed pages, inspired, as I told you, by only three days spent in Sicily.

Did the novel's success change your relationship in any way?

No, but Elsa felt more confident, because, before, she had the impression that I rather took her for granted. It wasn't true, but she had that feeling. Actually, my opinion meant a lot to her because she loved me; but at the same time perhaps she would have loved me less or even not at all if my opinion hadn't been, as it was, extremely favorable. Elsa was something of a totalitarian: either you were with her or against her. Fortunately, thanks to her great human and artistic qualities, I managed to be sincerely "with her" all her life. At this point I must say that she was not always like that toward me. Sometimes she wasn't "with me." And this was so perhaps because I am almost completely lacking in that amour propre that was so strong in her. For me it was and still is today easy to accept negative opinions on my work. With her, you had to be careful.

In what sense?

In this sense: Elsa possessed remarkable critical gifts, but with her own work she tended to have a passionate relationship.

She was competitive?

She was, in the sense that she had a poetics of her own and anyone who criticized that poetics was automatically wrong. In short, she was intransigent in an almost religious way. In this connection I remember that when she read Joyce's *Ulysses,* though she recognized the importance of the work, she covered the pages with unfavorable comments. Joyce didn't fit into her poetics. So you can't really talk of competition: it was a matter of literary ideals.

Did you live up to her literary ideals?

This will seem strange to you, but Elsa and I rarely talked about each other's work, and if anything, I talked more than she did. For instance, she loved me from afar, not knowing me, when I was known only for *Gli indifferenti*. But she never talked to me about that novel. So even now I wonder if the novel had any importance in her love. At the time when she was writing *La storia*, I remember that she said to me, with sincerity, "Among all the books I've read about the war, *La ciociara* is the one that holds up best." At this point I'd like to sum up: I wasn't a part of her poetics, but she loved me and perhaps for her love finally was more important than literature.

Was she part of your poetics?

I've never had a poetics and I have always thought, or rather felt, that poetry isn't a personal matter. It's there or it isn't, whoever the poet may be.

Your relationship with literature isn't one of passion?

The relationship has a long story, like the relationship with a woman you've lived with all your life. I'll simply say that in this relationship I have slowly moved from what literature says to how it says it, still remaining faithful to the initial idea, namely, the idea that literature must say something that is found outside of literature itself.

You didn't have the same poetics, but you admired the same writers and poets?

Here again the question of professionalism arises. Elsa and I were absolutely not a professional writing couple who read each other's manuscripts, talk about books, debate the virtues and faults of the authors they are reading. We were really a man and a woman involved in a very difficult, very personal relationship. Yes, we talked

about books now and then, but no more than any ordinary cultivated married couple.

Did you have some masters in common?

As a boy my master had been Dostoyevsky: for Elsa, it was Kafka.
We both loved Rimbaud very much, she with a passion that ap-
proached brainwashing: she cherished a picture of Rimbaud with
an inscription "To Elsa, Arthur." *L'isola di Arturo* is another clear
reference. As for Kafka, she later changed radically, preferring
Stendhal. This was for strictly personal reasons: Elsa was quarreling with an aspect of her own personality that she defined, a bit
like Simone Weil, as *pesanteur*. Kafka at a certain point obviously
seemed to her too "heavy." Stendhal, on the contrary, along with
Mozart in music and Rimbaud in poetry, represented for her that
ideal of lightness to which she aspired all her life. This was explained very well by Cesare Garboli in an essay of his on Elsa.

But what is this pesanteur? *A Jewish quality that she inherited
from her mother or a Sicilian characteristic that came from her
father?*

In persons of genius you can't talk of heredity or determinism. It
would be like saying Leopardi was a pessimist because he was a
hunchback. I would say rather that Elsa's impassioned nature always had female origins. I mean, her rejection of *pesanteur* was
more than anything else an incipient feminism. For her, passion,
or *pesanteur*, was not a historic, ethnic, religious fact, but a fact of
nature; in a certain way she would have liked not to be a woman,
though she was one and, what's more, an exemplary one. Now, I
must underline that these are conjectures, because she and I never
discussed the matter, but it is a fact that she couldn't tolerate the
unquestioned though obscure relationship between woman and
nature. Let me repeat, however: these are pure conjectures.

What do you mean then by "nature"?

Elsa oscillated in the psychological and cultural sense between a
creatural, premoral, and therefore physiological concept of

human life and an idea of lightness, angelic, or if you prefer, demonaical — in any case, not physiological. This, in my opinion,
was her drama, and she could never make up her mind to chose
definitively one concept or the other. Nature was physiology,
sometimes approved as innocence, sometimes accused of *pesanteur*. Ariel and Caliban, if you like, but an Ariel as incapable of
ridding himself of Caliban as Caliban of Ariel.

*What you say doesn't suggest any intimate relationship be-
tween you.*

There was a dialectical relationship, deeply felt and hence intimate; but it was an impassioned intimacy that constantly risked
being transformed into its opposite. In plain words, we argued all
the time, our arguments were sometimes heard even in the
Bolognese, the restaurant below our apartment, in Piazza del
Popolo, and our fights had made us famous in our own world of
artists and intellectuals. But I repeat, they were hardly ever personal quarrels; if anything, they were caused by two views of the
world that, before becoming complementary, could seem irrec-
oncilable. To oversimplify: I loved reality with all its warts, and
Elsa, on the contrary, felt for reality about as much fondness as
her numerous cats felt for water. The curious thing, however, is
that, whereas in my novels, characters and situations are invented
on the basis of general personal experiences, in Elsa's novels,
without even much transfiguration, you find Elsa herself and the
people in her life and her relations with these people. What I'm
saying is that realism is a very imprecise word, and in our case, the
realism that so horrified Elsa took its revenge in her surprising
ability to depict everyday and autobiographical reality.

Wasn't this about the time when the review Nuovi Argomenti
was born?

Nuovi Argomenti was founded in 1953. Alberto Carocci, a Florentine lawyer and literary figure, who had been for many years editor of *Solaria*, in the early 1940s had founded a review entitled
Argomenti, along with Giacomo Noventa, a poet and writer from

the Veneto. Then, like so many other things, the magazine was swept away by the war. After the war, Alberto Carocci opened a legal office in Rome and suggested to me that we publish a magazine together, *Nuovi Argomenti*, in fact. He suggested it to me probably because I was, or rather he considered me, the exact opposite of the contributors to *Solaria*, especially in the literary sense. The idea was to create a left-wing review like Sartre's *Temps modernes*, which would be alert to the reality of Italy in an objective way, not lyrical like the reality of neorealists on the order of Vittorini and Pavese; and at the same time, it would try to break the dogmatic shackles of Marxism.

Who financed the magazine?

Adriano Olivetti, who was a client of Carocci's. The review, in my opinion, had a certain importance, even though it didn't print a lot of copies. A run of two thousand was exceptional: that happened when we printed an article by Palmiro Togliatti on Krushchev's revelation of Stalin's crimes. The review also published some special numbers of a strictly documentary nature, one, for example, on the Fiat, and one on the bandits in Sardinia, as well as questionnaires about different aspects of literature and Italian social life and literary works of every trend. You just have to remember that the first poem we published was "Le ceneri di Gramsci" by Pier Paolo Pasolini. At present the review is edited by Francesca Sanvitale.

Who were the other contributors? Did Elsa write for the magazine?

Elsa didn't write for any magazine. She sent answers to our questionnaire on the novel. Her contribution to magazines and papers was very short-lived and was all before the war. Our contributors, however, included anthropologists such as Ernesto De Martino, writer-painters such as Carlo Levi, and writers such as Italo Calvino, Carlo Cassola, Paolo Volponi, Mario La Cava, Pier Paolo Pasolini. We published the first chapters of Vittorini's *Le donne di Messina*, a story by Franco Lucentini, pieces by

Leonardo Sciascia. We published, that is, all the new literature that represented the cultural terrain of the postwar Italian novel.

Was Bassani a friend of yours?

Yes, he was our friend, though with reservations on both sides. For the magazine he offered us "Gli occhiali d'oro," a very beautiful story, probably his best, in which there is a very lucid comparison of the "difference" of the Jew and the homosexual. We accepted it, but he wanted to be paid, and since our review had no money, he gave it to *Paragone*. I felt friendship for him; he didn't always feel it for me. He occasionally attacked me in unforeseen and unforeseeable ways. Once in a newspaper he wrote that I wasn't worthy of representing Italian literature. Another time a Belgian TV team came to Rome and they asked him, "Did Moravia have any influence on you?" He answered almost as if he'd been insulted.

Carlo Levi, on the other hand, was really your friend.

Carlo Levi had a beautiful character. Solar, in a sense. He was very vain, as was Bassani for that matter, but their vanities were very different. I remember that a newspaper decided to publish on its literary page some texts of great European writers introduced by Italian writers. Bassani was offered Svevo, and he replied that he would do it, but he wanted also to be presented as a great European writer himself and he added the titles of his books translated and published abroad. Carlo Levi, on the other hand, answered, "I'll introduce anyone you like, but who is introducing me?"

Let's talk about La romana.

La romana is a novel of 550 pages written in four months, between 1 November 1946 and 28 February 1947, after I had begun with the notion of writing a little three-page story to tell about an episode in my life from 1936 that lasted probably no more than an hour.

What episode?

I was with Leo Longanesi in Largo Tritoni, after an evening of customary Roman boredom, and I suddenly saw a woman who was walking along as if she were a streetwalker. She looked no more than twenty and was very beautiful. I said then to Leo, "I like that girl. I'll leave you now." And I went up to her, "Where shall we go?" "To my house." She took me to a small, humble apartment in a narrow street behind the *Messaggero* building. As we went in, I realized she lived in this house with her family. At a certain point she was naked; she had a splendid body. I remembered a strange story by Henry James called "The Last of the Valerii," in which there's a man who falls in love with a statue. Then suddenly an old woman came with a pitcher of hot water and a towel, and she said proudly, "Tell me, where did you ever see a body like that . . . I ask you, have you ever seen a body like that?" The girl and I made love in a simple, normal way. Afterward she said to me, "The woman who brought the towel is my mother." This is the story of my encounter with the girl who ten years later was to inspire the character of the woman of Rome.

At this point I'd like to say something about inspiration and its power of irradiation. As I said, my encounter with that girl lasted at most an hour, but the sentence "that woman was my mother" lasted no more than a few seconds. This may be a romantic notion, but what if it is? That sentence had the duration and also the efficacy of a lightning flash during a storm; it revealed to me what you might call an entire human landscape, for which a sociologist, to explain it and illustrate it properly, would need a book of reflections. More simply, I would say that the sentence "struck me"; that is, it traumatized me. Then inside me that phenomenon that psychoanalysts call suppression must have taken place. The suppression, as I said before, lasted ten years and broke down on the morning of 1 November 1946, when I sat at the typewriter, thinking to turn out a little story on a relationship between mother and daughter of the Roman working class. Instead I continued for four months, typing every morning, and on 28 February 1947, I had a novel of 550 pages which I entitled *La romana*, a title suggested by Elsa. Now I must add a final thought. This novel is what it is; I won't go into its literary merit. I want only to say that its success, undoubtedly considerable, not only confirmed the almost forgotten, taken-for-granted success of *Gli indifferenti*, but also had secondary results. Though these had nothing to do with literature, they showed the book's power of penetration: first a movie, then, many years later, another movie, countless translations, paper-backs, and so on. Briefly, the story of the success of *La romana* is the history of a minimal event, a sentence uttered by chance that then, through mysterious paths, provoked increasingly big and distant effects, as a stone thrown into the water makes ever-widening rings.

How is this moment of success connected with Gli indifferenti?

The link is very simple, through the same literary trend of which my first novel had been an early fruit: the existentialist movement. *La romana* is a novel of existence, neither more nor less than *Gli indifferenti*. Even though in the traditional sense it is fairly consciously inspired by Defoe's *Moll Flanders*.

Can we then say that La romana *is your third important novel, after* Gli indifferenti *and* Agostino?

Yes, that's right.

Did you know Beppe Fenoglio?

No, I didn't know him. *Gli ultimi giorni di Alba* is a good book.

Also Il partigiano Johnny?

Less so. Fenoglio's anglicisms bother me a little. But Vittorini's dialogues and Pavese's speech also betray an imitation of American writers, including minor ones like Saroyan and Cain.

Was the influence of American literature in Italy very great in those years?

Very. It had begun before the war, with the famous anthology edited by Vittorini, *Americana*, to which I also contributed. I translated a story for it. But I continued being an existentialist; I didn't become a neorealist like Pavese and Vittorini. I still am an

existentialist. Italian neorealist writers borrowed the worst faults
of the Americans: while Hemingway remains within the confines of direct speech, the neorealists create a new rhetoric according to the atavistic tradition of Italian literature in every age.
Calvino also began that way. If today you reread Calvino's first
book, *Il sentiero dei nidi di ragno*, you can hardly get through it
because of the mannerism that then seemed almost natural and
today is obsolete. On the subject of this dated character of all
mannerisms, I remember Berenson saying to me, "A book lives
in the moment it appears because of how it's written; later it
lives for what it says." Of course, the neorealists had things to
say; if anything, their trouble was they lacked things to think.

Does neorealism present the true Italy of that time?

Italy was a poor, defeated country, but full of generous passions, at
least among the people who had taken part in the Resistance. In
this sense neorealism surely reflected the mood of many Italians.
But it was mirrored, as I said, without the filter of a premeditated,
organized political and cultural thought. Politically, the neorealist
writers were almost all Communists, but they didn't feel like accepting the propaganda art created by Maxim Gorky and approved and supported by Stalin. The closing down of Vittorini's
literary review, *Il politecnico*, and the expulsion of Vittorini himself from the Communist party represented the most important
episode in this conflict.

How could Vittorini reconcile Hemingway and Il politecnico?

With lyricism, or poeticality.

Yes, but in those years Communism —

Communism had become very strong, but also the bourgeoisie,
while fearing it, very quickly recovered: the Communist Party
couldn't take over the government, because America would never
have allowed that. The bourgeoisie had the support of America
and the Vatican. In 1948 the Christian Democrats won an elec-

toral triumph, and after that the Communists were never part of a government.

Malaparte had become a Communist?

Malaparte was capable of becoming anything. As I said, what mattered most to Malaparte was not this idea or that. In the postwar years he became a Communist, then he became Malaparte again. Nothing but Malaparte.

And Elsa?

Elsa certainly was concerned with politics, but in her own way, passionately and, in any case, putting politics in second place, well after literature. She was interested in politics, but didn't attach much importance to it. She sympathized with the Communists, the Left, yes. But no more than that. She would never have gone so far as to write propaganda, political articles.

Did you and she like the Americans or not?

I did, certainly! They had liberated us!

And Stalin?

I hated Stalin mortally. I hated him more than Mussolini, as much as Hitler, but in a different way. Hitler was, and pronounced himself, an antisocialist. Stalin, on the contrary, had been a socialist and had done socialism the greatest possible harm. We were liberated from Hitler, but we'll never be completely liberated from Stalin.

Were the Italian Communists also Stalinists?

They certainly were! I had a furious argument one evening, in Guttuso's house, because a high official of the Communist Party insisted that Trotsky was already a traitor at the time he was commanding the Red Army. How was he a traitor? The man answered, "Objectively," which is a magnificent adverb of Stalinist jargon, like "unconsciously" is an equally magnificent adverb in Freudian jargon.

Did you travel during those years?

Yes, I traveled with Elsa, who was always recalcitrant, always quarreling with me. I remember that, after the war, I went with Montale and Elsa to London, invited by the British Council.

How did you find London after the war?

There was nothing to eat. I remember still, because it made a deep impression, that we went to a very elegant restaurant, with Doric columns, red plush, that sort of thing. I ordered a shrimp cocktail, and they brought me a single shrimp. We were off to a bad start. Then I ordered *canard à l'orange.* A very stylish waiter arrived, with a metal tray: it wasn't silver, but that was the effect. On it was an oblong dish, in which there was the breastbone of a duck. A bone, a genuine bone, brutally presented as duck. Then we ate, or rather didn't eat, and went out, and at a pub I bought a paper cone of fish and chips.

How did you happen to be with Montale?

He and I had been friends since the days at Forte dei Marmi.

What sort of friendship was there between you?

I admired him. He — who knows? Once, maliciously, he said I was like Mascagni, the composer of a single opera. But on other occasions he was affectionate. Montale most of all wanted to be first; he wasn't pleased if someone else, a novelist perhaps, had a success. I realized this later when he wrote some dismissive remarks about Elsa's *La storia.* I also remember that, after my marriage to Elsa, I introduced her to him. She had a face as fresh as an apple, under a cap of splendid white hair. I said, "This is my wife." He looked at her and then said, "Fresh bread for you; moldy bread for me." Near him was Mosca — that was her nickname — who had been the companion of his whole life. And I was afraid she had heard.

Who was Mosca?

Mosca was the aunt of Natalia Ginzburg, the wife of the art critic Marangoni, and the mistress of Montale.

And he loved her?

Yes, of course. He dedicated many beautiful poems to her. He loved her, but at the same time he made her an emblematic figure like the wall bristling with bits of broken bottles in a famous poem of his. Montale loved squalor because it was the perennial source of his poetry. He loved it and in a sense he cultivated it.

What did Montale look like? How was he?

Montale looked like a humanist, sensual monk, with thick, blondish hair that grew halfway down his forehead, blue, mild eyes, faintly delirious, and a big mouth with greedy lips that sagged over a dimpled chin. There was something monklike about him, but nothing ascetic: a refined, bookish friar. In a café he would never talk, he would only hum, or sing softly, because he had studied voice. But he never went from his low warble to full song. At least, I never heard him.

Did he smoke?

Yes, he smoked. He dressed simply, like a petty bourgeois, in gray, with laced shoes. He was, in fact, the typical person he described in *Ossi di seppia*, saying, "How all life and my travail is in this following a wall that has sharp bottle fragments along the top."

Was he aware of being a great poet?

He was already considered that generally. It seems to me unlikely that he also wasn't convinced of it himself. Everybody thought so. I thought so, and I still think so now. In London, during the trip Elsa and I made with him, we called on Eliot. He offered us tea at Faber & Faber, where he worked, amid piles of books, old and new. Eliot said of himself in a poem, "How unpleasant to meet Mr. Eliot!" He said he resembled a bishop, and in fact he resembled a Protestant bishop and perhaps he was also disagreeable. This said, he was the favorite poet of my youth, along with Rimbaud.

Were you struck by postwar London ?

No, no. London was exactly the same. Nothing had changed. I had been there in 1930; everything was still the same. The great cleanings of the following years, which would give the city a Georgian whiteness, hadn't begun. The city was still Victorian and sooty. Rationing continued after the war, which had just ended. For example, I remember that in the Greek restaurants we had to be wary of the moussaka because at one time it had been made with spoiled egg powder and could cause temporary blindness.

Was London the only place you went that year?

No, I made a trip to Zurich to interview Carl Gustav Jung for *L'europeo*. I went to see Jung in a rich suburb of Zurich. Looking for the villa along the main road, in heavy rain, I couldn't help thinking of the American novelist Scott Fitzgerald, the singer of the previous postwar era, and of a beautiful novel of his in which he described with great precision the psychoanalytical circles of Zurich. An American millionaire, worried about his daughter's mental health, takes her to Zurich, to a clinic among the most famous and expensive. There they discover simply that the daughter was seduced at fifteen by that same, doting father. The daughter falls in love with the doctor who is treating her, she marries him, and goes to live with him on the Riviera.

But there I was, finally, at number 228 Seestrasse, the lakeshore drive. The rain was beating down on the yellow leaves of a straight allée at the end of which the entrance of a villa could be seen. I rang; Jung's secretary came to the door; a few minutes later Jung himself entered the little vestibule and showed me into his study. Jung was an elderly man (he was seventy-four) with a heavy physique, a strong face that seemed reddened by the constant flames of a welcoming fireplace, with a white mustache, piercing eyes, white and disheveled hair. A bourgeois-looking gentleman, dressed in heavy woolens, like a sportsman, a bit breathless and corpulent. Pipe in hand, he waved me to an armchair, facing a bright lamp, whose light almost blinded me. Meanwhile, perhaps out of psychoanalytical habit, he sat opposite me, his face entirely in shadow, as if he wanted to examine me without the risk of being examined himself at the same time. So, with me bedazzled and him immersed in darkness, our dialogue began.

We talked in French, which Jung spoke excellently, though with a rather thick German accent. The first questions and answers were awkward. Then, no doubt because the study of my face had made a favorable impression, Jung warmed and began speaking more freely. The subject naturally was the theories and books of Jung, which I knew very imperfectly; and in particular the theory expounded in his latest book, *Symbolik des Geistes*. In some disorder, Jung expounded ideas from his last book to me, connecting them with the doctrine that had made him famous. In the new book the most important part was devoted, apparently, to an "attempt at psychological explanation of the dogma of the Trinity." That book had already caused great commotion in Switzerland, precisely because of this Jungian interpretation of the Christian Trinity. Briefly put, according to Jung, Christian dogma would be a symbol of the collective psyche; therefore the Father somehow symbolizes a primitive phase, the Son an intermediary phase, and the Holy Ghost a third phase which is a return to the first phase, but enriched by the intermediary reflection. In his book Jung added to this Trinity a fourth person, thus transforming it into a Quaternity, so to speak. This fourth person, then, opposed by the clear and conscious function of the first three, had an obscure, unconscious function and, again in Jung's thought, was the devil. To make this idea of the Quaternity comprehensible, Jung linked it with his familiar theory of the psychology of the unconscious. He reasoned more or less in this way: In ancient times the devil, that is to say the unconscious, was in direct relations with the spirit, the conscious. This relationship was supremely beneficent in that the light of the conscious was fed by the darkness of the unconscious, its positive nature by the negative of the unconscious instinct, its rationality by the instinct of the unconscious. The ancient religions knew of these relations between conscious and unconscious; indeed, they favored them. Jahweh, for example, besides being God, was also devil. But with the beginning of Christianity, and especially with the Reformation, the unconscious — the devil, in other words — was more and more opposed, repressed, forgotten, obliterated. With Luciferan pride, northern Protestantism believed it could do without the devil. And then, gaining strength in fact from the very excess of this repression, the unconscious at times exploded in different diabolical and destructive ways.

This, Jung said, explained the clear demonaical and suicidal tendency of European civilization on the eve of World War I. At that time the devil, or the unconscious, too long repressed and forgotten, avenged himself, driving mankind to yearn for destruction and death, wooing them lustfully. At this point, Jung recalled with picturesque words the trains crammed with exultant recruits, the locomotives decked with flowers, as they left Berlin for the front in 1914, and he defined this joy at the imminent massacre as the joy at the wedding finally achieved, with blood and death, with the unconscious. Jung offered the same explanation for the monstrous and automatic cruelty of the Nazis during World War II. This time, too, he said, the lack of genuine relationship with the devil was the origin of an explosion of inconceivable destructive fury. So, he concluded, it was necessary to restore as quickly as possible this relationship; and if it was necessary, to create deliberately the Quaternity. After he had expressed this strange wish — for that matter, quite suited to what I would call the villa's Faustian atmosphere — I said good-bye to Jung. Outside, it was still raining. In the rain I headed for Zurich.

What happened politically in Italy between 1945 and 1950?

In 1948 the question was raised as to which direction Italy would take, whether it would go to the Right or the Left. The Communist Party was very powerful, but it couldn't achieve more than it already had, because it was forced to confront the bulwark of the Atlantic Treaty. Before 1948 there was the attempted assassination of Togliatti, which nearly caused a revolution: I remember that Italo Calvino came to Rome and informed me that the revolution was really about to come. I had never seen him so excited. I, on the contrary, was skeptical of the possibilities of a revolution in Italy, and in fact, a little later De Gasperi went to America and the Communist Party quit the coalition government for good. Elections were held. I was sure the Christian Democrats would win, because Italy is a pendulum: many Italians voted for the Communists, but they didn't want communism to take over. Even now, it's the same thing with the Communists. If it's a question of voting for abortion or divorce, people vote for the Communists. If a few women have abortions and some couples divorce, it doesn't change anything much, does it? But when it's a question of the Chamber of Deputies, they don't vote for the Communists. I'll never forget something said to me by the chauffeur of an English friend of mine, a former officer, in 1948, when it was announced that the Christian Democrats had won. "The colonel should have told me the Christian Democrats were going to win: I'd have voted for them."

Now, with De Gasperi's victory, a kind of regime began. Why do I call it a regime? Because the Christian Democrats, until then, had been just another political party. With the election, which was virtually a plebiscite in their favor, the coalition ended and a so-called monochrome government took over: a regime, pratically speaking. Now, what distinguishes parliamentary governments from regimes is that the opposition not only exists but can also replace the government. Instead, with the Christian Democrat regime in power, nobody could take its place, and furthermore the Christian Democrats made it quite clear that they didn't want anybody else to succeed. So, as I said, a regime began, and finally, it wasn't very different from the Fascist regime, in my opinion. Fascism had been a totalitarian regime; now there was a parliamentary regime, but the immobility of the CD transformed the government into a regime. The Christian Democrat regime lasted until the death of Moro.

It took the Red Brigades —

Maybe it took the Red Brigades. They acted rather like the scorpion: they used to say it bit you, then died. The Red Brigades died after biting the Christian Democrat Party. But the result is that there is no longer a regime today. The five-party coalition isn't a regime, or at least not yet.

It seems to me that it risks becoming one.

No use bandaging your head before it's wounded. I distrust prophecies also because somehow, as I've explained, lacking a past, I tend to make them.

For the intellectuals was the Christian Democrat victory of 1948 a defeat?

No, they didn't take it greatly to heart, it wasn't a defeat. The intellectuals were also Italians, they voted for the Communist Party, but they were afraid that communism might come. To understand the situation of the intellectuals, and of the Italians in general, you have to realize that they had hated Fascism because it was a dictatorship of the bourgeoisie: a contradiction, in other words. The bourgeoisie is either liberal or it's nothing. But from that to go to communism, to Stalin, is a great step, too big for the Italians at that moment in history.

I get the feeling that for you those years were very boring.

I'll tell you again, once and for all: to me years are not public, they're private. And in general my years are marked by the presence of a woman. The years of the war and the immediate postwar were characterized by the presence of Elsa Morante. When Elsa Morante went, Dacia Maraini arrived. When Dacia Maraini went, Carmen Llera arrived. These are my years. The fact that Mao assumes power in China, that the state of Israel is born, certainly interests me very much, but not as much as my private events. This is a general thing, it applies to everybody, absolutely everybody, because life is private, not public. We can't get away from this. Life is so private, in fact, that for politicians, who are public individuals, politics is a private fact.

In talking about your writer friends, we've overlooked Guido Piovene.

Piovene was a friend whom I never saw.

We haven't talked about Ennio Flaiano.

Flaiano was another friend I never saw. Piovene lived in Milan. When we met we were very cordial to each other. I liked Piovene very much. Only he did something incomprehensible and contradictory during Fascism.

What?

He supported the regime with an anti-Semitic article. Then he married Mimì Pavia, who was Jewish. Piovene explained this and other philo-Fascist acts in a book entitled *La coda di paglia*, very lively and basically honest.

And Flaiano?

Flaiano was a little man, originally from the Abruzzo, dark and stubby, with a core of pessimism, of negativeness. He was witty, and he knew he was, with keen intelligence. You know what Pascal says about the witty?

No.

"Diseurs de bon mots, mauvais caractères." In the sense of his fundamental sadness, Flaiano had *mauvais caractère*. When I saw him, we were very affectionate with each other, but he wasn't someone I saw often. As a writer, he oscillated between surrealism and a British black humor. He also did an imitation of Queneau's *Exercices de style*.

Queneau and Perec were the writers Calvino admired most.

Yes, because they were very different from him. Calvino was a humanist; they weren't.

Were Calvino and Pasolini friends?

I don't know. They may have been. Calvino was particularly close to Citati. He didn't live much in Rome. He went to Paris very early.

We've talked about your friends in the 1930s: was Chiaromonte among them?

We were close friends; then he went to France and, after the Nazi occupation there, to the United States. At the end of the war when he came back to Italy we never managed to be close in the same way. Perhaps it was the basic political difference between someone who stayed in Italy and someone who had gone into exile.

What was Chiaromonte like?

He was a man of the south. In Italy the great difference is between north and south. Even central Italy counts for little in this basic difference. Chiaromonte was a southerner, first of all physically, with a handsome dark head, round eyes. And then mentally, with a distinct tendency toward philosophical speculation. And finally, psychologically, thanks to a certain number of typically southern complexes. I think any Italian man can look at home in ecclesiastical garb. It's only a question of what rank he should be: a cardinal, a bishop, a Jesuit, or a monk? It was easy to imagine Chiaromonte dressed as a country priest. In his temperament and his physical appearance, he bore some resemblance to Silone, also easily visualized as the pastor of some little village in the Abruzzo.

How did Chiaromonte become so well known?

He was an intellectual of the Socratic type, with an authority, that is, based on the word, on ideas. Especially in the United States, in New York, he was much respected in the left-wing literary circles, *Partisan Review*, the *Reporter*, and so on.

Besides Flaiano, who else used wit as a safety valve to release the basic discontent during the years of Fascism? Is it true that in Rome there was a group of anti-Fascist wits?

Yes, it's true. In the atmosphere under Fascism, Roman wit was the equivalent of the pasquinades against the pope during the period of the Papal States. These anti-Fascist wits always gathered in a café and found satirical nicknames for everyone. For example, I was called "Amaro Gambarotta," the name of a bitter cordial, which means literally "Bitter Broken-leg"; the poet Vincenzo Cardarelli was called "the decadent" because he had only ten teeth. Savinio, who always wore a beret (a *basco*), was called "La bella addormentata nel basco" (instead of *bosco*, "wood"). A certain woman writer, whose name I won't mention out of respect, was known as "Virginia Vulva"; and so on. Naturally there were also anti-Fascist bon mots. For example, "You can't be Fascist, intelligent, and honest at the same time. Because if you're honest and intelligent you're not Fascist, if you're Fascist and honest you aren't intelligent, and if you're intelligent and Fascist you aren't honest." Among these wits you must include also Leo Longanesi and Mino Maccari, who, like Flaiano for that matter, were real artists.

Wasn't Longanesi a Fascist, however?

Yes, he was a Fascist, but he was an intellectual and an artist, and hence aware of the above-mentioned impossibility of being at the same time Fascist, intelligent, and honest. Probably the origins of Longanesi's Fascism were similar to those of the Fascism of the farmers in Emilia, his region, who reacted with gangsterlike physical violence to the naive verbal violence of the populace. But then Longanesi came to Rome, and his Fascism became like that of all the Italians who didn't want trouble or else were dependent somehow on the Fascist state: it was only a pose, in other words. Longanesi was a craftsman of genius: he left an important mark, for example, on journalism and on Italian graphic taste. When Longanesi was growing up there was only one weekly in Italy, *La Domenica del Corriere*, old-fashioned, popular, mid-nineteenth-century almost. Longanesi created *Omnibus*, the first of many cultural and news weeklies that today are so numerous. Furthermore, Longanesi was a very original engraver and cartoonist. Finally, there was an artisan quality about him that has always been characteristic of artists of all ages in Italy. Longanesi belonged to the old Italy, full of humors and fragrances, individualist and anarchic. When he died, I said of him that he was an antagonist by nature, unable to feel at ease in any positive political and social situation. Anti-Fascist under Fascism, he became a Fascist under anti-Fascism, and so he doomed himself to an inevitable economic failure.

And Maccari?

Maccari was a complete artist, who, despite an early participation in Fascist violence, was less connected to political events than Longanesi. He was an extraordinary caricaturist, and throughout his life he satirized the tics and habits of a certain Italian bourgeoisie of the Fascist period and also after Fascism.

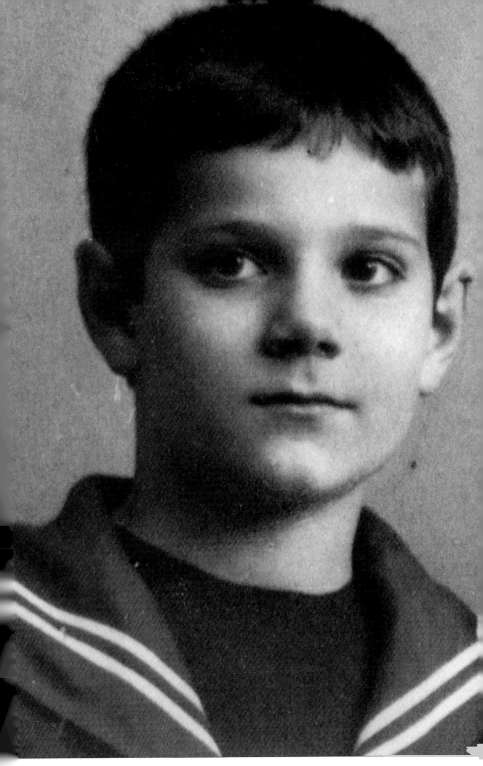

Portrait of the young Alberto Pincherle. *(Archive of C. Cecchi/Alberto Moravia Foundation)*

ABOVE: Alberto Pincherle with his parents, Carlo Pincherle and
Teresa De Marsanich. *(Archive of C. Cecchi/Alberto Moravia Foundation)*
BELOW: Alberto Pincherle at seventeen, during his convalescence in the
sanatorium at Cortina, 1924–25. *(Archive of C. Cecchi/Alberto Moravia Foundation)*

ABOVE: Alberto Moravia and Elsa Morante at Capri, 1948.
(Archive of C. Cecchi/Alberto Moravia Foundation)
BELOW: Moravia with Carson McCullers at Villa i Tatti,
Florence. *(Archive of C. Cecchi/Alberto Moravia Foundation)*

ABOVE: Moravia in Capri at Villa Malaparte. In the center of the photo is Curzio Malaparte. The two women are Elsa Morante (left) and Palma Bucarelli. *(Archive of C. Cecchi/Alberto Moravia Foundation)*

BELOW: Moravia with Pier Paolo Pasolini and Maria Callas in Mali, 1970. *(Photo by Mohammed Melehi/Alberto Moravia Foundation Archive)*

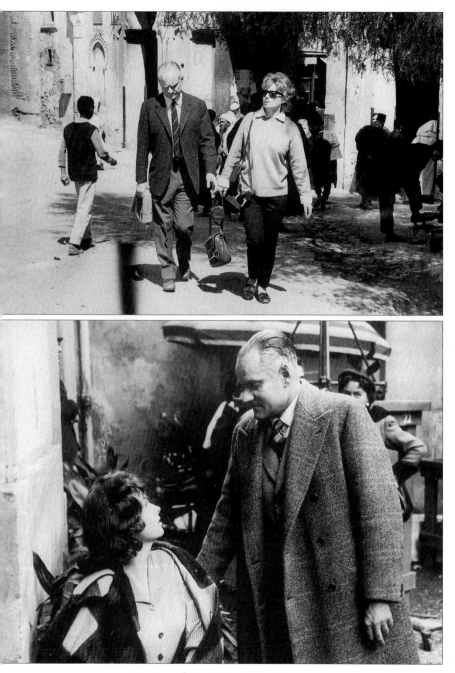

ABOVE: Moravia and Dacia Maraini in Morocco, 1975.
(Photo by Mohammed Melehi/Alberto Moravia Foundation Archive)
BELOW: Moravia and Gina Lollobrigida on the set of
La romana, Rome, 1958. *(Alberto Moravia Foundation Archive)*

ABOVE: Moravia with Federico Fellini, 1987.
(Photo by Marina Colonna/Alberto Moravia Foundation Archive)
BELOW: Moravia with Citto Maselli, Ingmar Bergman, and Liv Ullman. *(Alberto Moravia Foundation Archive)*

ABOVE: Moravia at his typewriter. *(Photo by Alain Elkann)*
BELOW: Moravia with Alain Elkann. *(Photo by Alain Elkann)*

Moravia at his desk. *(Photo by Alain Elkann)*

I I

ALAIN ELKANN: When did you go to America the second time?

ALBERTO MORAVIA: In 1955. I didn't go earlier because they wouldn't give me a visa. The Russians wouldn't give me one because they said I was too Atlantic, and the Americans because I wasn't Atlantic enough. Apparently in Washington there was a kind of scandal and a question raised in my favor in Congress. In 1955, at the same time, I received both the American visa and the Russian. I chose to go to America, at the invitation of the State Department. It involved a tour of the United States from New York via Chicago to California and back. At this point, I'd like to talk about Elsa again. In that period, though I continued to love her, our life together had become rather a blind alley.

Did you have other women?

No. Occasional encounters, commercial perhaps, which for me, however, were not really commercial because my novelist's imagination was capable of giving an adventurous cast even to the most banal aspects of daily life. Anyway, I didn't have a mistress, but I had encounters from time to time.

You told me that you loved Elsa but were never in love with her. For you what's the difference between loving and being in love?

Falling in love is an existential catastrophe that involves us radically, even though in a completely obscure fashion. When I say it's obscure, I mean that while we're in love changes occur of which we are not aware — changes of all kinds — for example, in an artist, mysterious changes of inspiration. Love, on the other hand, is a conscious feeling, not at all catastrophic, at times solid and profound.

Which of the two feelings do you prefer?

Because of its existential impact, I prefer falling in love.

How do you react to it?

I experience it totally.

But did you suffer at this lukewarm relationship with Elsa? Were you bored when you were with her?

No, I wasn't bored with Elsa; I was never bored with Elsa, because basically she was a very fascinating person. Perhaps the only thing that disturbed me was her competitiveness. Elsa considered herself the greatest writer — as all writers do, for that matter. But she didn't hide this belief; in fact, she made a point of declaring it. It was explicable as an affirmation of herself, but I thought that with me it shouldn't have been necessary.

Are you also competitive?

No, not at all. Perhaps it's no merit of mine, but rather my early success. I had a success very quickly. I knew quite well what it was, and I didn't care in the least about competing. Of course, I would always have liked — and still would like — to be a better writer than I am, but this isn't being competitive. It is simply the fact that my ambitions have been and still are beyond my strength.

What are your ambitions?

To express myself completely as all the writers we consider great expressed themselves.

At a certain point, when Elsa's Il mondo salvato dai ragazzini *appeared, Elsa became a myth. Why?*

It's true, but as with all the myths of literature, the origin of the Elsa myth wasn't literary. She created it herself with her "world-view," declared, indeed flaunted, on every occasion in her life. Besides being the writer of genius we know, Elsa was also a character with a considerable talent for acting and performance.

In this sense, you're also a myth.

Any one of us can be a myth for someone else. I remember meeting a poor man, perhaps a humble clerk in a city office in Rome, who was, however, a myth for his concierge, who spoke of him as the Fascists spoke of the Duce. There is no limit to a human being's mythmaking capacity. In this sense I can agree that I am also a myth, but I don't believe I was ever a performer like Elsa.

Performer only? Or also sincere?

Elsa had a great sense of the tragic. When she learned that her lover Bill Morrow had committed suicide, she staged a great mourning scene no less sincere than the grief displayed in southern Italy by bereaved widows and mothers. I'll talk about this mourning later, at the proper moment. But here I want to underline that Elsa was a character because she "felt" she was one. The performance came spontaneously.

Was Elsa a character also in your private relations?

Less so, but in a sense always ready to become one.

When did you win the Strega Prize?

In 1952 with the story collection entitled *I racconti.* In other words, the complete collection of my stories from 1927 until 1950. I was voted unanimously in protest against Pope Pius XII, or at least against the Vatican prelates in charge of the Index of Forbidden Books, who had banned my book. I was put on the Index the same day as André Gide. I remember that on the same page of the *Osservatore romano* there were two columns in Latin, one on one side, one on the other: one concerned me and the other concerned Gide. My books were condemned as *fabula amatoria*, whereas Gide was condemned for his "immoralistic" theories. There was a reaction of solidarity around me, especially from what we could call the liberal part of our culture. Since the prize was in the hands of this part of the culture, I was awarded the prize unanimously: a unique event. Gadda, who was in the running for the prize with a book of his own, took the whole thing as a plot against him organized by me, whereas actually, until the last minute, I knew nothing of the papal ban or of the Strega Prize, and Gadda wrote Gianfranco Contini an extremely offensive letter about me. This letter is all the more surprising as Carlo Emilio Gadda had written a beautiful critical article on *Agostino*, and this letter is evidence of the well-known and painful neurosis of that extraordinary man.

On the subject of the Strega, I'd like to tell here an anecdote that, if Gadda were still alive, would disprove the tendency to intrigue that he asserted. When I published *La disubbidienza*, in 1948, it was immediately clear that the book could easily have won the Strega prize. So easily that one morning there came to my house a delegation of writers, led by Vitaliano Brancati, who asked me to withdraw from the competition so another candidate could win: Angioletti, whose daughter was to be married. On such an occasion, the prize money would have come in very handy for him. I withdrew, though I didn't have a cent myself; and I'm saying this only now and only because Gadda's letter to Contini was recently printed in the volume of correspondence edited by Contini himself. The same *La disubbidienza*, which I consider one of my best books, was sent by Vittorini to compete for the Saint Vincent Prize, but only to act as counterweight to the book of a disciple of his, who in fact won the prize. What should I say of literary people in general? Better to remain silent.

You consider yourself a man of letters?

That "also," but I would feel very sad if I were "only" that. At least in those circumstances, Gadda and Vittorini were "only" men of letters.

But Gadda was an artist?

Of course, a great artist, when he was one.

After the war did you start traveling again?

The first journey I made was with Elsa to Egypt, the Holy Land, Turkey. A journey with disastrous moments, because of Elsa's character.

When was that?

I believe it was in 1954.

Why disastrous?

Because Elsa was a very difficult traveling companion.

In what sense?

In the sense of a constant, obsessive affirmation of her own personality and independence even on the most trivial occasions. I'll give you an example. I left for Egypt by ship, to do something different from usual. Elsa was to follow me by plane. I arrived in Cairo and found it was very cold, I was carrying only a raincoat, so I wired Elsa asking her to bring my overcoat. Unfortunately for me, I thought, "Perhaps they don't know she lives there, that she's my wife." I addressed the telegram to Elsa Moravia. Elsa received the telegram, took the overcoat, came to Cairo, and the moment she arrived began a scene that lasted three days, because I should have written Elsa Morante. Practically speaking, this scene, so cruel and unjust, cast a pall on our whole journey, which for me was anything but amusing. And as soon as we were back in Rome, I told her it was the last time I would make a trip with her.

What does "cruel" mean?

It's hard to explain. There is a cruelty of the tone of voice as there is in words chosen deliberately to offend. Elsa was cruel in both senses.

On what level did she offend you?

Oddly enough, never on the literary level, the public level, that is. Always on the private. For example, my family, my friends, my social activities, and also on the defects or presumed defects of my character.

For example?

I have an almost pathological capacity for not taking offense, either because I identify and almost agree with the offender, or because I completely forget the offense. In Elsa's case, certainly, I didn't manage to agree with her, but I would go out, take a walk, and when I came back, I had already forgotten or at least, as they say, I had swallowed the pill. I don't remember nor do I want to remember what she said. I want only to tell you an anecdote. During those years we went to Paris and we stayed at the Hôtel Pont Royal. Once in our room, Elsa all of a sudden began to moan and then fainted. I tried to bring her round with some little slaps and damp cloths, but it was all in vain: Elsa lay motionless, stiff, her eyes closed. In the end, frightened, I decided to call a doctor. I knew three in Paris; I called all three, but since it was Sunday, I didn't find anyone in. Meanwhile, time was passing and I didn't know what to do. I sat on the bed, looking at Elsa, motionless and stiff, obviously unconscious, and I tried to remember the name of some acquaintance in Paris I could ask for help. At this point, all of a sudden, she opened her eyes and started laughing, but not a childish, joking laugh, as if at a successful trick; it was a really mean laugh and her eyes were equally mean.

Why do you think she played this joke?

I've never known, because she wouldn't tell me. Obviously during the journey, which had been normal and calm, I had said something to infuriate her, and she avenged herself with the joke.

Did she know you well?

I've never figured that out. She said I was innocent, ingenuous. She said that there are three great, basic characters in the world: Hamlet, Don Quixote, and Achilles. Achilles is the man of the earth, who lives out his passions. Don Quixote is the man who fights for his dreams, and Hamlet is the one who doubts everything. I was, in her opinion, a bit Achilles and a bit Hamlet, with nothing of Don Quixote.

And she was Don Quixote?

She said that characters of the Don Quixote type include, for example, Madame Bovary and, naturally, herself. She was very brave and, in her way, very generous, but not good. Elsa always used to say to me that I have a form of incurable detachment that I can't break out of. This detachment is probably due to a form of defense of an intellectualistic nature.

You told me you had written Il disprezzo *in an excess of irritation with Elsa?*

Yes, there were days when I would have liked to kill her. Not just separate from her, which would have been a rational solution, but kill her, because our relationship was so close, so complex, and finally, so alive that crime seemed to me easier than separation.

Why did you want to kill her? What had happened?

Absolutely nothing new had happened, but at certain moments I couldn't stand it any longer.

You couldn't stand her character any longer?

She had been too cruel, practically sadistic. If you read carefully *La storia*, this cruelty strangely combined with her creatural and pre-moral pity, will seem obvious to you. For that matter, pity and cruelty are only two aspects of a relationship with reality more physiological than intellectual. In any case, the idea of killing her was transferred almost immediately into a novel, *Il disprezzo.* In the first outline of this novel the protagonist, reacting against his wife's unjust attitude toward him, was to plot and carry out her murder. But this idea of a crime faded as the novel was written. The wife dies in an accident; the protagonist of the novel I actually wrote no longer has anything to do with the character I had thought of at the very beginning.

Did Elsa recognize herself in the book?

No, how could she have? In the book I ended up not writing, only one thing would have been connected to our lives — the murder. All the rest would have been pure invention. What might have made her suspicious was the very clear love-hate association that is the true theme of the book. But Elsa really wasn't all that interested in seeing if I spoke about her in my books or not. And this was because she knew quite well that in my novels invention always predominates.

Did Elsa speak of you in her books?

Elsa is infinitely more autobiographical than I am, but only in the recreation of adolescence. When I started living with Elsa, her adolescence was long over. As a result, she never spoke of me in her books.

From Il disprezzo Godard made one of his best films. Do you think the film is superior to the novel?

As I said before, I consider the writer and the director as two distinct artists, unrelated to each other. In the case of Il disprezzo no connection is possible thanks to the indisputable originality of Godard. If he had been less original, perhaps he would have been faithful; but he was very original and therefore completely unfaithful. Godard said once that Il disprezzo was a novel to read en chemin de fer. This rather disagreeable definition indicates the typical attitude of directors who make use of a novel as if it were a fait divers.

You don't consider Il disprezzo a novel to be read on the train?

Absolutely not. I consider it one of my best novels, because it is at once deeply felt and completely invented, which I consider the best combination for writing a good novel.

How did you get on with Godard?

I didn't. Godard is a man of genius who has revolutionized cinema, but he is a person with whom it is difficult, or rather virtually impossible, to communicate. I have written critical articles on almost all the films of Godard, but on the very day I first met him, in a Roman hotel, I gave up any idea of getting to know him. Curiously, the extremely literary character of Godard's films, a cineast's literature, that is, prevented me from explaining myself to him, the few times we met. I think it's easier to get along with less literary directors.

Were you fascinated by Godard?

By his film expression, yes. By his literature, not so much.

During those years you also wrote Il conformista. *The novel became the masterpiece of Bernardo Bertolucci. What was your relationship then with Bertolucci?*

Then and on other occasions, I have always had very friendly but sporadic relations with Bernardo Bertolucci. In other words, Bernardo Bertolucci is a friend I see infrequently.

What do you think of him as a director?

I think he is first of all a film animal, as I am a fiction animal. This said, Bernardo Bertolucci is fairly closely descended from Luchino Visconti: sensitive cultural and sociological observation, sensationalism, critique and depiction of the bourgeoisie and its ills, left-wing sympathies. But Bertolucci's talent is characterized by an extraordinary capacity for reliving the past. Whether of Fascism or the Chinese Empire.

You were saying that in 1955 you went to America. How was the trip?

In 1955 I went to Washington, where I was invited to a dinner by some professors, one of whom, I remember, said, "You Italians always look at women's behinds when they go by. Take care not to do that here."

It was in Washington that you suffered homesickness?

Yes, a TV crew came to film me for a whole day. That evening I had nothing to do. I asked the girl who had interviewed me if she would like to have dinner with me, and she said, "But I have a boyfriend." I spent the evening alone. The next morning, in an access of boredom and loneliness, I sat at the window and realized that I was thinking about something totally stupid: that a button had come off my jacket and I didn't know how to sew it back on again. I also realized that I was crying, as I looked at the landscape. Then I took off my shirt and saw that I had a line along my chest. I went to a doctor, who said, "This is homesickness." The same as in Mexico, in 1935. Then I went to that disastrous dinner with the American professors, who seemed to me very disagreeable. Finally I left for Chicago with Saul Bellow.

Did you already know Saul Bellow?

No, or rather I had seen him only for a few days. He was going to Chicago, and he offered me a lift. It was an excellent trip; we stopped at Buffalo to see Niagara Falls, then once we arrived in Chicago, we went our separate ways.

What impression did Saul Bellow make on you?

A very keen intellectual who, however, didn't talk about literature but rather about commonplace, normal things. He also seemed to me a great neurotic, of an undefinable kind. In Chicago I had an experience with a black prostitute, whose lover was a young white from the South who didn't have the courage to marry her. He stayed at the bar drinking, and the woman and I, with his consent, went out to find a hotel. I remember that she had a very beautiful body, with a very fine-grained skin the color of roast coffee. She did all the usual things, enter the room, look around, undress, but with the severe attitude of the Puritan she actually was, and so I said to her all of a sudden, "I'll pay you, but we won't make love. Tell me your story instead." She told me her story then, about the lover who loved her but didn't dare marry her and every evening, while she prostituted herself, got drunk all alone in the bar. Then we went back to him and the three of us drank together. That was all.

Again, as in China, you preferred not to make love with a prostitute. Why?

Because that was how it was. There aren't any explanations, or at least I can't find any. I left Chicago for Denver, for a curious reason: I knew that in the museum of natural history there was a famous dinosaur. I went to a hotel you could call very patriotic. There was a big staircase with many American flags hanging from the different floors. At the bar there were some men with short boots, spurs, and big felt hats. I came out of this hotel, took a taxi, and gave the address of the museum of natural history, and once there, I paid and got out. I entered the museum, looked at the dinosaur, truly impressive, three or four meters high and twenty-seven meters long. Then I came out and there were no taxis. I had to walk twenty kilometers. Along the streets you could see only the Denver families out for their Sunday drive. Wife, husband, child, and the man's jacket on a coat hanger inside the car. The next day I left for San Francisco by train, the Trans-Pacific, almost empty.

During that trip did you telephone Elsa?

No, never.

Did you write her?

No. Actually, our good-bye had been very cold. I must tell you that in 1954, the year before, I had made a trip in Spain with a couple of friends, an Irishman with an American wife. Before leaving, I said to Elsa, "I'd like to write you." She answered, "Write poste restante. If I feel curious I'll read your letters. Otherwise I won't." I wrote to her poste restante; she never collected a letter. You see, this was typical behavior on Elsa's part, at least at that moment.

Where was Elsa then?

In Rome.

And what was she doing?

Writing, writing, writing.

You never told me the impression Spain made on you.

It was purely a tourist trip. I was particularly struck by Cordova, and the bridge over the Guadalquivir. An impression of grandiose decadence and social immobility. It was a fascist country, therefore very sad.

What did you like most in Spain?

Besides Cordova, the plain of Castile, and naturally the museums with great Spanish painting: Velazquez, El Greco, Goya. But also trivial things, like a picnic under an oak, with garlicky salami and a flask of red wine black as the blood of the bulls in the corridas. In any case, to get back to the trip in America, from Denver I took the train for San Francisco. I went to the dining car to eat, and a gentleman, not very young, very respectable, said to me, "What country are you from?" I said, "I'm Italian." His curiosity was immediately frozen. He thought I was from who-knows-what-other-country. Italians were considered worthless.

We're talking about 1955, and we haven't yet mentioned Hiroshima. What was its effect on you?

The news of the Hiroshima bomb in 1945 didn't have on me the effect you might think, and for two reasons: The first, shared by everyone, was that our joy at the end of the war surpassed the horror that should have been inspired by the means used to end it. The second reason was that I can arrive at a thorough understanding of events like the atom bomb only through an intellectual process, what you could call personalization. In short, I need to consider public events as personal acts, felt and understood personally.

When did your concern with the atom bomb come?

It came after a long trip I made in Japan with Dacia Maraini, on an invitation from the Japan Foundation. Oddly, after the ritual visit to Hiroshima, I was no longer capable of considering all the aspects of Japan and writing a few articles, as I had planned to do originally. Instead, for *L'espresso* I wrote just one article, only about the atomic bomb. Then I tried to understand what had happened. I understood the following things: One, the atom bomb is not a weapon of war. On the contrary, it could almost be called a weapon of peace, because it abolishes the possibility of war. Two, the atom bomb is, you could say, the technological expression of a death instinct present in the West (including the Soviet Union) at least since the second half of the nineteenth century, that is, from the triumph of the Industrial Revolution on. In other terms, it is a perfect means for the suicide of the human species. Three, though I used the metaphor of indifference, I had been speaking about this death instinct inherent in Western culture since the long-ago days of my first novel. Finally, the visit to Japan opened my eyes to the connection I had till then ignored between my writing and the temptation of the species toward suicide.

You said to me that the first postwar years were grim also because of the Cold War.

No, they were grim because somehow my relationship with Elsa, which basically I had always considered one of love, though of a very special kind, was transformed into a relationship of simple cohabitation, more or less friendly. Elsa fell in love with Luchino Visconti in 1955, during my trip to America. In fact, when I returned from the trip and arrived home, she, with her usual emotional severity, didn't even allow me to embrace her. I already knew about this relationship, though I thought it hadn't gone beyond the initial phase, that of an affectionate courtship, in other words. I had realized it just before leaving for America, because Visconti had sent Elsa a present, an owl in its cage. I said absently it was very kind of him, and Elsa answered that he was kind because he loved her. From the tone of her answer I had the distinct sensation that she returned this love, and in a burst of anger I broke my plate with both hands (we were at table). I slammed it once and the plate broke into two perfect halves. Then I left for America. On my return I found the cold welcome I mentioned, and I realized that what I had previously intuited had now happened.

What had happened?

Our situation was stabilized, as I said, into a kind of friendly co-habitation. In the morning Elsa went to Luchino Visconti's house and stayed there all day, taking part, as I imagined, in his life. At night she came home; as a rule she found me awake, and then she would sit at the foot of the bed and talk to me about Visconti and the ups and downs of her passion. I listened to her with the objectivity of an affectionate friend.

But wasn't Visconti homosexual?

He was, but sometimes he wasn't. For example; at the time I met him before the war, he had already had an affair with a famous Fascist film actress.

But was he also in love with Elsa?

Elsa said he was and described him with great precision and many details as a man in love. She said, for example, that when he looked at her his legs trembled, he was so moved.

How did you react to these nightly stories of Elsa's?

I didn't react. True, I felt a bit embarrassed, but it was also true that we hadn't had any physical relations for several years. While on the one hand, Elsa's confidences made me aware that everything between us was really over, on the other, they didn't alter the feeling that still united us and that couldn't really be called mere friendship. A singular feeling, basically of existential symbiosis. It was this feeling that enabled Elsa to tell me the story of her relationship with Visconti and enabled me to listen to her. I must again say something I will repeat later. What unites a man and a woman is not reciprocal fidelity but in fact this existential symbiosis, which can comprehend everything, even infidelity.

How long did the love between Elsa and Luchino Visconti last?

It lasted two years and ended, as far as I know, in the following way: Elsa informed me that she was leaving me to go and live with Luchino Visconti. But on the day and at the hour when they were to meet for the definitive decision, he didn't show up. So in the space of a few hours I had two very different sensations: that Elsa was leaving me forever and that, on the contrary, she was going to stay forever. The idea of her going away grieved me very much, more than I would have thought; but it wasn't possible for me to rejoice at the fact she had stayed, because her disappointment embittered her to such a degree that she became almost unbearable. I remember we left for Venice for the contemporary music festival, and since there were no rooms at the Danieli, I went to stay in a furnished room at Rio Cabalà. In a way I preferred that little room to the Danieli because Elsa, though I saw her every day, with her usual tendency to display and dramatize her own feelings, didn't conceal but rather flaunted her sorrow, adding to it a kind of aversion to me. It was a very cruel period, after which her feelings toward Visconti passed from attraction to rancor. This rancor was all the more remarkable in that her earlier feeling had been one of complete subjugation, to such a degree that she had actually changed her accent. She, born in Rome in Via Giulia, adopted the Milanese accent of Via Montenapoleone.

Didn't all this make you suffer?

I probably suffered, but I realized it only afterward. At that moment I endured this suffering, so to speak, like so many others in my life. Perhaps I should say at this point that I have a great capacity for tolerating any physical and moral suffering because as a child I was obliged to tolerate the sufferings of illness and solitude.

Those were the years of the Cold War. What did that mean?

A great boredom that lasted practically until Gorbachev and Reagan. It began with the so-called "Berlin air lift," and it was certainly a very serious thing for the countries that were directly

involved in Eastern Europe and in Asia; but in countries such as
Italy, away from the front line, it brought paralysis and boredom.
For that matter, the expression "Cold War" tells the whole story.
After what could be called the hot war, against Nazi Germany,
instead of the peace we had hoped for, a kind of hostility had en-
sued, and with it, extremely boring propaganda. The Cold War
was a war of mass media and secret services: that should suffice to
explain my boredom. Tantamount to saying a war in which it's
difficult for an intellectual to participate. I had hated Fascism seriously. Now I was called upon to hate either the Americans or
the Russians; they were the two great countries that had won the
war and had liberated us from Fascism. I didn't feel like choosing
a side. I saw the faults of the Americans and the faults of the Russians, but also their virtues. And above all, I was irritated by the
propaganda from both directions. For that matter, I was very indifferent to politics. I felt a great uneasiness, because, while I had
sincerely sided with the Allies during the war and had drunk the
health of the Russians, in their embassy, sincerely, with feeling,
now I didn't feel like taking part in the nonsense of their reciprocal propaganda. I had chiefly the sensation that there were a lot
of lies in the air. More propaganda than truth.

*Between 1955 and 1956 you made a trip to America, then a trip
to Russia. What was your impression of the two journeys?*

In America the sensation was of a great country in which the Italians counted for nothing. America wasn't at all the way Vittorini
and Pavese had conceived it. I like the American people: they are
likable. The dominant class, less so. The dominant class in
America, the so-called Wasps, often seemed to me inhuman and
for this reason also a bit dangerous politically, because they were
uninformed and tended to replace reality with formulas no less
ideological than the Communists'.

Luckily, the mechanism of American democracy is real. It is
the only real democracy that exists in the world, in my opinion,
thanks perhaps to the continuing extraordinary economic fortunes of the country. There are two kinds of democracy: that with

delegated powers and that without. Democracy without delegation, direct, in short, is the democracy of Mussolini or any other
dictator who speaks from a platform to a hundred thousand
people from whom, obviously, he expects no criticism but only
applause. Democracy with delegation is the West's kind, especially America's, which I consider preferable. Delegation means
this: parliamentary mechanisms, congress, representatives, sena-
tors, and so on. And no speeches from a dictator on a platform.

Do you believe that real freedom of the press exists in America?
Real freedom of the press never exists, not in any country.

In any case, there is honesty in the newspapers.
No. "Freedom of the press" is a legal, historical term. It isn't the
truth. But in the West there is always more of it than in the totalitarian countries.

Were you in America during the McCarthy years?
I must say I didn't give it much thought. After Fascist terror, Mc-
Carthyism seemed and was only a distortion of parliamentary
democracy. Needless to say, it was a persecution to be condemned without reservation.

Tell me now about your trip to Russia?
The trip to Russia proceeded in an official manner.

Who went with you?
I went alone. Invited by the Russians, naturally. By the Soviet
Union, that is. As a guide they gave me an Italianist named Breitburd. He was amazingly informed about Italian literature, but
about nothing else. If I mentioned Cocteau, Breitburd had never
heard of him. Short, plump, considerate, indeed heartbreakingly
affectionate. I think I was told later that he belonged to the KGB, but
he was always extremely kind to me. I remember, for example, that,
on arriving in Moscow, I discovered I didn't have any nail scissors,
and I asked him for some. I didn't realize, in that period devoted

exclusively to heavy industry, tractors, and not to nail scissors, that I was asking the impossible. He then went all the way to his home in a very distant suburb and brought me a pair of women's nail clippers, so I could cut my nails.

What was your impression of Russia?

A fascinating people, a great revolution. But at the same time, poverty and squalor. Plaster statues of Lenin and Stalin, separate or together, were everywhere. Speaking to my guide, I made fun of all these propagandistic statuettes, and he pathetically protested and said I was cruel. I made an endless journey into the Caucasus, the Ukraine, Central Asia, Siberia. On all sides I saw the same hard conditions borne with an admirable and mysterious resignation, which on the one hand oppressed me, but on the other gave me the sensation of the unusual spirituality of the Russian people.

How long were you there?

A month and a half, I think. On my return I wrote a book entitled *Un mese in* URSS, in which, basically, I said that the Soviet government was careful not to promote light industry because it needed the savings of the workers in order to spend them for heavy industry and armament. Therefore the scantiness of light industry products was in a way deliberate and artificial, due not so much to the inability of the Russians as to the will of the government to make sure that the Russians would be unable to buy anything, neither a pair of shoes nor an automobile, so they would put their money in the bank.

Did your impressions of Russia and America remain the same over the years?

I am still more favorable toward America than toward Russia. I could live in America, not in Russia. However, human relations are often more agreeable in Russia than in America. The Anglo-Saxons are always rather stern toward others because they are stern toward themselves. In the Third World you would say that poverty makes people more indulgent toward themselves and others. The Third World is more cordial.

After your first two journeys, in 1955 to America and in 1956 to Russia, you've been back to those countries several times. Have your ideas changed?

No, the first impression — which, after all, is always the best — has been confirmed.

In your opinion are Russia and America approaching each other, resembling each other more and more?

They're approaching each other, yes. Russia's great ambition is to resemble America, and perhaps one day, perhaps through perestroika, Russia will succeed. At least as far as life massified by technology is concerned. Naturally, the United States and the Soviet Union have different ideological origins. But it's significant that both began in the Age of Enlightenment, in the second half of the eighteenth century.

Russia, however, isn't a democratic country. The Russians have never known democracy.

Russia is a military country, but that doesn't prevent the Russian ideal from wanting to imitate American democracy. In my opinion, classes, genuine classes, exist especially in Europe. England is a typical class-ridden country. There are actually several degrees: middle class, lower middle, upper middle, and so on. And these are not only nuances of language. But today the class culture is tending to disappear. So class differences, really, amount simply to differences of income.

PART III

12

ALAIN ELKANN: *Getting back to writing, what changed in your work during those years?*

ALBERTO MORAVIA: The real travail that transformed me, as I said, was in the period between *Gli indifferenti*, published in 1929, and *Agostino*, published in 1944. The most difficult moment involved the writing and the failure of *Le ambizioni sbagliate*. In my career as a writer *Agostino* marked my return to the vein of *Gli indifferenti*, but enriched by a more mature literary experience. A second crisis, but much less profound, accurred between *La ciociara* and *La noia*.

What caused this second crisis?

I suppose it was due to the collapse of the national, working-class myth that had led me to write *La romana*, *La ciociara*, and *I racconti romani*. Or rather, it wasn't a personal collapse, since I went on writing and publishing. It was only the loss of the creative energy inherent in every myth. I remained faithful to the left-wing political ideas I had always had, but I didn't feel like writing novels and stories in the genre of those I had written just after the war. Perhaps this crisis was more profound than it seems to me now. In fact what emerged from it was *La noia*, a novel that can seem to be a break after the novels and stories of the working-class myth. But that isn't the case. In reality the boredom described in the novel of the same name (*La noia*), like the indifference of *Gli indifferenti*, stood always to indicate that anguish of living that I am convinced is the foundation of the existentialist current to which I know I belong and from which, I believe, the contemporary novel is to a great extent derived. Having said this, I would only add that boredom is not a new subject in modern literature from the nineteenth century to today. You have only to remember the famous pages of Schopenhauer, not to mention the "spleen" of the decadents. Perhaps there was something new to be found, as I feel I did in my novel — in discovering *noia*, ennui, boredom, also in language and therefore in the impossibility of establishing, through language, any relationship with reality. I owe this new aspect in part to my reading at the time of the works of Wittgenstein, which however acted on me more as analogical stimuli than as a direct philosophical influence.

Did you think all these things before writing, or are they reflections you made afterward?

As I've told you, these are things I say after the fact, as a critic might do in examining a writer's work. I am a critic of myself.

In what sense?

When I write, as I've said, I always start out from individual situations. For example, I write a story about a man who loves a woman, or doesn't love her. What he feels. This is an existential start. I start with existence; then, without willing it, going deeper into the story, I arrive at its meaning. In humbler terms we could say that I tell of an event in life and then, as I depict it, I arrive at the culture. Culture today means Freud, Marx, Nietzsche, perhaps Wittgenstein, perhaps Heidegger, and so on. But artists have always behaved like this: they told stories that in the end proved homologous with the culture of the time.

When the story is finished, you ask yourself, "What have I really written?" Is that it?

Yes, exactly. You've put it very well.

Perhaps we should go back a little. In 1957 you published La ciociara.

Shortly after writing *La romana* in 1947, I thought about writing a novel whose theme would be the war and whose story would be the one I lived through with Elsa. I invented the character of Cesira and dashed off, I believe, about eighty pages, but then I stopped because it seemed to me there wasn't yet enough distance from the events that I wanted to narrate to allow what we could call contemplation. So I put the eighty pages away and instead wrote *La disubbidienza, Il disprezzo, Il conformista*, and many short stories. Probably *Il conformista*, so imaginary and invented, inspired me with the desire to write a novel that, though its characters and situations were invented, would be based on a generic personal experience of mine. I took up the eighty pages again and finished the novel, which I entitled *La ciociara*. With *La ciociara*, though I wasn't aware of it, I was bidding a definitive farewell to the national working-class myth that had led me to write *La romana* and *I racconti romani*.

Is it true that in those years you were afraid you had cancer?

This is what happened: At the age of fifty it occurred to me to have a checkup. So it was that I went to a radiologist. The moment he looked at the X-rays, the radiologist, in great fright, told me that he had seen a shadow in my stomach that could be a cancer. Naturally, I took this diagnosis seriously and with my X-rays trudged from one doctor to another, including the most famous ones in Rome. All of them more or less advised me to have an operation, so in the end I resigned myself. I started looking for a surgeon to perform the operation. I discovered to my surprise that it isn't easy to find the right man in such a situation. Every surgeon had a positive reputation, but also a negative one. To give you an example, of one of them I was told, "He's very good, but his wife's unfaithful, he's terribly jealous, his hand might shake." Everyone, however, agreed in recommending Valdoni, and so, in a spirit of contradiction, precisely because everyone recommended him, I chose another who was very well known and headed a clinic with an excellent reputation. On the phone I asked him one favor: not to keep me waiting in a waiting room, but to receive me promptly. Politely, he replied that I was not to worry, I would be the first.

On the established day I turned up accompanied by my regular physician. I entered a crowded little reception room. I was told to wait, like all the others. Infuriated by this unkept promise, I left the room and went straight to Valdoni, who operated on me two days later. The morning after the operation, Valdoni came in and said simply, "I cut away a centimeter and discovered that you had nothing and that the radiologist's shadow was from a misplaced pancreas — an anomaly that is found perhaps once in a million cases, and completely innocuous. However, I took advantage of the laparotomy to reach over and snip away your appendix, while I was about it."

You can imagine my state of mind: I was in bed feeling as if I had a truck wheel on my stomach and he tells me I had nothing. And that isn't the end of it. A few days later I discovered that my ill temper had saved me from a terrible danger. I learned in fact that the surgeon who had failed to keep his word had already decided, after consulting the famous Bastianelli, who had examined me before, to remove my entire stomach and connect the duodenum to the esophagus, thus making me a chronic invalid for the rest of my life. It was a mistake, something that any professional in any profession can make. But while it seems natural for a lawyer or an architect to be wrong, the mistake of a physician strikes us in a special way, because basically, since our life is involved, we want the doctor to be infallible. I wonder why. Perhaps because we don't have a spare life at hand.

You also had nervous disorders in those years, didn't you?

During the time with Elsa strange things happened to me. There was a period when I couldn't move my right arm. Then I became allergic to cat hairs.

They were all psychosomatic ailments?

Psychosomatic, yes. Then I suffered phenomena of locomotor ataxia. One day I wanted to walk to the right, and instead my legs carried me to the left. Finally I suffered a rather terrifying phenomenon: I felt my legs were being attracted toward the ceiling as if by some dire magnet. Further, at least a couple of times, I developed, I believe for psychosomatic reasons, the skin infection called impetigo. In other words, I was always a bit ill, but with illnesses that came and went for no evident organic reason: psychosomatic diseases, in fact. Finally, in those same years, I suffered from all sorts of allergies. I did nothing but sneeze and cry.

Before you and Elsa separated you made a trip to Iran in 1958 and one to India in 1960 with Pasolini. What were these journeys like?

I believe, in general, that traveling is a fundamental test of a person's character. I've never understood why this is so, but it is a fact. Perhaps travel somehow requires a complicity that refers to other, similar complicities in life. When these complicities are absent, a journey is a revealing touchstone. Now, with Elsa this is how things went: though she was in love with me, she had no sense of complicity. I've already told you what happened during our trip to Egypt, but I saw it confirmed on three other trips: one in Turkey, one in Iran, and one in India. Today these episodes could seem comic, but in reality, especially when they were happening, there was nothing comic about them. In Iran, Elsa, who had the habit of sending postcards to friends during journeys, refused to have them mailed by the hotel desk clerk as I advised. "He'll steal the money and then not send the cards. We'll go to the post office." We went to the post office, and naturally the woman who sold stamps spoke only Farsi. Instead of accepting the situation or perhaps trying to make herself understood to the woman, Elsa blamed everything on me. Naturally, a large crowd gathered around us, and I resigned myself to waiting till she calmed down. A similiar incident took place during our trip to India with Pasolini. We went to visit a temple. Pasolini and Elsa walked off and I waited alone in the taxi. Immediately a great number of beggars gathered to ask for alms, among them one man who could only be described as a monster: he had a face like a lizard, was probably blind, and he stuck his head into the taxi just like a reptile endowed with a long neck. Then I lost patience and shouted in English for them all to go away. At that moment Elsa arrived, and also on this occasion she held me responsible, guilty of not having been patient with the beggars. She went to the hotel in a fury and immediately began packing. Then, thanks to my pleas and Pasolini's, she calmed down and we continued the journey.

How did you meet Pasolini?

Pasolini met Elsa first and then me. Elsa talked to me a great deal about this poet, who had told her about the slums where he then taught and which later were the setting of his poems, his novels, and his films. It must have been about the time of the trip to Persia or even earlier. In any case both Elsa and I became his friends. Pasolini, as you know, gave *Nuovi argomenti* a long poem, "Le ceneri di Gramsci." It was the first poem to appear in the magazine, which until then had published chiefly nonfiction and fiction. We saw Pasolini almost every day because we were in the habit of eating out in a trattoria in the evening and he would join us. Or else, later, I would see him in the house of Laura Betti, his friend, his actress, and after his death the person who has done most to make Pasolini's work known abroad.

And Enzo Siciliano? When did you meet him?

I became friends with Enzo Siciliano much later, toward the end of the fifties, at the debate in the Einaudi bookshop over the For-mentor Prize, which I'll talk about later. I remember he was there with Garboli. The most important thing about my friendship with Siciliano is that we telephoned each other every day, and I say this because for me a friendship is measured especially by the number of telephone calls the two friends make. Telephone calls, in my opinion, are the thermometer of a friendship today as letters were in the eighteenth century. If I am someone's friend, I feel the need to telephone him every day to talk about everything: this for me is friendship. At least at the beginning.

Who were your telephone friends then?

Enzo Siciliano, as I said, then for a long period Lorenzo Tornabuoni, and lately Dario Bellezza.

What other writers and poets were intimate friends of yours?

There was never a clan, except in the imagination of the literary gossip columnists. But I felt friendship, affection, and respect for some writers. I've just talked about Pasolini and Siciliano. I'd like to add at least Parise and Brancati. The latter was my friend before Parise, and he died young.

What was Brancati like?

He is an important writer, author of that little classic titled *Don Giovanni in Sicilia.* I was very fond of Brancati, who was a man at once sweet and ironic, shrewd and sensitive, and all this with a strong Sicilian tone, which to me seemed, as it really was, a sign of authenticity. He was short, tiny, with a Saracen head with long eyes, sweet and smiling. He had a great success, but just as he was about to enjoy its fruits, he died. His death made a deep impression on me but didn't surprise me, because it was caused by a botched operation, and I've had to do with doctors all my life. Brancati had a benign tumor. A famous surgeon, who was his friend, convinced him to undergo an operation. Since the tumor was very big, the surgeon decided to perform the operation in two stages. But once he had opened the body of the writer, who had been put to sleep with anesthetic, he changed his mind and decided to remove the whole tumor. It was the idea of a brilliant surgeon who, being fond of Brancati, wanted to spare him a second operation. But Brancati's body had adjusted to the presence of this tumor and couldn't tolerate the sudden void that followed its removal, so Brancati died on the table. This premature end caused me great grief.

Your friendship with Goffredo Parise?

There was a curious literary analogy between Parise and Brancati: what Brancati had done for Sicily, transforming it into a literary myth, Parise did in some of his books for the Veneto. But the analogy ends there. Parise was an adventurous man, restless, and at times also bizarre. I once wrote of him that he had made so many journeys to prove to himself and to others that "all the world is *not* kin." He had a head rather like a pirate's, with big, melancholy eyes. His work, at the end, in a significant way, returned to his beginnings. He had begun with the Veneto in *Il ragazzo morto e le comete*, and he ended with the Veneto in the two volumes of *Il sillabario*. His first and last books are his best.

But what Brancati did for Sicily and Parise for the Veneto, Bassani has done for Ferrara; Natalia Ginzburg for Turin; Sciascia for Sicily; Gadda, Pontiggia, and Arbasino for Milan; Siciliano for Calabria; Calvino, Pavese, and Fenoglio for Piedmont; Pratolini for Florence; Volponi for the Marches; La Capria for Naples; and so on. What does all this mean, in your view?

I mentioned Parise and Brancati not so much because they were writers but because they were two people of whom I was very fond. As for the writers you've named, and for many others, what it means is this: the unity of Italy, as Goldoni says in his comedy *Il bugiardo*, is a "witty invention." After its unification, Italy has remained disunited and, what's worse, with a capital that isn't a capital, but the main city of the Lazio region. If anything, it's the capital of the Church.

You used to spend the afternoon walking around Rome. What did you think about?

I didn't think about anything. I walked from one street to another, looking, nothing else. As much as ten kilometers a day. About thinking, at this point, there's something I'd like to say: probably because of my long isolation due to my illness, most of the time my head is completely empty. I'm in a state of contemplation or, if you prefer, of totally spontaneous distraction. They say this is one of the aims of those who practice yoga. I've never done yoga, or else I've done it unawares. In any case, walking helps you not to think, among other things. I would walk alone, stop for a long time at shop windows, or else I would follow people, shadowing them to see where they were going. I'll give you an example of a walk of mine. For many years I lived in Via dell'Oca. I would leave Via dell'Oca, take a bus, and go to Via Veneto. Then, on foot, I would walk to the bottom of Via Veneto, down Via del Tritone to Piazza Venezia, then the length of the Corso, which would bring me back to Piazza del Popolo [and Via dell'Oca]. Or else I would do the opposite. Or else I would go out to some outlying district, Testaccio, or the Ponte Milvio area, or Trastevere.

Did you go to the movies every day as you do now?

I went to the movies, yes, but only when there was a good film, which for me can only be a "film d'auteur."

Elsa didn't go to the movies?

Yes, but when she was working, she wouldn't go anywhere. Then there were periods when she wasn't doing anything and she would come.

Would you like to talk some more about Elsa?

About Elsa there would be many things to say; I'd never finish. Twenty-five years together are no trifle. Elsa was a person who, at heart, was unhappy all her life. In conflict with reality. With one consolation, however, an enormous and satisfied amour propre. For she believed, and she was right to believe, that she was a great writer. So she had an unhappy relationship with reality, counter-balanced by a good relationship with herself, as far as writing is concerned, that is. The opposite of me. As I told you, I'm pro-foundly dissatisfied with my books and with myself. Perhaps more with my books than with myself.

Who were the writers you respected at that time?

Gadda, especially.

Why?

Because he was a writer who had a keen, though anguished sense of the comic. Something very rare.

You like the comic, don't you?

Yes, very much. I like to laugh when I read. I don't know why.

Do you like Flaubert?

No, Flaubert isn't comic.

What about Bouvard et Pécuchet?

No, it's not comic at all. *Bouvard et Pécuchet* is a perfect fiasco. James Joyce, in *Ulysses,* carried out the comic operation that Flaubert failed to perform. I want to tell you something: good serious novels number in the hundreds. Good comic novels, on the other hand, you can count on your fingers.

You like Dostoyevsky very much, and he isn't comic.

In the first place, Dostoyevsky *is* comic. Just think of *The Double,* which is a genuine comic masterpiece. For that matter, wherever there's poetry there is comedy.

When is Gadda comic?

Always. Even in a horrifying book like *La cognizione del dolore.* Moreover, he had a great writing ability. A narrative flaw in Gadda, I feel, is that he loses himself in digressions. But perhaps it's not a flaw. Think of the constant "digressions" of Sterne in *Tristram Shandy.* It's a trait. In any case comic writers are my favorites. I've reread many times Rabelais, Cervantes, Dickens, Gogol, Carroll, Collodi, and so on.

Palazzeschi is also a comic writer!

In fact, I've read and reread all his works, from the Futurist poems to the last novels.

And did you admire Landolfi?

In his personal life Landolfi somehow had something in common with Malcolm Lowry, the author of *Under the Volcano*. Malcolm Lowry destroyed himself with alcohol. Landolfi was possessed by gambling, less destructive than alcohol, true, but more obsessive. Landolfi lived in Florence. I was told that in the winter he would go and eavesdrop outside the doors of bakeries, since bakers are the only ones who stay up past dawn. He would then look in and say, "A little game, anybody?" And he would start playing amid the loaves and the sacks of flour. But apart from gambling, which certainly had an influence on his life, Landolfi perhaps never gave everything he could have given (he could have been the Italian Bulgakov) because in a significant way he possessed and imposed on himself creative limits, through a singular procedure, which consisted of showing disbelief in what he was saying at the very moment he was saying it. On the other hand, oddly, his writing suggests a somewhat ironic return to nineteenth-century narrative forms, similar to what Elsa Morante did in her novels.

And Calvino?

He is a writer of another generation, with whom I had no affinity and few personal encounters. Of his work I particularly like *I nostri antenati*, which seems to me a happy encounter of writing with what I would call personal ideology. Some stories, too, of what you could consider the realistic period seem successful to me. Calvino's shyness was proverbial, and at the same time, in a singular combination, he was an important literary catalyst. I liked him, and he indicated his liking for me on several occasions, especially when I was threatened by right-wing terrorists and he wrote an article about me in the *Corriere della sera*.

There was much talk of Beckett in those years. What did you think of him?

I thought that he was an important writer of genius. But I also thought that, like Borges and Kafka, he was for the Western bourgeoisie what the Americans call a "fad," a passing fashion based on some commonplaces. The fashion for Beckett can be demonstrated by the following joke. Two Milanese meet and say to each other, "Have you gone to see *Godot?*" "Yes." "Any good?" "I don't know, but you mustn't miss it." Personally, I prefer Beckett's novels to his theater.

Did you know Sartre in those years?

Yes, fairly well. I saw him every time he came to Rome. He was a man of extraordinary mobility and intellectual voracity. Small, with cross-eyes behind his glasses, he reminded me of those fish in aquaria that dart here and there devouring everything in their path. He is perhaps the most ambitious intellectual I've ever met in my life.

Did you like talking with Sartre?

I liked listening to him.

Did you meet Camus?

Yes, I met him two or three times. I saw him once at the *Nouvelle revue française;* then I made an excursion with him and Chiaromonte to Hadrian's Villa, outside Rome. Since as a rule he's coupled with Sartre, if for no other reason than their common existentialist roots, I would say that he was more of an artist than Sartre, but in the final analysis, Sartre occupies a more important position than Camus in French culture.

Is the Camus myth justified?

No myth is ever justified. I believe he's a bit overestimated. As a writer, his best narrative work is *L'Étranger.* Sartre wrote at least one story, "L'Enfance d'un chef," that is comparable to the books of Camus.

Did you know that L'Étranger *is the best-selling book on the Gallimard list?*

I reread the book when Luchino Visconti made a film of it. It didn't have on me the effect it has on the French: namely, that it's a classic. For me a classic is a book you reread often. *L'Étranger* has its defects: the murder of the Arab, for example, is focused on the glint of the sun on the blade, pretty much as D'Annunzio might have done it. For this reason, at least for me, it isn't a book I reread with pleasure.

In the years between the end of your marriage with Elsa and before you began living with Dacia you did a lot of traveling. Did you meet figures of international importance?

I met Nehru, Tito, the king of Afghanistan, Fidel Castro, and, later, the shah of Iran, Arafat, Ceausescu, and others.

What are your memories of these very different characters?

I saw Nehru during one of my journeys in India. The Italian ambassador wanted me to meet Nehru formally. I had been introduced to the president of the Indian republic the day before and Nehru kindly agreed to receive me. I had been warned, "After about an hour Nehru's eyes will begin to wander around the room in boredom. That will be the moment to leave." Whether because of this warning or because the invitation had come quite suddenly, I went to see Nehru with no preparation, and at least for me, that visit was completely without interest. Of course, it was my own fault. I was received in a large room filled with ivory objects. I was much struck by Nehru's elegance: he was wearing a white silk tunic buttoned to the neck and jodhpurs. He had a red rosebud, absolutely fresh, in the buttonhole of his tunic. They told me he changed it every two or three hours. As I said, I was unprepared and what's worse, for some unknown reason, my mind seemed to go blank. I could have talked about all sorts of things: relations between British and Indians, Gandhi, Indian religious philosophy, the industrialization of the country, and so on. Though I wasn't an expert, I was sufficiently knowledgeable to ask interesting questions. Instead, we literally talked about the weather, and at a certain point I realized that the moment of boredom had hit me even before him. We dragged along for a few more minutes and finally, exactly one hour after I had come in, I saw the famous and fascinating man's eyes wander, vague and bored. Then I took my leave.

And Tito?

With Tito it was the exact opposite. I was sent as special corre-spondent of *L'espresso*, and I flew with Dacia Maraini during the mid-August holiday. I thought it would be a short, unmemorable flight. Instead, we ran into a summer hurricane, the instruments conked out, and the airplane actually swerved to the south and car-ried us over Bosnia. On the island of Brioni, where Tito lived in the summer, I was expecting to find a Mediterranean landscape, rocky and sun-baked. On the contrary, Brioni is a rather melan-choly island, without rocks, with great green meadows sloping down to the sea and distant forests, dark and thick, where does and stags roam. Brioni seemed sparsely populated, deserted in some places. Tito received me, as arranged, at nine in the morning, in the presence of some officials and his wife, Jovanka. I have a very distinct impression of him as a man in whom the contrasting char-acteristics of the worker and the soldier were happily blended. In fact, this is what Tito was: a metalworker (he descended from a family of smiths) who, from the time he was a simple soldier in the Austro-Hungarian army, had had a special interest in the problems of war. That morning he was wearing a marshal's uniform, but his face was a proletarian's. A maid brought us a tray with glasses of whisky and cups of coffee. The interview was lively and commu-nicative, the opposite of the one with Nehru. At a certain point I said to Tito, "You've had a beautiful life." He answered me, "Beau-tiful, yes, but hard." The curious thing is that he was probably thinking of his political-military career, while I was thinking of his adventurous life as a young man, when he had been prisoner of the Tatars in Siberia and then an anonymous witness in the days of the 1917 revolution in St. Petersburg. After the interview Tito showed me his private zoo, full of animals given him by various Asian and African potentates. In short, it was a successful day, and it confirmed my idea that men of action, whoever they are, are more interesting that purely political figures.

And Arafat?

That interview was also organized by *L'espresso*. I flew to Damascus with a Palestinian friend, who was later killed by the Israeli secret services. From the hotel I went straight to PLO headquarters, a modest little building in an outlying district. They made me wait in a squalid office, and finally Arafat arrived. From what I could understand, he was coming from Amman and to reach Damascus, for fear of assassination attempts, had traveled along a secret route through the mountains. He wore the traditional kerchief on his head and shoulders, but he carried a pistol in his belt. The interview was about the future of the Palestinians. I seem to recall that Arafat proved very lucid and reasonable. In reality he expounded to me ideas he had already published in a book issued in France by the Éditions de Minuit. They were reasonable ideas, or so they seemed, but their application obviously required drastic changes on the part of both the Israelis and the Arabs. In fact, as of today nothing has been done about them. I don't have many opinions on the Palestinian problem for the very good reason that, like the South African problem, at least at present I consider it a problem without a solution. But after all, why must every problem have a solution? There are problems that don't. As for Arafat, my impression of the man was one of a great coldness that I have noticed also in other Arab figures: a quality that paradoxically often accompanies fanaticism. Something, that is, which doesn't exist in Europe, where as a rule either you're a fanatic or you're coldly rational, but not both things at once. Also in the case of Arafat, as in that of Tito, I felt a curious liking for him precisely because he was a man of action.

And Castro?

I was invited to Cuba in 1966 to the Tricontinental Conference, and I went there with Dacia Maraini. The conference was chiefly concerned, at least from what I seemed to understand, with political-military questions. It was, that is, a conference that allowed you to intuit, at least in a general way, Cuba's future armed intervention in many parts of the world. Among the delegates to the conference there was Régis Debray, then very well known thanks to a widely circulated revolutionary text: I remember that Dacia and I spent a day of sun and sea with him at Varadero, a holiday spot of rich American tourists before the revolution. At Varadero, besides the sea and the beach, there was a curiosity, a fake Spanish castle, residence of the billionaire Morgan family. I visited this castle with Debray and other delegates. It was all in Spanish style, inside and out, and all fake. I was particularly struck by the dining room.

Long black banners hung on the walls, arabesqued with golden letters. These banners bore one of the most famous texts of pre-Romantic English poetry: Coleridge's "Kubla Khan." At the end of the hall there was a big organ that was used for playing Christmas carols. The table was laid: the visitors could see how the American capitalists lived and ate. I asked the guide if it was better in the Morgans' time or now. He had been a Morgan butler. He answered enigmatically, "The same."

The other Cuban attraction, if you can call it that, was the Hemingway house. It was an old, unassuming house surrounded by a dusty park with a cement swimming pool, drained and full of stones. Inside, sofas and armchairs in flowered chintz, many books of light reading, impossible as this may seem, airport books. It was like being in the villa of a retired British colonel. Hemingway's presence was revealed largely by two collections of quite different objects: a rack with numerous guns and a great quantity of boots, for hunting, fishing, and so on, of unusual size.

As for Castro, I had two views of him, one public and the other private. The public view was during a long speech given by the dictator in the main square of Havana on a very special subject: rice. Communist China had stopped, or at least greatly reduced, the shipments of rice to Cuba, making it difficult to provide the island with its favorite cereal, necessary for the national dish, *cristianos con moros*, namely, rice and lentils; perhaps there were others reasons for discontent. In any case, Castro was protesting against the treatment of the small Communist countries by the big ones. We listened and at the same time we ate. Everyone was given a tray with a bottle of wine and a piece of meat. We were directly beneath Castro's platform; he gave me the impression of being a good orator, full of calm, rational authority. Just the opposite of Mussolini's epilepsy and Hitler's hysteria. The private encounter was very brief, during a reception at the government palace. Dacia and I were introduced to the dictator, and between him and Dacia the following dialogue took place: "How much do you think I weigh?" Dacia answered, "A hundred kilograms." "And how tall do you think I am?" "One meter ninety." "You came close." Castro was dressed in his usual fatigues; he smoked as usual a thick cigar. But seen like this, he made a strange impression on me, as if that beard, so famous and so widely imitated by his followers, served to hide some scar, some wrinkles, or other unusual facial defect.

Did you like him?

As with Arafat and Tito, I felt a liking for him because in him I sensed the man of action. Indeed, at that moment he represented the man of action par excellence, since the Cultural Revolution was overturning the old-line Marxist belief that thought must precede action. To this belief Cuba had replied, "First action, then thought," which was then the great novelty of the Marxism-Leninism of 1968. In any case, action — deeds — had always made me find likable those political figures who acted. Deeds are somehow sacred for me; words much less. Doing changes the world. Words, unless they turn into deeds, change nothing.

You've always told me you didn't feel any special attraction for political figures. Do dictators attract you?

No, as I said, I'm attracted by men of action. Dictators often aren't men of action. Mussolini was a journalist. Hitler was a beer-hall ideologue. Stalin was always shut up in a room in the Kremlin, he never visited a factory. He provoked action, yes. And this led him to make mistakes.

Then you feel a liking for Caesar, Napoleon, and figures of that sort?

An idea is an idea, and liking is liking. Ideas are general and can be discussed and explained. Likings are individual, not discussible, inexplicable. To give you just one example: I find Caesar likable, Genghis Khan, no, but I can't say why. At this point it occurs to me that I've never told you about my meeting with Léon Blum.

When?

Just after the war I went to see Léon Blum, sent by *L'Europeo*. I was aware of Blum's double character, a political figure of prime importance and at the same time an intellectual, a literary man of great refinement. But Italy's defeat in the war was too recent for him to take me into any consideration. He received me in great haste, and I doubt that he knew who I was. He was thin, with a professorial mustache, very elegant in a tight suit, the sleeves rather short, with shirt cuffs protruding, held by diamond cuff links. He said something to me about Italo-French relations. If I recall correctly, he said that undoubtedly these relations would improve in the future. After this self-evident truth I took my leave. On the same occasion I called on Malraux, an attractive and very vital man, endowed with an intelligence somehow more *mitteleuropäische* than French. Like Léon Blum, he foresaw better relations between Italy and France, but he expressed himself with a certain bombast, "I see a group of Italian partisans file beneath the Arc de Triomphe; with them I see a group of French partisans." All the time he was speaking Malraux made a constant noise with his nose, *en reniflant.* His conversation was nervous, darting, and finally very friendly. He knew me as a writer. I've been told that he once said of me, "Moravia wrote *Gli indifferenti* and then he died." In a literary sense, he meant. Another time I met him in Paris, I had lunch with him. After lunch he invited me to go with him to see Koestler, the author of *Darkness at Noon.* For some reason I remembered all of a sudden that Koestler, after having been a communist, had become an anti-communist, and though I was absolutely anti-Stalinist, I declined the invitation. I was probably wrong. But I was troubled by the prospect of an ideological sermon.

How did you meet the shah of Iran?

I had already been to Iran in 1958 with Elsa Morante. I went back in the seventies on the eve of the shah's fall. I went to Iran with Gianni Barcelloni, who was shooting a film for Italian TV. In 1958 I had visited the great monuments in Teheran, Isfahan, and Persepolis. This time I made a more detailed trip. We had made arrangements to film an interview with the shah, and he received us one morning in a salon lined with mirrors. We waited a long time, then he came in. I saw a man coming toward me in a blue chalk-stripe suit, his face visibly prepared with makeup. He had a sad manner, absent and weary, but he spoke with great confidence and in excellent French. The conversation touched on some timely questions: his ambitions for Iran, armaments, relations with the Soviet Union, the internal situation, and so on. From this conversation I formed a very precise idea about his political position: granted all the differences due to the fact that Iran was a Third World country and also Asiatic, it can calmly be said that the shah was a fascist, but not a street fighter or a demagogue like Mussolini or Hitler. Rather, he was organically fascist, in competition with communism to modernize and industrialize his own country, naturally for the benefit of the traditional ruling class.

He had, however, one thing in common with Mussolini: a rhetoric that totally excluded religion, Islam in Iran and Catholicism in Italy. The shah, like the Fascists, harked back to a mythic empire of the past. But there was also a big difference: the Italians are not a nation of fanatics, and the church was accommodating. Whereas Iran is perhaps the most fanatical country not just of Asia but of the whole world, and the mullahs did not forgive the shah. In other words, the shah made the mistake not only of modernizing Iran, industrializing it, but also of westernizing it in fashion, in customs, in daily life. To put it simply, he didn't understand that airplanes, factories, and arms didn't contradict Islam, but the abolition of the veil for women, licenses for nightclubs, and

movies did. With this, we mustn't forget that the shah commanded a cruel and detested police and, further, was unaware
how general the corruption of the government was. I remember I
asked him many questions and he gave typical answers, such as,
"What is a king for his people?" "He is a father, a judge, a priest."
I recognized also the fascist atmosphere in a certain megalo-
mania, "Teheran must become a great capital, like Paris or
London. Powerful countries have great capitals." "But don't you
think that transplanting so many peasants to Teheran could create
some social imbalance?" He answered, "On a pensé à cela." Two
years later the shah went. *Il n'avait pas pensé à cela.*

**Did the shah belong to that category of chiefs of state you found
likable thanks to their capacity for action?**

Absolutely not. He was a monarch in a blue chalk-stripe suit who
gave orders to his ministers, kept in touch with the bazaar, and
promoted the so-called white revolution. A false palingenesis, in
other words, based on the bureaucracy. But I repeat: he competed
with communism in industrializing his country. He reached the
point of importing an entire factory from Czechoslovakia, he
aimed at building the world's fifth largest army, but he overlooked
Islam. In short, he was anything but a man of action.

What sort of impression did the man make on you?

Oddly contradictory. At once sad and presumptuous. Downcast and
megalomaniacal. He seemed to be acting the part of shah on a bet.

And the king of Afghanistan?

Kabul was one of the stops on what you might call my honeymoon with Dacia Maraini, a trip around the world. My brother-
in-law was first secretary of the Italian embassy, and we stayed
with him. I asked to be received by the king, and etiquette de-
manded that ten days pass between the application and the audience, so we spent nine days in Kabul. It was a little city of peasants
and bureaucrats, totally lacking in interest. Among very beautiful
mountains. We made some excursions, we went down to the

Khyber Pass, we climbed up the road that leads to the Soviet Union as far as the Hindukush Pass. On all sides you could see with absolute clarity that the Soviet Union had taken Britain's place as dominant power. The Soviets had their barracks, their kindergartens, their movie theaters, but they kept their distance exactly like the so-called imperialists. The king basically governed for the Soviet Union. The question I've always asked myself is this: Why did the Soviet Union allow the king to be dismissed and a Communist government to be established? The king guaranteed the continuity of the religious tradition, of old customs, but once the Communists were in power, a good part of Afghanistan revolted. They say the Communist coup d'état took place to save the immense investments made by the Soviet Union in Afghanistan and to ward off a coup from the opposite direction, but who knows if that's true? After the nine days the king received me in a palace all in fake Louis XVI style. He was silent, sober, discreet, perhaps sad. He gave me a red carpet, very beautiful, which I still have.

Do you remember other chiefs of state?

I also interviewed Ceausescu for *L'espresso*. I went to Rumania and spent three very boring days in a hotel in downtown Bucharest. It was a Soviet-style hotel, but without that oddity and those anachronisms that make Russian hospitality pleasant. It was like being in a third-class hotel in Ostia. On the ground floor there was a nightclub, also provincial and melancholy. I sent twenty-six questions to Ceausescu; he accepted only six, the most banal. Finally I went to the government house, and after going through an endless succession of secret service bureaucrats, I was introduced into the dictator's office. Now I will tell you something almost incredible: of that encounter I remember *nothing*! Perhaps because of the boredom of the long wait or the uncommunicative and extremely cold reception by Ceausescu. I don't even remember his face very well, or his physical features. I remember only the expression on that face, distrustful and malevolent. I left Bucharest with great relief! In other words, the whole trip was a big mistake.

I had been in Rumania before, with Pasolini, in the city of Dr. Aslan, the woman who discovered Gerovital, a product supposed to maintain eternal youth. Both Pasolini and I wanted to be examined by the doctor, but they sent us away saying we didn't need it. On that occasion I saw a lot of some young Rumanians of both sexes; I had the impression of a country that was not only not communist but was anxiously awaiting the return of capitalism.

Leaving aside famous political figures now, I'd like you to talk to me about Bobi Bazlen and Emilio Cecchi.

I don't remember when I met Bobi Bazlen, but it was surely in the fifties. He was a Triestine, so his culture was not so much Italian as middle European, an Austrian background. Now it has been proved that in the period between the two wars perhaps the truly important European capital was not so much Paris as Vienna. Think of Freud, Wittgenstein, linguistic philosophy, dodecaphonic music, Musil, and so on. Which is tantamount to saying that Bobi Bazlen was the more or less conscious importer of a dominant culture into a country that in some ways was provincial. This, in my opinion, explains the unquestioned influence he had at a certain moment in Italian culture. Just one example: he advised Einaudi to publish Musil. The relationship between Trieste and the Italian culture of the period was, in other words, the contrary of the relationship between Trieste and Italy. For Italy, Trieste was an "unredeemed" city that then was "redeemed." In reality, Trieste was the redeemer of Italian culture, as is shown not only through Bazlen but also through Svevo and Saba. Bobi Bazlen was little, very ugly, with one shoulder higher than the other. Elsa said he had spent all his money on a psychoanalytic cure after which his right shoulder had become higher than his left, whereas before the cure the left was higher than the right. The fact remains, however, that when psychoanalysis was completely unknown and quietly banned in Italy, Bobi Bazlen had experienced it, knew it, and understood it. Bobi Bazlen never wrote anything; the only thing of his I ever read was a poem he showed to Elsa, and she said of it, "Obviously, he's not a poet." He was a man full of snobbish tics, which concealed a difficult rapport with reality. On the subject of tics, I remember that after a long conversation with Elsa he went off, saying, "I'll come back tomorrow and I will speak to you of the letter B." He often spent his time with couples on the verge of separating, and he devoted himself altruistically to the lives of others trapped in conjugal bonds. I remember him always as if in flight through the streets, a little peripatetic Socrates in a constant hurry.

And Cecchi?

During the Fascist period Cecchi was one of the central cultural figures in Rome. He was Tuscan, with a working-class physique and background. In Florence and its environs it is easy to encounter men resembling Cecchi. In a way he was very representative of the virtues and the defects of "post-grand ducal," "post-Risorgimento," "present-day" Tuscany. He had the great bursts of enthusiasm that characterized the intellectual ambition of the most illustrious region of Italy and the same time the limitations and, if you will, the pettiness indicative of this same region's decline. The result was a very refined figure, very cultivated, very precise and prepared, who for all his life wooed poetry without managing to seduce it. He was originally part of the *La ronda* group, but he didn't share their idea that the true Italian prose was that of the 16th century, edited and revised by Leopardi, and later by Cardarelli. If anything, Cecchi's style reflected the tail end of art nouveau, or rather art deco, with quite a few examples of elegant Tuscan superiority. It would be facile to say that he and his friends of *La ronda* hated and denigrated the novel because they weren't able to write one. The fact is, nevertheless, that for about twenty years the writers of Cecchi's group, also for economic necessity, favored the literary article for the daily paper, the piece then known as the *elzeviro*. Baldini, Cecchi, Barilli, Cardarelli, and others published in the newspapers but were not newspapermen. That is, they used the papers to make good literature, or at least what they considered good. Unfortunately, the limitations of the form, literary and otherwise, are perceptible today; the genre is dated. When I met Cecchi he was already fifty and I was twenty. Indeed, I remember a joking remark of his, "When are you going to stop being twenty?" He was a friend, but not without some ambiguity of the sort that, in his day, before the war, had earned him a famous attack from Giovanni Papini, with an unjust and disagreeable, but not entirely unfounded article entitled "La sora Emilia." As for me, the ambiguity emerged when *La ciociara* was published. He asked to meet me. He said that instead of a critical article he would write a dialogue between the two of us. Then, a few days later, instead of the dialogue, the *Corriere della sera* published a traditional hatchet job. On other occasions, however, he spoke well of my books, especially of *La disubbidienza.*

Tell me now about the end of your marriage with Elsa.

I could say that it collapsed on its own, in the sense that more and more Elsa and I were simply living together, but both alone, with our separate lives. After 1955, more or less, we weren't companions, as they say today. But not so strangely, given my character, I would have continued living with her if I hadn't fallen in love with Dacia Maraini. Why do I mention my character? Because my natural tendency toward change is found only in my writing. In life I prefer, before breaking up an association as important as the one between Elsa and me, to find another, equally important, to replace it. I've already told you that from 1955 for about two years Elsa practically lived with Luchino Visconti. Immediately after that the young American painter Bill Morrow came into her life. Meanwhile, I met Dacia Maraini, with whom I fell in love in the only way I am capable of: very slowly, beginning almost with indifference and ending with passion. And it was then that, almost without realizing it, I found myself separated de facto. Here something very strange happens, which I'll try to make you understand. No matter how hard I try, I can't remember at all the day when I actually left Elsa.

Many years later, more or less the same thing happened to me when I had a very bad car accident that forced me to stay in bed for three months with a fractured femur. I remembered the moment I left the house and the moment when I regained consciousness in the smashed car, with the broken leg, but the shock had caused a phenomenon of total repression that is called retrodated memory. It's the same with my separation from Elsa. I remember very well how on my birthday, in Via dell'Oca, she came into my study and clumsily threw a bunch of flowers on my desk and I thanked her, but I wasn't able to be really affectionate. From that moment my memory actually leaps to the apartment on Lungotevere della Vittoria that I bought in order to live there with Dacia. Between my birthday and the beginning of our life on Lungotevere della Vittoria I remember very little, and yet several months must have passed. From this void the only thing that emerges is my trip to Africa with Dacia and Pasolini. I had suggested to Elsa — this I remember — that she come to Africa with me and she refused indignantly. Then I went with Dacia. During the night, as we were flying out, I was awake and was trying to look down at the shadows of the Sahara. And then all of a sudden I felt a sense of absolute physical liberation. As if I had rid myself of something heavy, like a plaster cast. But the separation was never entirely complete. For years afterward I felt intermittently a horrible sensation of being abandoned. In short, I've come to the conclusion that our life is other people, and being separated from them for whatever reasons, or by their death, is substantially a kind of death for us. The others go away and take a great part of our life with them.

Did you have a legal separation?

Nothing of the sort; we were separated only topographically. I went to live with Dacia on Lungoteve della Vittoria; Elsa remained in the apartment in Via dell'Oca. As far as the economic side was concerned, I suggested that instead of giving her the usual bourgeois monthly allowance, I open a bank account in her name, where she could have her own checkbook and could draw out whatever she needed. Elsa was always very modest, and after the success of La storia, she used the account much less.

So you left Via dell'Oca and went to live on Lungotevere della Vittoria. You left Elsa and went to live with Dacia. Did you realize you were beginning a new, important period of your life?

In life the beginning of important periods is usually concealed by everyday routine. In the case of Dacia, I actually did realize that everything was changing for me. In particular I realized it because of the journeys I made with her.

Why?

With Elsa I had made some trips: Egypt, Middle East, Iran, France, Switzerland, England, India, and so on. But I have to say this: every character has its moment of self-expression, and as I said before, Elsa's expressive moment had come in the terrible difficulties of the period during the war. Elsa gave the best of herself in exceptional situations, in emergencies. But in traveling she had the habit of bringing with her the psychological relationship that is proper to everyday life. We could go to the other end of the world, but it would still seem we were in Via dell'Oca. Elsa didn't travel; she altered her surroundings, that's all. With Dacia, on the contrary, I really traveled, in a sense somehow adventurous that isn't composed so much of adventures but of complete oblivion of the steady, well-defined world left at home. I traveled the way you dream; by this I mean that for many reasons, the chief one being the cosmopolitan personality of Dacia (she spent her childhood in Japan and for many years had spoken Japanese more than Italian), I finally traveled with abandon and discovery. It is not without significance that to celebrate our union we decided to go around the world. Maybe it was a kind of challenge; in reality it was also, especially, a hunger for space and freedom, finally satisfied. This is shown, if by nothing else, by the fact that, returning to Rome after two months of constant traveling, when I tried to write some newspaper articles I realized I had nothing to say. Everything I could have said concerned that hunger for space that I had borne inside me for so many years. The years with Dacia were, however, marked by a great discovery.

What discovery?

It sounds like the title of some book by one of the explorers of the so-called dark continent: the discovery of Africa. After our first journey there with Pasolini, every year Dacia and I made a trip to Africa. It isn't easy for me to define this discovery. I've published three books on Africa citing a kind of slogan: the greatest and most noble monument that nature has erected to herself. And also: in Europe nature is weaker than man; in Africa it's stronger.

What else do you think marked your transition from Elsa to Dacia, from Via dell'Oca to Lungotevere della Vittoria?

It's something that everyone who changes life knows about: life with Elsa finally had literally come apart. Our relationship had fallen into the void, on its own, like a ripe fruit. With Dacia I felt I was regaining vigor, starting over both in small things and big. It's a very common expression, but still strange and over-whelming: why does life disintegrate at a certain moment and then miraculously resume, when you change companion and habits and residence? I don't know. I know only that I was able to live with new energy in the years between 1960 and 1978, when the relationship with Dacia broke off. Thanks to this energy I remember those eighteen years as the best in my life. For the rest, however, there were very few evident changes. I had lived till then with a writer, amid books and literature; I was still living with a writer amid books and literature. I hadn't changed friends: they were the same as those of the period with Elsa. The only novelty was the fact that Dacia couldn't lead a solitary life with me as Elsa had done on Capri. Dacia was not only a writer; she was also involved with the theater, with feminism, and was socially very committed in Rome.

Did Dacia have the same working habits as Elsa?

No, Dacia works every day, like me. Elsa could go years without writing; then, once she started working, she literally wrote all day long.

Is Dacia a very ambitious woman on the literary and intellectual level?

I would say yes. She has written many poems (which, in my opinion, are among her best things), a fair number of novels (the latest, *La lunga vita di Marianna Ucrìa* is, along with her first, *La vacanza*, the one I prefer), about twenty plays, and many stories, articles, and so on.

What are the things you and Dacia have in common?

I believe that in a conjugal relationship it isn't the things in common that matter but rather the complementary nature of different or even opposite characters. As in the case of Dacia and me, in fact. We are very different, but our union had the originality of two diversities that completed each other.

13

*A*LAIN ELKANN: *On that first trip to Africa with Dacia and Pasolini, what was your immediate impression?*

ALBERTO MORAVIA: The revelation of a land where I should have gone much earlier. Instead, I went there very late in my life. I was by then fifty. I should have gone twenty, thirty years before. I didn't, I don't know why. I regret that. For me Africa is the most beautiful thing that exists in the world.

What was the first country you came to?

Ghana. We landed in Accra, and I saw black Africa for the first time.

Was it the first time also for Dacia?

Yes.

Also for Pasolini?

Also for Pasolini. In Accra I saw for the first time how much black Africa loves colors. You could see enormous black men dressed in multicolored cottons, manufactured for the most part in Holland or England apparently; the patterns were very modern, deco, nouveau, and so on. Often around the edges of these fabrics you could read moral sentiments, for example, "The best path in life is that of virtue." Simple, puritan-style morality. In Swahili, however, not in English or in Dutch. The Africans seemed to fall into two categories: very thin or very fat. Very often you could see corpulent men and women, wrapped like ancient Romans in several yards of highly colored cotton, one end flung over the shoulder. They strolled along, wearing turbans made of the same fabric as the dress. Dacia bought some of these fabrics and wore them on the beach, for bathing. It was a different kind of New Year's for us: in the hotels there were Chistmas trees with all the lights that blinked on and off and, at the same time, those Africans with bare arms and bodies wrapped in wondrous fabric.

What was Pasolini like to travel with?

Delightful, very. He talked little and was extremely alert: an excellent traveling companion. He had a fairly well developed sense of humor, but I remember that on one occasion he lost it perforce. We were all pleased on our first night; we did nothing but sing the praises of Africa. The next day, when we came down, I stood on the sidewalk by the car to make sure they put all our suitcases in it.

Where were you going?

To the airport, to continue the journey. When I saw all the luggage was inside, I got into the car. Anyone would have done the same. But the porters exploited that one moment to steal our luggage. We went to the airport; a case of mine and one of Pasolini's were missing, as well as my typewriter, a brand-new Remington. My traveling companions didn't know what to do, but I decided at once: back to the hotel. At the hotel, the manager, a Greek, replied that he knew nothing about our bags. We visited all the rooms, one by one, and I managed to recover the two suitcases but not the typewriter. Pasolini was beside himself: no more singing Africa's praises! Then, belatedly, the police arrived, looking like huge ants, with black uniforms and huge black

glasses. But the things had been found; all the same, the policemen asked us for money, as if they had been the ones to recover our luggage. After that incident we left Ghana and
continued the journey as far as Togo: fifty kilometers of beautiful
landscape, with great white, deserted beaches, shaded by very tall
palms. I remember that as soon as we arrived in Togo, we all
threw ourselves out of the two white-hot Land Rovers and flung
ourselves into the ocean just as we were, not with bathing suits
but in our underwear. From Togo we went to the north of
Nigeria, to Kano, which is a typical city of the Sahel, the pre-
desert zone, a city all of red clay, the walls of the houses windowless, and palms jutting above the garden walls. A Muslim city,
therefore hermetic.

At this point I'd like to say why Africa holds such an appeal for
me. In my opinion, the African landscape often has nothing special about it, it can even lack completely those picturesque details
that so attract us in Europe, and yet, more than in any other part
of the world, you feel that it has a strange soul of its own, inarticulate, monotonous and yet mysteriously noble and eloquent. Africa
speaks to us in its way of ages that have vanished forever, whether
through its marvelously monotonous plains (a bush, an acacia,
and so on and on for a thousand kilometers) or through its eroded
mountains, like tables. Among the grasses of those plains and
under the barriers of those mountains it wouldn't be surprising to
see the great reptiles of the Quaternary shambling along, dinosaurs, brontosaurs. Africa is the most primitive and wild continent of the earth, and yet nature, perhaps not by chance, has
given it an order and a pattern that seem due to man's conscious
intervention. All Africa is in parallel stripes, like the bathing suits
in Mack Sennett comedies. A first stripe is the temperate zone of
northern, Mediterranean Africa; the second is the Sahara; the
third is the Sahel, or savannah; the fourth is the tangled woods
without any tall trees. The fifth is the tunnel-like, virgin forest.
Below the region of the forests it all begins over again: first the
brush, then the savannah, then the so-called Kalahari Desert, and
finally the temperate zone of South Africa.

In that part of Africa where you went the first time, were there many animals?

There were no animals at all — not for some centuries, in any case, I would say. In the parks some lions and some elephants survive, but it's hard to see them. Animals are found chiefly in East Africa — Uganda, Kenya, Tanzania, and so on. West Africa for four centuries was colonized by the Europeans, East Africa for less than a century. Further, the destruction of the fauna was largely carried out by the ephemeral kingdoms and empires that succeeded one another in West Africa. The destruction of the fauna was accompanied by the destruction of ethnic groups carried out by the slavers: the entire black population of the United States and Latin America comes from there. Now to the destruction of the fauna and the decimation of whole peoples there is being added, perhaps more grave than anything else, the destruction of the flora carried out by European consumerism. West Africa in some way demonstrates that the end of the world, the topic of so much talk surrounding the atomic bomb, has already begun at the ecological level. The forests of the Ivory Coast, of Nigeria, and below them, of Zaire and Gabon, are being destroyed at a frightening pace. I myself, during that journey with Pasolini and Dacia, crossed in Benin a solemn and shadowy forest like a cathedral. Barely ten years later there was nothing but countless stumps and, now and then, a big sign testifying with consumeristic pride to the massacre of nature, KLEIN, PARIS. Almost all the prized wood used in Europe for furniture, window frames, and building comes from Africa. The damage is perhaps more irreparable than what so-called civilization has done to the fauna and the people: animals and humans can reproduce themselves rapidly, but certain arboreal colossi take centuries and perhaps even more. The majestic forest is followed by bush, and in those thickets the giants of the forest have a hard time growing, or don't grow at all.

Why did Africa make such an impression on you?

I already hinted at it when I said that the African landscape suggests the presence of the dinosaur. Africa fascinated me because to me, a European, aware not only of the history of Europe but also of Asia and the Americas, Africa appeared a prehistoric continent, a land where the rapport between humans and nature is not mediated by history. On this question of Africa's being prehistoric or, rather, without history, I had a discussion, not to say a virtual quarrel, with a Kenyan writer, Ngugi Wa Thiong'o, author of many anticolonialist novels, including the very well-known *Petals of Blood.* Ngugi is a radical nationalist who, after having written a number of books in English, did the opposite of Conrad, who replaced Polish with English, that is, replacing his national language with an imperial language. Ngugi, on the contrary, replaced imperial English with a national language, Kikuyu. This explains also his insistence during the debate, in which he asserted I was mistaken, that Africa was inside history and had a history of its own. Ngugi was referring to the history of northern Africa and in particular to that of Egypt, but I was considering what I regard as the real Africa, black Africa. In this Africa there is no written history, no cultural critique of the past. Or else it has been written by foreigners, by Arabs, French, English, and so on. But there exists an oral history, which I, however, consider not history but epic, handed down from one singer to another over centuries in the form, in fact, of epic poems sung and recited in public, such as those that described the glory of the Bambara Empire. Ngugi didn't agree with me: the usual attitude of nationalists, who have a notorious tendency to universalize the particular. All this happened during my last visit to Kenya. But to return to my first trip in Africa: our whole band was transported to Khartoum, and there Dacia and I left Pasolini. He went into southern Sudan and we set off for Aden.

You had been to Aden before, when you went to China in the thirties?

Yes. I went back. I said to Dacia, "Let's go to Aden, which is a fine place with splendid beaches." In Aden I began walking through the streets. At a certain moment I ran into an Arab, who said to me, "I've been to your house, in Rome. I'm a Yemenite revolutionary;

why don't you come to see the revolution?' In North Yemen a revolution against the imam had, in fact, broken out just in those
days. "But I don't know how to go there; you have to have a visa,
surely." He answered, "I am the representative of Yemen Airlines.
I'll give you both tickets and you can go. As a passport all you need
is my calling card for the revolutionary committee." So we accepted, more out of the spirit of adventure than from genuine curiosity, and we left. Yemen Airlines consisted of two old Dakotas,
full of peasants with baskets and bundles. Unforeseen, unprepared, that was truly one of my most beautiful experiences in those
years: Yemen was a country stupefying in its conservatism and immobility. Just think, their currency was still the eighteenth-century
thaler of Maria Theresa. I went to a bank to change a traveler's
check. They invited me to be seated, offered me coffee; there was
a garden full of pomegranates and jasmines, with a fountain
playing. The Orient, in other words! Then, at a certain moment, a
man arrived with a big handkerchief, full of heavy silver thalers
with the portrait of Maria Theresa, the empress of Austria.

That was the local currency?

It was the currency of the Red Sea, both in Arabia and, on the
other shore, in Ethiopia. The Vienna mint continued to strike
those coins for the potentates of the area. At that moment
Yemen was occupied by Nasser's troops, whom you could see
stationed everywhere, all wearing a red band on their sleeves.
We took a Land Rover with a driver who spoke only Arabic, we
went as far as San'a. In San'a we lived in a makeshift hotel set up
in a former Turkish fort; with us at table, in the dining room,
was the entire provisional government. We were served by
beardless waiters, adolescents, wearing enormous turbans, right
out of an eighteenth-century opera buffa: red, green, yellow.
From time to time, beyond the window, cannon fire was heard:
boom, boom, boom, the cannons went on all day. It was the first
time I was seeing the Arab world in its pure, totally pure state.
We had turned up in the midst of a real revolution against a
regime that had lasted for centuries; but as they say, life went on.

The country was split into two parts by the civil war: the north was still in the hands of the imam, the south in the hands of the rebels, assisted by Nasser. You could hear the cannons and see the effects: enormous gaps here and there in the walls of the buildings. Everybody chewed *qat*, the national aphrodisiac. It's a green plant, which they sell everywhere. They take the leaves, crush them into a ball, pop it into their mouths, and chew with swollen cheeks for hours and hours.

Did you try it, too?

Yes, but I didn't feel anything. I remember that at the door of the royal palace there were two sentries, both with their cheeks bulging with *qat*; a colonel came by, also with a wad in his cheek. One day I also saw an entire artillery regiment stop in a town famous for its *qat*. The whole regiment went to buy *qat*, abandoning their cannons in the middle of the road. We visited all the part of Yemen that wasn't in the rebels' hands: a beautiful, very beautiful country. Then we went back to Khartoum, because from Yemen you couldn't fly to Italy. I had been thinking the whole time, "I'll never go back to Khartoum again." Instead, I've been back five times in my life. It's the last city where anyone would want to go, ugly and squalid, but it's a very important air junction. This was my first encounter with black Africa as well as Arabia. The fact that this journey was a kind of adventure influenced all my later journeys in Africa and the Middle East and led me often to reflect on the deep theme of the adventurous character of such journeys. I finally concluded that adventure is not only cultural but also physical. It puts us in contact with different cultures through tests, more or less unpleasant or in any case new, of our bodies. For this reason journeys to such countries as the United States or Russia are without doubt journeys but not adventures. The body doesn't suffer, isn't put to the test. In 1963, the following year, we went to Tanzania, and it was a beautiful journey. We set out from Dar es Salaam and went all the way to Lake Tanganyika. We traveled with a Roman movie troupe who cared very little about Africa. They kept looking for spaghetti and

Frascati. Their big problem was, Will we find spaghetti for dinner today? Pasolini, on the other hand, was seriously seeking out locations for a projected black Oedipus film that he never made.

Did he like Africa?

Very much. He even saw in it a solution to his personal problems. He would say, "Africa, the last hope."

What do you think he meant by that?

Pasolini, in his way, was a disciple of Rousseau. Basically, he believed in the noble savage, as in the good slum boy and the kindly policeman. Africa, the last hope, however, indicated his incipient disappointment in the European proletariat.

During this second journey did Africa make the same impression as it had the first time?

Always, the same impression, and for many years afterward. I have committed follies because of my enthusiasm for Africa. Once I left Rome at five in the morning; I flew and flew, all the way to Abidjan, all by myself. I slept three hours, then took a Land Rover and went to the north of the Ivory Coast into one of the wildest places of Africa. The day before I had been in Piazza di Spagna. I still remember the joy I felt on waking in Abidjan at five in the morning, when I smelled the odor of Africa and, looking out the window, saw the monumental African housewives hurrying toward the market. The smell of Africa is something you never forget.

Is it different from the smell of Asia?

They're different because the nature is different. Look at the map. Black Africa has a hydric system comparable to the vein system of a human being: there is water everywhere. Asia, on the other hand, is the continent of deserts; consequently, the African washes often, the Asian doesn't. The absence of water in the Muslim world reaches the point where they make their ablutions with sand. On the other hand, it must be said that the African, even the cleanest, has a special, strong odor. I remember carrying from one place to another, in our Land Rover, some Pygmies from the Ituri forest and some Elmolo in the country around Lake Rudolf. Well, both times, I was struck by an odor that was the smell not of unwashed skin but of a special skin, African skin, in fact. For that matter, odor is one of the most important aspects of the human body. I don't know where I read that Don Juan stunned women with his odor. That said, on the subject of odors you must also remember the difference in cuisine: the *pili pili* or capsicum in Africa, and curry in Asia.

Is Africa a dangerous place?

The animals are never dangerous; the diseases are sometimes, if you don't take proper precautions. If anything's dangerous in Africa, it's the lack of infrastructures — roads, railways, and so on — which are at the origin of the so-called mystery of Africa and which make travel in Africa, as I've said, a continuous adventure. Also Africa can be, I won't say dangerous, but particularly difficult for reasons of tribal politics. You mustn't forget, in fact, that there are hundreds of tribes and every tribe has its army, large or small, and is determined to impose its will through arms. Finally, among the dangers of Africa you have to include the nationalism imported from Europe, which means that the Africans have gone from the ancient innocence of their relations with Europeans to suspicion and at times even hostility. An example of this European-brand nationalism is an incident that occurred during another journey of mine with Pasolini. In a remote village of Tanzania they wanted to arrest us for espionage.

What happened on that occasion?

Pasolini passed around sweets and smiles to the inhabitants of Kasulu, a wretched little village in Tanzania. Some so-called Green Guards arrived, the equivalent of the Chinese Red Guards, and they incited their compatriots to lynch us because we were suspected of being spies. Imagine! Spies in Kasulu! We were saved by the police, who took us away, pretending to arrest us.

Did you experience many adventures during your travels in Africa?

Not really. African adventures are almost always caused by lack of roads, of lodgings — as I said, of infrastructures. My most adventurous journeys, on the contrary, all took place in Asia, precisely because, whereas it is rare to have rapport with the Africans, in Asia you can communicate with the people fairly easily and especially with the women, who are everywhere bearers of adventures, perhaps only mental.

Have you ever suffered what is called mal d'Afrique?

Just once. Dacia was in the Ivory Coast making a film on African women, and I was in Rome, bored. I felt a horrible desire to leave and join her. I telephoned her and left. It was a record; in a very few hours I reached her in a village in the center of Africa. I went immediately to the table and ate hardtack and canned food. That night I slept on a bed without a mattress, but I was happy. I suspect, however, that I was happy not so much to be in Africa as to be with Dacia.

14

ALAIN ELKANN: *Let's go back to Italian literature. I wanted to ask you what you thought of the fact that Dino Buzzati was for many years the Italian writer best known in France.*

ALBERTO MORAVIA: From the point of view of his writing, which is after all what counts when you're talking about a writer, Buzzati is basically a journalist, and as everyone is aware, the prose of journalists has little to do with that of real writers.

Why?

Journalists' prose is informative; writers' is creative. Still, Buzzati had, of his own, a genuine sense of death, and to the extent of his powers he tried to express it. An imitator of Kafka at the outset, he transferred this sense of death into the expectation of the war that was about to break out in Europe, in his *Il deserto dei tartari*. The book enjoyed a popularity precisely because the success of Kafka, a true writer, had prepared the ground for the work of his imitator.

What do you think of Umberto Eco, who many years later had a great success abroad with Il nome della rosa?

Umberto Eco isn't a journalist like Buzzati. If anything, he is an erudite academic, a popularizer of genius. His prose isn't journalistic; I would say, as I've told you, that it is more communicative than connotative. But in his books there is an interpretation of reality that you would seek in vain in the Kafkesque Buzzati.

The Italian writer best known abroad is Pirandello. What are the cultural reasons for this success? Did you have any dealings with Pirandello?

I saw him a few times. Once, in Rome, he was sitting in a Via Veneto café, and I sat down with him. We talked for a moment about politics, or rather — taking a liberty — I asked him why he had joined the Fascist Party in 1924. He answered with candid sincerity, "Moravia, if you only knew how disgusting Parliament was." Then he said something strange, "What times we live in! Imagine, Moravia, the Principessa di Piemonte has been artificially inseminated." These two sentences don't say much, but they say fairly clearly what was then the truth: Pirandello, who could have been my father, was a bourgeois of the nineteenth century, but in the great edifice of Western culture of that century he had been able to discover the crack that would later cause its collapse. The crack was the discrepancy, or if you like, the contradiction, between the social man and the real man, the former provisional and debatable, the latter doubtful and sophistic. Pirandello, basically, never consoled himself for the fact that the Commendatore wasn't really a Commendatore, as a stepson wasn't really a stepson, a stepfather wasn't a stepfather, and so on, according to *Sei personaggi in cerca d'autore*. This famous play was originally going to be a big melodrama in nineteenth-century style, with incest, suicide, and so on. Writing it, Pirandello discovered it didn't work. He realized all of a sudden that it didn't work not so much in society as in his own head. And so his "theater of the theater" was born, a kind of touchstone that Pirandello used at first to demonstrate the lability of so-called reality. Basically, the scene of the "six characters" should be not this or that bourgeois house but the interior of a cranium, Pirandello's. As to his success abroad, obviously Pirandello said something that everyone was waiting for, at least within the confines of Western culture.

Was Pirandello a great writer?

In some ways he's the opposite of Manzoni. Manzoni was a great writer and a mediocre novelist. Pirandello was a mediocre writer and a considerable narrator and man of the theater. The last time I saw Pirandello was in the dining car of a train bound for Paris. In the dining car there were just the two of us, him and me; I remember asking him why he was going to Paris, and he answered that he had an apartment there where he could work in peace. We talked about literature from the philosophical point of view, which Pirandello preferred. He repeated the familiar Pirandellian formula about life and art and made a gesture with his hands, as if to wash them, as if to say, "Everything's resolved, there's nothing more to say." He gave the impression of taking himself very seriously, but with sincerity and without any vanity.

Did you also know Italo Svevo, who in those years was also discovered in Paris, thanks to Valéry Larbaud, Crémieux, and James Joyce?

I didn't know him. His mother's name was Moravia, like my paternal grandmother's, but we weren't kin. I consider Italo Svevo the greatest Italian narrator after Manzoni and Verga. Svevo is another proof that after the unification of Italy the peripheral writers made their mark, those belonging to the south and the north, and the hegemony of central Italy, of Tuscany, began to fail. Svevo is a modern novelist in the sense that he anticipates the shift of the novelist's attention from social life to the interior life. In other words, an existentialist novelist long before European literature was talking of existentialism. Svevo writes very well, even if sometimes incorrectly. His Triestine bourgeoisie has no rivals in the rather poor and too often autobiographical land-scape of the Italian novel. But the quality of the great writer that Svevo supremely possesses is the mysterious and all-seeing indulgence, tempered by an almost imperceptible irony, which is the sign of born writers.

You've known many poets. We've already talked about Montale. What others?

I met Ungaretti quite early, I mean early for me. He was a man you couldn't help liking, even when you didn't approve of what he was saying or doing: temperamental, a bit childish, sardonic, impetuous, probably passionate, he had unforgettable eyes, like two slits in which his blue pupils moved. I saw him often; we would walk together through the streets of Rome, talking of literature. He was a Fascist and made no secret of it; he had dedicated poems to Mussolini. "When the war breaks out," he would repeat, frenetically, under the arcades of the Piazza Colonna gallery, "we'll sink the Home Fleet." One day, in Via Nazionale, he said to me, "I am, and I can say it without vanity, the greatest European poet." Then, to pique him, I countered, "There's another who has the same claim." Worried, he asked me, "Who's that?" I said, at random, "Blaise Cendrars." It wasn't true, but I felt a great yen to contradict him and punish his childish vanity. In fact, he frowned and changed the subject. The day the Nobel Prize was awarded to Salvatore Quasimodo, I happened to be at a party at the Soviet embassy. Ungaretti was jumping from one little group to another, shouting, "They've given the prize to the parrot!"

Was Ungaretti as important a poet as Montale or Saba or Penna?

Certainly he was. *L'allegria* is a very beautiful book of verse, comparable to Apollinaire's *Alcools*, which it resembles in some ways and whose echoes you can notice often. Moreover, Ungaretti had a considerable importance for his way of "making poetry." So essential, quite different from the D'Annunzio atmosphere of so much poetry produced at the time. A poem like "M'illumino d'immenso" contains more lyric feeling than certain lengthy D'Annunzian poems that want to say the same thing.

How do you recognize poetry?

How do you recognize beauty, in your opinion? The beauty, for example, of a woman, that mixture of loveliness and originality? You don't recognize it, you feel it. But I'd like to say this: you infallibly recognize poetry, especially after having read it and enjoyed it very much. Perhaps you have to be a poet to recognize it at first sight without any previous education. For myself, I will simply say that a beautiful poem moves me to tears, something that doesn't happen with a novel. Even the most beautiful novel rouses in me more admiration than emotion.

Elsa Morante was notoriously a great admirer of Saba. Are you?

I haven't had a great deal to do with him. He was a very sweet man, tormented, ambiguous. In his poetry, unlike what happens with the works of Montale and Ungaretti, there are great unevennesses of poetic level. But the beautiful poems are really beautiful, in an atmosphere of existential evocation that later was to characterize also Sandro Penna.

And what was Sandro Penna like?

I was a friend of Sandro Penna. I consider his poems as inseparable from his life as they are from the years in which they were written. Sandro Penna was a poet of the Alexandrine genre, like those of the *Palatine Anthology*, but with something more impressionistic, momentaneous. He went around Rome, quick, elusive, insinuating, with a fluent and homogenized eloquence, like a sound track that embodied everything, reflections, memories, opinions, judgments, anecdotes. Sandro Penna lived with his mother and trafficked in pictures by painter friends. He was very poor, but I must say at this point that it wasn't a pose of his, as some said toward the end. Under Fascism poverty was the normal condition of artists.

Where do you place Pasolini?

The most important Italian poet of the second half of the century, Montale being that of the first half.

Why?

Italy has a long tradition of civil poets, in the positive sense, beginning with Petrarch and then continuing with Foscolo, Carducci, D'Annunzio. These poets were civil because they had a humanistic background that led them to exalt the kinship between the Italians and Rome. Pasolini is the contrary; he is a civil poet because he doesn't exalt in the least the Roman origins of the country, but mourns its catastrophe. For him the Italians are not ancient Romans, they are if anything the Italians of the year 1000 who still speak a language spiced with Latin, but above all they are the Italians of the present, of Fascism, anti-Fascism, the lost war, and the wretched postwar. Pasolini's tears for the fatherland are not rhetorical because the fatherland really is vanquished and destroyed. Pasolini said all this and many other things in poems that have the fascination of the half achieved, of transition, the passage from one epoch to another. This poetic gift for rendering reality, or rather, the present as it develops, is witnessed by Pasolini's inspired use of the *terzina*, which once was called only Dantesque but now must be called also Pasolinian.

What attracts you in poets?

What attracts me in poets is poetry. Poetry is like the water in the depths of the earth. The poet is like a dowser; he finds water even in the most arid places and makes it gush forth.

But you've spoken of some poets in a rather limitative way.

Poets are poets only on the page, because on their pages they are never alone. They are there with their demon. In life they are alone, without demon, and then they are men like anyone else.

Who was Pasolini's master?

Pasolini's master was the great European poetry, such as Rimbaud, for example. Pasolini was European already in Casarsa, when he wrote verses in Friulan dialect.

In 1963 Dacia won the Formentor Prize, is that correct?

Yes, it was at once a victory for her and a great test for our relationship.

Why?

To make you understand what happened, first I have to explain how the prize was set up. There were two juries: the first comprised five publishers, from France, Italy, the United States, Germany, and Britain, who awarded a prize for the best unpublished novel. The publishers were committed to paying a sum of money to the winner and to publishing the novel at the same time. Then there was another prize, with a jury of writers, for the best novel published during the year. I was naturally a member of the second jury, along with Vittorini and many other writers. Between the two juries there was no connection of any kind concerning the two prizes. The publishers worked in absolute secrecy, and so did the writers. In any case it was absolutely impossible to exert influence on either prize, not least because of the great number of judges. The publishers' prize for the manuscript of an unpublished novel went to Dacia. The writers' prize went to the German novelist Uwe Johnson. That's the whole story. The prize took the name of Formentor from the place in the Balearic Islands where it was awarded the first time. The firm of Einaudi decided to hold a public debate on the two prizes. I thought it would be useful if I took part, as I had been on the jury, and I gladly accepted. Apparently, however, a group of writers, headed by Giuseppe Berto, had met secretly in a Roman bookstore and had decided to attack me during the debate, saying that, with my influence, I had been the one to have the prize go to Dacia, with whom everyone knew I was in love. So it happened that after I had made a brief statement, Giuseppe Berto stood up and accused me of having brainwashed five big publishers from five important countries in favor of Dacia. There was a great uproar, and I discovered they were all against me. I reacted with what was later called arrogance, but which was instead the indignation of one who finds himself unjustly accused. Dacia was very distressed, got into her car, and fled, driving all the way to Siena in the night. Afterward we made up, but as I said, it was a very severe test. You always have to keep an emotional rapport well away from professional questions.

Why did Giuseppe Berto have it in for you?

His resentment dates back to a prize established by the Automobile Club for a story that somehow involved an automobile, and strangely, it was also connected with the death of Hemingway. The Automobile Club asked me to be a member of the jury. I accepted without attaching much importance to it. In fact, I forgot about the prize almost at once. The prize consisted of a Fiat 1500. Days passed and suddenly I was summoned for the prize. I took part and found it had all been settled in advance. A well-known critic stood up, slammed his fist on the table, and said, "The prize goes to Signora xz." A bit dazed, I left the room. I encountered Carlo Levi, who said to me bluntly, "You're a pig. The prize should go to me." In this situation, I resigned from the jury, which then reached a typically Italian compromise. Two smaller cars were awarded, one to Signora xz and one to Carlo Levi. Giuseppe Berto, with whom, I should say, I was fairly friendly, wasn't given anything, and he never forgot it. A little later Hemingway died, and I wrote an obituary that some people found "reductive." I went by Rosati's and encountered Giuseppe Berto, whom I hadn't seen since the Automobile Club prize, which, as I said, I considered insignificant. I saw Berto had grown a huge beard, and I asked him innocently, "Why the beard?" He snickered but said nothing. Then I learned that Berto was a Hemingway fan, that he was mad at me because of the Automobile Club prize, and that the beard was meant to be a sign of affection for Hemingway and hostility toward me. I'd like to add just one other thing about Berto. He conceived a manaical hatred of me after a friendship that, for my part, had been sincere but a bit ambiguous and whose ambiguity he probably sensed. Unfortunately, while I found him likable as a man, I liked his books much less. Moral: never make a friend unless you respect what the friend considers the most important thing in his life. It's true that I was a friend of Malaparte though I didn't admire him as a writer, but Malaparte wanted to be not so much a writer as a protagonist; perhaps unconsciously, he didn't consider writing the most important part of his life.

Those were the years of the Nouveau Roman in France and the Gruppo 63 in Italy, weren't they?

More or less. In both cases, the Nouveau Roman and the Gruppo 63 (which, however, is quite another thing from the Nouveau Roman), there was little homogeneity. Both Gruppo 63 and the Nouveau Roman involved writers who had little connection with the ideas of the group itself. You could say they were two power groups, literary power, that is. Between Nathalie Sarraute, Butor, and Robbe-Grillet there was nothing in common except the fact that they firmly rejected the formulas of the traditional novel, including the existentialist novel of Sartre. They were all in their various ways experimental, but differently. Robbe-Grillet carried out a kind of dismantling of narrative volumes in a somewhat cubist fashion; Butor did rather the opposite. He proceeded through accumulation and complication. Finally, Nathalie Sarraute raised the commonplace to the level of poetic soliloquy. There was also the idea of "boning" the narration, eliminating any rational structure, transforming it into prose poem; but the prose poem requires brevity. A prose poem of three hundred pages is illegibile. I'd say that the Nouveau Roman won the game because, finally, when all is said and done, the writers of the Nouveau Roman often achieve a degree of compelling readability, and this is no small praise. As for the Gruppo 63, it's not my fault if I saw it chiefly as a literary power group rather than as a literary group, period. Still, both on

the level of criticism (structuralist) and on that of poetry, they un-
deniably influenced Italian literary developments, at that time
splitting into two very different currents, one toward social and political protest and the other toward the most formal Italian tradition. On the level of the novel, however, the Gruppo 63 had less
fortunate results, for the reason I believe I've already mentioned:
poetry is always avant-garde; the novel, not.

*What was your position toward these two movements? You knew
some of those writers: what did they think of you?*

I have never had positions to defend or to assert. In fact, my position is to have no positions, except the one that was created, so to
speak, with *Gli indifferenti.* I was part of the *Novecento* group because I had a great liking for surrealism and *Novecento,* for better
or worse, represented it in Italy; but I wasn't the least bit interested
in Bontempelli's magic realism. In the case of the Gruppo 63 and
the Nouveau Roman I liked everything that seemed to me interesting and successful from the literary point of view. For example,
in France, I liked some novels by Robbe-Grillet, Nathalie Sarraute, the first novel of Butor. At the Formentor Prize I spoke in
favor of Nathalie Sarraute, and in fact she won it. The avant-garde,
any avant-garde, interests me, amuses me, and stimulates me. As
for what the two avant-garde groups thought of me, I believe they
didn't love me either, because for the avant-garde, everywhere in
the world, anyone who isn't with them is against them. In any case,
the Italian neo-avant-garde wasn't completely hostile toward me as
they were, for example, toward Bassani. Edoardo Sanguineti even
wrote an essay on my work, but it is also true that he came to see
me and said to me, "Novels like yours can't be written anymore."
Apropos of avant-garde, I remember a curious incident. I went to
Palermo to meet Dacia's grandmother, but it was said that I had
gone for the congress that the Gruppo 63 was holding there in
those days. Everybody thought I was running after the neo-avant-
garde. I made an excursion to Segesta with Sanguineti, Malerba,
Colombo, Guglielmi, and others. Sanguineti spoke of Pasolini in
these terms, "It's really the worst possible way of writing poetry." As

for Dacia's grandmother, a Principessa Alliata of Chilean origin, she said, "Because of your books you'll go to hell." I remember a strange story about this princess. There were these two Chilean sisters, both very beautiful and wicked, and they married two angels; one was Dacia's grandfather and the other an English baronet. The latter, in despair, decided to kill himself, leaving a letter in which he said his death was due to his wife's wickedness. He turned on the gas and shut the windows, but the gas rose to the floor above and killed also his wife.

How did you live in the years before 1968?

Traveling with Dacia, which, as I told you, was for me a fundamental experience. And writing various books, from *La noia* to *La vita interiore*.

Does it seem to you that in those years your creative capacity was in some way changed?

No, not at all. Seen from outside, my life as a writer could even give the impression of a certain monotony. In reality, it wasn't like that: life — mine, at least — is a constant travail, alternating between the destruction of the old and the creation of the new, and this travail in me has always been difficult, filled with anguish, even if also fascinating. The only thing I'd like to say at this point is that I spent not only those years but my whole life in rejecting, more or less consciously, achieved results while essaying new experiments. This tendency toward the new wasn't the result of clear, abstract decision; it was the effect of boredom. Boredom has been my great inspirer. At a certain point, certain subjects, certain ways of dealing with them, inspired in me an intolerable boredom, and so I then tried to change them.

You say you had nothing to do with literary groups. But it is said that you, Elsa Morante, Pasolini, Siciliano, and others were really a group. Is that true?

It's nonsense. Groups publish their magazines, hold congresses and meetings, plan their action, issue manifestos, and so on. I simply had some friends whom I saw on occasion in restaurants. Chiefly Pasolini. The review *Nuovi Argomenti* perhaps had a distinguishable tendency in the immediate postwar period. By this time it had become eclectic and published anything that had literary value. We never issued manifestos and never held meetings or congresses. In fact, there doesn't exist a group with our name or any name, and this is perhaps the clearest proof. The literary group is a trademark.

15

ALAIN ELKANN: When did you go to Japan for the first time?

ALBERTO MORAVIA: At the end of the fifties.

How did the trip come about?

In Tokyo there was the congress of the Pen Club, and I took the place of Ignazio Silone, who couldn't go.

Did you know Ignazio Silone well?

I had seen him first in 1933 in the Engadine, where I was spending the winter in a little hotel at Celerina. Ignazio Silone was living abroad and had already left the Communist Party. I was in bed with a temperature of 103 degrees, he looked in at the door, said hello. That was that. Then I saw him again various times in Rome, after the war. He was a tall, heavy man, with a grave, some-what rustic face, like a country priest. I had read a book of his about his Communist experience in Russia, *Uscita di sicurezza*, and *Fontamara*, which I consider his two most successful works. Silone in some ways makes me think of Solzhenitzen: *Fontamara*, like *One Day in the Life of Ivan Denisovich*, is one of those unique books based on a unique experience felt and expressed directly, in fact, as experience. Later Silone wrote other books in which the ideological element prevailed over experience and revealed some less timely and convincing aspects of his writing.

What is the reason for Silone's great fame?

There are two reasons: the fact that he was an important figure in the Italian Communist Party and then left the party, and secondly the fact that I already referred to. *Fontamara* is a peerless document and also valid as literature, a bit like certain stories by Verga about analogous Sicilian situations. But his writing belongs to an Italian tradition, that of naturalism, already outdated.

So you went to Japan for the first time. How many times have you been to Japan?

I've been there three times, and each time I have had important experiences. The first time I went, as I said, at the invitation of the Pen Club, to its congress in Tokyo. The second time, about ten years later, I went with Dacia; that was when we also went to China and Korea. The third time I went back with Dacia in the seventies. The first time, the encounter with Japan, not always pleasant, was totally new for me. The second time, I met many writers and intellectuals, including Yukio Mishima, and I had the opportunity to understand Japanese life more profoundly; on the other hand, the Japanese experience became mixed with those of China and Korea. Finally, the third time I visited also the Japanese provinces, I went as far as the island of Hokkaido, and in particular, after visiting Hiroshima, I decided to devote myself to the antiatomic campaign.

What made you come to this decision?

Apparently it was casual, like all the profound things in life. I had already written many articles on Japan and I didn't want to repeat the same things. Then, after placing a wreath on the grave of the victims of Hiroshima, I invented a questionnaire about the atomic bomb, which was circulated among politicians, religious figures, and intellectuals of every kind. The result of this was some articles in *L'espresso*, but especially it made me realize that the subject of nuclear warfare was in complete, even if subterranean, accord with my most authentic inspiration. As I've said, the temptation of atomic war, still today very strong in the West, is for me simply the extreme expression of that death instinct present in European culture against which, unconsciously, I had begun writing with *Gli indifferenti.* In short, there is no gap between my books and my antiatomic convictions.

Let's talk about your first two trips to Japan.

Among the participants in the Pen Club congress were some English intellectuals, including Stephen Spender and Angus Wilson, whom I saw often during my stay. Stephen Spender is a poet I admire very much, of the generation of Auden and Isherwood. He is a man of great charm mixed with a somewhat cynical, typically Anglo-Saxon sense of humor. I remember he had to make a speech but didn't have the required dark suit. A Japanese tailor cut and sewed him one in a single night. He was traveling with the novelist Angus Wilson and also had in his party a young Japanese actor, who was very attached to him. They were quite pleasant traveling companions, and with them I made a trip to Osaka. Then, on the way back to Tokyo, I had a rather disagreeable adventure. One evening I went to a nightclub, one of the best in Tokyo, and the evening ended in a very elegant brothel with one of the girls from the nightclub. I remember the house very well: it was a wonder of harmony amid a great diversity of kinds of wood, used on the walls of the stairs and the bedrooms. I have also another memory, a rather strange one; the girl had a pretty face, with tiny and perfect features, like a doll. At the moment of making love, I saw that face decompose profoundly, assuming the features of one of those frightful masks sometimes seen in Japanese Noh drama. A few days later, this novel experience revealed an unpleasant aspect. I discovered that, in my association with the woman, I had contracted a venereal infection.

Naturally, I treated it, but I had a lingering suspicion: what if, beside that superficial ailment, the taxi girl had also had syphilis? I decided to get to the bottom of the matter, and so I went back to the nightclub accompanied by a Japanese doctor. I had the taxi girl called, and she arrived at once, assuming an expression of happy surprise; she was certainly expecting me to repeat the evening in the house with the walls of rare woods. She sat at our table very coyly, and then, as the doctor explained, I had the unpleasant sight of her smile gradually turning to bitter, painful dismay. But in the end it all came out for the best. She agreed not only to allow herself to be treated at my expense but also to take the test for syphilis. The result was negative, and I came back to Italy. Before leaving, I made some purchases. With my royalties I bought a celadon dish from the T'ang dynasty, as well as a magnificent necklace of cultivated pearls for Elsa. I still have the plate. Elsa quickly sold the necklace the moment we separated.

And the second journey?

The second journey was really a journey to China and Korea, with a fairly long stay in Japan. Between the first journey and the second, my life had changed, as I have told you. I no longer lived with Elsa Morante; Dacia Maraini was my new wife. I say "wife" even if we were never married. At that time the law allowing divorce in Italy didn't exist, and further, Elsa Morante, for what I presume were religious reasons, was not pepared to legalize our separation. At this point I must say that for many reasons the years I spent with Dacia were the happiest of my life.

Why?

Partly because of Dacia Maraini's character, which makes her what I would call an ideal life companion, in the sense that she has a somewhat English character: self-control raised to the highest degree. It is perhaps banal to say so, but self-control seems to me the best guarantee of good relations between a couple and also in the manifestations of reciprocal feelings. Naturally, self-control by itself can lead to aridity, but this is absolutely not the case with Dacia Maraini, who has a particularly sweet and affectionate nature.

But that isn't why you loved her?

I loved her for all the usual reasons one loves a woman.

What does this mean? That you were really in love with her?

Yes, she is one of the four women in my life with whom I have been in love.

What does life as a couple mean for you?

It takes four things: love, affection, common interests, and reciprocal tolerance. In our relationship these four things existed to an extraordinary degree.

You're a man with a vocation for life as part of a couple?

If you look at my life, you would say yes. Twenty-five years with Elsa, eighteen with Dacia, and already nine with Carmen. It's almost a record.

But loves end.

Love isn't everything, but at least for me it's almost everything. In fact, I have moved from one wife to another for reasons almost exclusively connected with love. For example, I would never have separated from Elsa if I hadn't fallen in love with Dacia.

How did your second journey to Japan go?

I went there with Dacia in 1967. In China it was the year of the Cultural Revolution. Passing through Canton, I wrote a letter to the Chinese foreign minister, Chou En-lai, reminding him that I had already been in China in 1936 and asking him to see the new China. Then we went to Tokyo, to a good hotel that had been the private house of a member of the imperial family, and there we waited for the answer from China. This time I led the life of a tourist, also because, though Dacia had spent two years of her infancy there, Japan was new also for her.

Why?

Dacia's father, Fosco Maraini, who is a Japanese scholar, on the eve of the war had been given a fellowship to go and study the Ainu, a white-skinned people who survive, in a small number, on the island of Hokkaido, but when Italy entered the war along with Germany and Japan, Fosco Maraini and Dacia's mother, Topazia Alliata, had to choose. The Japanese asked them, "Are you with the king or with Mussolini?" They chose the king. But Maraini hadn't foreseen that the Japanese would put not only him but also his wife and his three daughters in a concentration camp. Dacia was six, and she spent two years in a concentration camp. This forced stay in Japan involves an episode that has all the harshness of the war experience. The camp authorities gave them very little to eat; the Marainis were hungry, so Fosco Maraini decided to beat the Japanese on their own ground. He knew that if you cut off a finger and throw it at someone of whom you are asking something, that person feels obliged to grant your request. One morning Fosco Maraini took a hatchet, a wad of absorbent cotton, and some alcohol; he cut off his finger and threw it at one of the guards. At first he was simply beaten, but then the guards satisfied his request and gave him a nanny goat to provide milk for his daughters. Getting back to Dacia, all she knew of Japan was the concentration camp, because as soon as the war ended, the Maraini family was promptly repatriated. A curious fact: perhaps because of the trauma of imprisonment, Dacia, who spoke Japanese perfectly and also the dialect of Kyoto, forgot everything as soon as she arrived back in Italy. In any case, for her Japan was genuinely new.

What did the two of you do?

First of all we went to visit Dacia's old nurse, who lived in the mountains, where she ran a student hostel. We found an extremely affectionate woman who, the moment we arrived, after duly kissing and hugging Dacia, took her away to give her a boiling hot bath, Japanese style. I remember also that, two days later, when we left again for Tokyo, the same nurse accompanied us to the train, leaned in at the window, and with streams of tears, recommended us to the care of the other Japanese travelers. After visiting the nurse, we turned to cultural tourism. We attended a great deal of theater, we saw films by Japanese auteurs, we went to museums, we witnessed various traditional ceremonies, we took part in a wedding, we met writers and cultural figures.

Among the writers I remember especially Yukio Mishima. We called on him at his house. He had two houses: one in Japanese style, where his parents lived, and one in English style, Edwardian, where he lived with his wife. In the garden, in the midst of an English lawn, he had a statue of very white Carrara marble of a naked woman. The house, as I said, was in English style, high and narrow, with two rooms per floor. He received us in his study, amid a great disorder of papers, unusual in a Japanese house. Among all these papers a great photograph of Mishima was prominent: he was seen naked to the waist, gripping a sword. Mishima was small, well proportioned, athletic, with a perfectly oval head and very regular features. He granted me an interview, which was published in the *Corriere della sera*. Mishima expressed himself with sarcastic brutality on a number of his colleagues. For example, "What do you think of x?" "A fool." "And Y?" "A scoundrel." "And what about z?" "A coward," and so on. There was something military about Mishima, but it was probably more assumed than congenital. Judging by his books, actually, you would say that the militaristic attitude was a mask and concealed an excessive and very special sensitivity. It has been said that Mishima was a fascist, but the definition is not exact. If anything, he was a nationalist, conservative, decadent, a bit like certain writers of the monarchist wing in France, Maurras, for example. All sorts of things have been said about Mishima after his death, which was so terrible and theatrical, but few observers have borne in mind the fact that this decadentism of his was grafted onto the trunk of a very complex tradition, very remote from that of the West. So the references to Nietzsche, for example, made by Yourcenar, seem in his case rather gratuitous.

From decadentism, he derived, above all, a negative characteristic, rather serious for a writer: a lack of common sense. A lack
that is found, for example, also in D'Annunzio, whom he admired
very much and whose *Saint Sebastien* he translated. He was very
polite and invited us to supper in an elegant restaurant, where we
went in his American car driven by his wife; but he talked very
little and seemed pensive.

Before traveling in China, I was in Korea for a few days —
South Korea, naturally. This was before the boom that made
Korea one of the most productive countries of East Asia. I remember several things of varying degrees of importance from that
trip in Korea: the extroverted agitation of the Koreans, so different
from the composure of the Chinese and the reserve of the
Japanese; the ginseng shops, one out of every two shops in the
streets of Seoul; an excursion to the border strip between the two
Koreas; and finally, above all, a stupendous statue of Buddha.
There's no point in talking about the first two things. The trip to
the border and the Buddha, on the other hand, were very interesting. The two Koreas are divided by a narrow demilitarized
strip, a no-man's-land. It was a beautiful day. The no-man's-land
seemed invaded by flourishing vegetation, and yet the two countries, in that sunlight and over that vegetation, spied on each
other. I reflected on that occasion that the principle of nationality,
so important in nineteenth-century Europe, today is no longer
fundamental. There are two Koreas, two Chinas, two Irelands,
and so on. What happens? Almost always nothing. The divided
countries even reveal a certain economic vitality, and in any case
it doesn't seem that they are prepared to fight a war to be reunited.
As for the Buddha, it is a colossal statue of white marble erected
in a shrine at the end of a peninsula, facing the ocean at no great
distance from Seoul. It is the most beautiful Buddha I've seen in
my life. The path that leads to the shrine allows a lovely stroll
under huge, ancient trees. The artist was able to blend in the
statue the two chief principles of Buddha: to play on words,
serene despair and desperate serenity. A final observation about
Korea, which, however, concerns me and not Korea: at the Seoul

airport there was a furious wind storm, and getting off the plane, I
was almost blown to the ground. Curiously, I had a great sensation of freedom, as if it had been not the plane but the wind that
had carried me there.

What happened in China?

One day I received a telegram from Peking, inviting me to be
ready to enter China via Hong Kong. I had already been to Hong
Kong in 1936 and had stayed at the Hôtel Mandarin, which then
was the finest in the city. This time, however, I wanted to stay near
the border and went to a hotel in Kowloon, which is Hong Kong's
Chinatown. We thought we would be entering China at once,
but we were wrong. We waited a week for the heralded pass from
the Chinese consulate. We went to the consulate frequently, and
they kept telling us to come back. On that occasion I was able to
observe a ritual of the Chinese Communists: delegations and
tourist groups entered the consulate clapping their hands, and the
functionaries then replied by clapping their hands.

Finally, one morning at six we were informed that we should
pack our bags, and so we left. The train from Hong Kong to
Canton is a deluxe train with a dining car, but it stops at every
little station. This was the period of the so-called Cultural Revolution. Dacia and I were seated in the dining car having tea; at
every station the platforms were invaded by a hostile crowd,
shaking their fists and baring their teeth: we were capitalists, and
they wanted to show us that they were communists. The journey
proceeded more or less like the first one thirty years earlier.
China had changed politically, but not in its external appearance
— on the contrary, I had the opposite impression during my
journey twenty years later, in 1986. I saw again the port of Canton
crowded with sampans, the Pearl River, the old overpopulated
and timeworn Canton. We were taken to the top of a semi-sky-
scraper by a young propagandist who was acting as our guide. He
asked me aggressively, "Whom do you write for?" I answered that
I wrote for everybody. "Even capitalists?" And I said, "Why not?
Don't you want the capitalists to read?" In other words, the air of

the Cultural Revolution was beginning — or rather, an aggressive and unpleasant wind that was to go on blowing till the end.
We took a plane to Peking, a British Viscount with all the notices
in Chinese and English. All the passengers at a certain moment
started singing a song in chorus, giving me the impression that it
was ideologically addressed. Someone came to ask me why I
wasn't singing and I had to explain in English that I didn't know
Chinese.

In Peking, the Cultural Revolution was immediately revealed
in the hotel where we stayed, the Hotel of Nationalities. The pro-
grams of our day were decided every morning by committees of
employees of the hotel itself, assembled on every floor. I don't believe these committees had much to do, because the hotel was
completely empty and the staff was overabundant: almost all the
maids spent their time leaning out the window to watch the
demonstrations of the Cultural Revolution. These demonstrations consisted of very long, very orderly, and very slow processions that headed toward the "objectives" of the day: embassies or
ministries. In the first case, to protest; in the second, to applaud.
As it was raining, all the members of the processions were wearing
raincoats that came down to their ankles. Heading the processions, as a rule, were two girls bearing a huge photograph of Mao,
framed with flowers. Behind the photograph came a dozen red
flags and then the crowd: it looked like a religious procession in
southern Italy. The Cultural Revolution was evident also in our
dealings with the guide, who showed us the city: he didn't speak
to us except to name the monuments. At mealtimes he ate at a
separate table. In short, the Cultural Revolution, for us at least,
meant lack of communication, if not outright hostility. The only
incident that occurred to us was when some kids at a certain point
spat on Dacia's skirt: apparently the skirt was capitalist, and the
slacks all the Chinese women wore weren't, unlike Europe,
where trousers for women were a sign of emancipation and skirts
of conformity.

The visit, as I said, proceeded just like the one thirty years earlier. The real novelty was not so much communism as the Cul-

tural Revolution, which, by the way, wasn't limited to processions and protests outside embassies but had also provoked a lot of destruction. During that journey I had a very limited view of this destruction and the tortures and persecutions, especially of intellectuals. This is what always happens in countries ruled by a dictatorship. So it had been in Hitler's Germany and Stalin's Soviet Union: the visitor was kept completely ignorant of the negative aspects of the regime. In China I noticed especially a lack of cordiality, an embarrassed and openly propagandistic air. Later, when I went back in 1986 and learned the truth about the Cultural Revolution, I couldn't help but agree with so many Chinese of every class and every region who constantly repeated in a mournful tone that the years of the Cultural Revolution had been a nightmare.

I remember two things especially from that journey: a visit to the Red Guards and another visit to a model worker. The Red Guards lived in a wrecked school. They were all students, from God knows what remote provinces. They were carrying out the Cultural Revolution, but their faces retained a rather jarring rustic simplicity. I was struck by their absolute poverty: instead of tea they offered me some hot water. The model worker lived in a little two-room apartment in a building for workers. In my view, this visit, from a propagandistic standpoint, shows that even the refined Chinese, when they set to making propaganda, turn crude. The worker was elderly and retired; dressed in his best clothes, he awaited us, seated at the window. The apartment was poor but not lacking a shelf with a certain number of books. We asked the worker what he did in the afternoon, if he went to the movies. He pointed to the shelf and gave us this surprising answer, "I read." But what did he read? "The books of Mao, Marx, Engels." Then, pursuing the conversation, he said he wanted to show us an object that was very important for him. He took us into a little kitchen: the important object was a kerosene stove, the kind called "Primus." We went away with the impression that the visit had been rehearsed and, furthermore, badly. Another incident that upset me about the Cultural Revolution was the day we went to visit the famous tombs of the Ming emperors. We visited one of an interest that can unquestionably be considered enormous: you have only to think that the funerary objects found in that tomb had filled an entire small museum. I then asked to visit the other tombs. I knew that there were fourteen in all. They answered me in an orthodox fashion, "We won't excavate them. One tomb is enough to show how the imperialist capitalist exploiters of the people lived." These and other similar events of a propagandistic nature marked my second visit to China.

When you came back from China what was going on in Italy?

As soon as I got back from China, I agreed to preside over the jury of the Venice film festival. Dacia and I went to the Lido and spent a month seeing films, then giving prizes. Among others, Susan Sontag was one of the judges. Several films of high quality were competing, including *La chinoise* of Godard and *Belle de jour* of Buñuel. I wanted to give the prize to *La chinoise*, more timely, although in general Buñuel, still my favorite director, seems to me superior to Godard.

Did you already know Buñuel?

I met him on that occasion, giving him the prize. He was deaf, with the likable face, alert and intuitive, that the deaf and persons of genius often have.

Why are you so fond of surrealism, of which Buñuel is a representative in cinema?

All writers at the beginning of their career take part in some avant-garde. I told you, mine was surrealism, which held an almost morbid interest for me. This interest was perhaps due to the fact that surrealism had discovered the unconscious, like Freud, and the unconscious was very important in the existentialist trend to which I belong. The surrealists changed our sensitivity; after them the depiction of the real became different and more complete. Very briefly, the surrealists completed wakefulness with dream. Surrealism existed all over Europe, but its historic roots and its greatest development were in France. Sade was a surrealist without knowing it, and so also was Lautréamont. Bréton actually made it a political-religious party.

To go back to 1968, what did you think of that period?

It has been said that the Cultural Revolution and widespread student protest were bound to each other; in reality, this was not the case, or rather, both were born without any direct connection, from a planetary phenomenon, the crisis of the Marxist left. In Europe, at least, student protest was born in Paris from so-called structural Marxism-Leninism. This current joined the German-American current of the Frankfurt school, Marcuse, Adorno, and so on. At this point I must say that for the first time in my life, I found myself more or less in complete agreement with a political movement and that this movement had very little that was ideological about it, even if there was an abundance of ideologies. It was basically a wave of feeling that came from a source not exactly clear and went no telling where, and it could be summed up with the exact opposite of the classical Marxist formula "first theory, then action." Protest, on the contrary, wanted action first and theory later. On this point all agreed, from Castro's Cubans to Marcuse's Americans, from Cohn-Bendit's French students to Dutschke's Germans.

What action? Thinking back, over a distance of so many years, I believe that the action had a revolutionary character precisely because it was action as an end in itself, which in any established order always represents something subversive. In a situation of order, on the other hand, all actions are planned, justified, and provided with an end. What you could call the protest movement will to act without theory produced, especially among intellectuals, some strange, even comic convulsions: they agreed to do something on the public level solely to reject it and to show that they weren't doing it. It was the period of denouncing all rules, from those of reason to those of grammar, from those of prosperity to those of ambition. Here I must say that the protest movement from the social point of view, the point of view of behavior, had a

great, undeniable utility. Especially in Italy, a country conservative and reactionary by vocation. The movement improved relations between parents and children, between teachers and
students, between superiors of every kind and dependents of every
kind: even its naïvetés were likable, and its violence never vio-
lated the existential limits of what twenty years earlier, rather
prophetically, I had called *disubbedienza* in a novel of mine. Unfortunately, the youthful and likable disobedience of the protest
movement directly gave birth to the grim and pedantic violence
of terrorism.

Did you know Feltrinelli?

I met him only twice, but those were significant occasions. The
first time I didn't see him in person, but I found his traces and his
memory: in Bolivia, where he had been shortly before I arrived
there, also to liberate Régis Debray. In Bolivia they talked a great
deal about him and not always favorably, in regard to the revolutionary plane on which he meant to move. In substance he was
reproached for something undefinable that was then not clear but
later became more and more distinct. A form of aesthetic dilettantism connected with and probably provoked by the sense of
guilt inspired in him by his great wealth. It can be said, in his defense, that he was a man in absolute good faith and that aesthetic
dilettantism is a constant of the Italian grand bourgeoisie. Think,
just to take one example, of how that same class in the time of
D'Annunzio adopted the poet's credo. Feltrinelli could have been
content with being a great publisher; his firm was then one of the
best in Italy. Further, we owe to Feltrinelli the most thorough
Marxist library in our country. What drove him to plant a mine
against the fatal pylon at Segrate, where he found death, was
something illusory and impassioned always present in men of action: you can smile at it only when it doesn't meet with success.
The success, on the contrary, that doesn't raise a smile is what you
read in the analogously reckless and "enacted" but mythical lives
of, say, Lawrence of Arabia or Che Guevara. Feltrinelli was never
a myth: this was where success eluded him. Yes, because in poli-

tics unfortunately only immediate success counts, a bit as in the theater: you must have a success on that given evening and not in a few days' time. Of this "acting out" aspect of Feltrinelli's terrorism I have a very precise memory: one afternoon in the garden of his villa in the country outside Turin, I was having tea with his wife, Inge, and Régis Debray, when all of a sudden Feltrinelli jumped out from a bush, dressed like the *barbudos* of Castro. This leap from the bush indicated that he was no longer living in his house with his wife and son but in a camper: he had gone underground. He embraced us all, drank his tea, then disappeared again into the bushes. Feltrinelli seriously shared Castro's idea: to kindle the fires of the revolution wherever there was a prerevolutionary situation — for example, in Sardinia. Something was lacking, as it was lacking really in all Italian terrorism, but it's hard to say what. My idea is that terrorist violence is neither useful nor practicable from below, from outside power; it works only from above, within power. In other words, by their acts of violence, the terrorists frightened the working class, who, mind you, were initially rather favorable toward them. Stalin and Hitler are two good examples of terrorism practiced on a wide scale, after and not before gaining power.

In 1968 you were both in Bolivia and in Africa. How and why?

It was the year of Che Guevara's attempt to export the Cuban revolution into Bolivia. Parenthetically, I'd like to make a general observation here. It is very difficult, if not impossible, to judge the greatness of a politician or a military figure, for the simple reason that, while the work of an artist, a poet, a painter, a musician, is based on two kinds of success, that of expression and that of appreciation, only practical success, achievement, creates what is called the greatness of politicians and soldiers. You can keep a novel in your drawer, knowing it's a masterpiece, but you can't keep in your drawer a war strategy or a revolution without putting it into practice. The greatness of soldiers and politicians depends, in fact, solely on success. For this reason I am very dubious about the greatness of Napoleon or Lenin. By this I don't mean that politicians and soldiers can't be great men. I mean that success or the lack of it is not a proof of greatness. Greatness is something interior, private, and it can also remain exactly that.

What politicians or soldiers had this greatness?

There is the old saying that no man is great to his valet. I would say the opposite: politicians and soldiers are great only to their valets.

In other words, you don't like them much?

That's true. I don't feel any great liking for those manipulators of men, politicians and generals.

Then why did you go to Bolivia?

Obviously because I thought I would have some influence on the fate of Régis Debray, who was a prisoner of the Bolivian government. Régis Debray, whom I had met, as I told you, during my trip to Cuba, had joined the disastrous Che Guevara expedition and had been taken prisoner during the same operation in which Guevara was killed. Many European intellectuals called for the liberation of Debray, but I was the only one to go in person to Bolivia. In Cuba I had found Debray likable, and besides, I was in a period of my life when I enjoyed committing myself to such ventures. At La Paz I had the Italian ambassador announce me to the head of the government, and I was received at once. The government was housed in a little two-story villa with a garden. In the rooms and on the stairs I encountered many uniformed officers. The chief of state, a general, also in uniform, embraced me and assured me he would do his best to free Debray.

Was Debray freed?

Yes, the following year, by a different chief of state, also a general.

Do you think your intervention was effective?

I don't know, perhaps it was. In any case, after that humanitarian visit, there was nothing left for me and Dacia but tourism, visiting

Bolivia, which we immediately found a very beautiful country, though sad and backward. One of those mornings we were informed that a plane was waiting for us at the airport to take us to Potosì, an old city very important in the past for its silver mines and its mint, which struck all the coins of Latin America. I thought we would find a regular flight at the airport. Instead, a tiny Cessna was awaiting us. The pilot informed me he had been made a lieutenant the day before. He took out a little elementary school notebook with a map of Bolivia and drew a line with a pencil from La Paz to Potosì. This was all his flight preparation, and then we left. The plateau of Bolivia is an immense expanse, dark and arid, all surrounded on the horizon by white, snowy mountain peaks. For a while we flew over the plateau; then we thrust among the peaks, slipping into the valleys between one mountain and the next. At Potosì we landed at an airport no bigger than a football field. Potosì reminded me of certain cities in the Mexican mountains; there was the same viceregal atmosphere, the same sullen decadence. We spent the evening in the hotel with the alcalde and the chief of police. The alcalde said to us, "Do you really believe the Communists are dangerous? You're wrong; the real danger is the Masons." The chief of police, for his part, told me he envied Italy the efficiency of her police. The next day we visited the greatest curiosity of Potosì, the old mint with its beautiful machines, all made of wood, for coining money. The silver mine is a sugarloaf mountain. Eight million Indios lost their lives excavating there. It is said that with the silver extracted from that mine a bridge could be built all the way from Potosì to Madrid. A few days later, from Potosì we returned to La Paz, and from there we flew to Dakar, in Senegal, where we had arranged to meet Pier Paolo Pasolini.

How was this trip?

Pasolini had shot *Medea* with Maria Callas, and they had become friends. So, in a totally unexpected manner, Dacia and I found ourselves traveling with the famous singer.

What was Callas like?

On the stage — for example, in Cherubini's *Medea* — besides
being one of the greatest singers who ever existed, she was actually
a great tragic actress. In private life, the life of every day, she was
actually a Greek bourgeoise with many characteristics typical of
her native country. She was very natural, direct, even ingenuous,
with a decided predilection for luxury in its most conventional
forms. During the trip, at table she would indulge in great eulo-
gies of capitalism, and then Pasolini would benevolently correct
her, saying in a reproachful tone, "Maria?!" She was very proper,
in a pleasant sense, without malice. She was also a prude, and she
had her own code of correct behavior. She said to me, for example, about Onassis, "You see, Alberto, a man can say what he
likes to a woman in private, but not in public. Onassis had the
habit of saying unpleasant things to me in front of everybody."
Her popularity was immense. At every airport we always found
delegations of admirers and little girls in school uniforms who
had her sign their records. At Abidjan the government put a heli-
copter at her disposal, with a French lieutenant who swirled us for
a long time over the virgin forests, scaring the life out of the buf-
falos standing in the marshes.

Did Africa interest her?

Not much. She liked most of all the grand hotels and the ceremo-
nious welcomes. A great bowl of fruit, which she found in her
room at the Hôtel Ivoire, a gift of the management, probably inspired a more profound feeling than the sublime solitude through
which the Niger River winds its way. With Callas we visited a Tu-
areg camp, and they played on her the old camel drivers' trick of
loosening her saddle the moment she was climbing onto the
camel, making her slump forward on the animal's serpentine
neck. And then, again with her, we had the equally inevitable experience of losing our way on the return from an excursion in the
area of Timbuktu. As a marker I had memorized a certain lake,
which the track circled at one point. Now, what I didn't know was

that in that region the Niger forms hundreds of such lakes. We were blocked for a while, unable to find the right road, as the sun was setting. All of a sudden, as often happens in such circumstances, we discovered that we were only two kilometers from Timbuktu.

What is the famous Timbuktu like?

It's nothing. Nothing fascinating, I mean. A very ugly little city of modern buildings, without style, squalid and unwelcoming, and the sand gets into everything. The streets were invaded by sand; when you ate the bread your teeth squeaked, it was so full of sand. There was a little hotel with a puddle and four palm trees. At that moment some fashion models, sent specially from Paris, were being photographed in the shade of the palms, while three or four camels were kneeling to drink. From Timbuktu, passing through the picturesque and magic land of the Dogons, made famous by the studies of French anthropology, we went as far as Mopti, which, unlike Timbuktu, has very beautiful buildings, in Saharan Sudanese style, of red clay, windowless, like fortresses. The journey ended at Abidjan, and from there we left for Europe.

Which legendary cities of Africa and Asia have been the greatest disappointments to you?

Timbuktu and Khartoum in Africa; Baghdad and Samarkand in Asia. But these cities owe their fame perhaps not so much to their beauty but to the fact that, on one hand, they had a historical importance and, on the other, they are at the edge of terrifying deserts. The traveler who arrives in these cities after long, dangerous journeys couldn't help but see them as earthly paradises. If you think about it, also the Eden of the Bible is probably made in the image of one of the many oases scattered about the Arabian desert. But it's impossible not to see these cities through the lens of myth. Perhaps I myself have made certain journeys so that I could then say to myself, "There, now I've been to Timbuktu, I've been to Samarkand, to Baghdad."

Returning to Italy from your journey in Africa you found your-
self much involved in student protest. How?

I found myself involved because the protest, among many other
things, was a generational movement, and I belonged to the
generation of those under attack. By then I was sixty. So I was
much attacked, often in the treacherous way, in bad faith, characteristic of the movement. I remember a very violent debate at
L'espresso. I was alone against a group of representatives of the
Roman protest movement, who accused me of fantastic sins of
which, to tell the truth, I knew nothing. I discovered that the
fact of being a certain age, in those days, was the equivalent of
being a leader to be hated and banished to the attic. At other
times it was almost amusing, and in any case I went with the
idea of amusing myself. In Florence, a whole theater was
yelling, "Corriere della sera! Corriere della sera!" In Bari, the
protestors shouted, "Ho Chi Minh! Ho Chi Minh!" From this
group I called one aside and asked him what his father did. The
Ho Chi Minh enthusiast replied that his father was a landowner.
I said to him then, "How can you cheer Ho Chi Minh, you, a
landowner's son?"

These were low blows of which, at heart, I was ashamed; but
that was the level of debate, and there was nothing to be done
about it. Then the movement made a very important discovery,
and I say this without irony: they discovered street violence. In
Valle Giulia, the students not only resisted the police charges but
charged back as well, thus realizing that after all a policeman
could also be beaten up. That memorable clash inspired a Pasolini poem that aroused much debate, since in it he sided with
the police, poor peasants brought to the city, dressed in rough and
heavy uniforms, against the students, all very bourgeois children
of well-to-do parents. I didn't agree with Pasolini. First of all, because the police were police, fighting for the status quo, and then
because the students wanted after all to change this status quo —
and in part, as I said just now, they succeeded. At my house I received a visit from the so-called Birds, also students, who didn't

talk but simply whistled; they were trying, as the expression went then, to "desecrate" family privacy. These extravagances, in other words, could always be reduced to a method. What made them irritating was not so much the extravagance itself but the senility of the culture from which the protesting students, if you looked carefully, were not at all liberated.

I have met German, French, and American protestors, not to mention the Chinese. Which most resembled the Italians? Strange to say, with their basically aestheticizing radicalism, the Chinese. The age of a country is not only a historic fact but also, so to speak, a flavor. The protest dish in France and America had an aroma that was completely missing in Italy and China. If you tasted Italian protest, or Chinese, you had the idea that the dish wasn't fresh: it was reheated. This was particularly evident in terrorism, the bastard child of the student protest. The terrorists' action was undoubtedly a new concept. For the first time terror was created by striking not an important figure (the Moro case was anomalous) but representative individuals, in order to terrorize a whole category. But the language of the Red Brigades was old and not without a counterproductive bombast. Why, for example, declare that "justice had been done," when they had simply murdered a poor carabiniere sergeant? This language, bombastic as I said, came from the depths of that same old, verbose Italy that the terrorists wanted to destroy, and that language probably did terrorism more harm than the actions they tried to propagandize. They introduced the idea of "justice" where instead there was only violence. Didn't old, feudal Bourbon Italy speak in the same way?

Let's talk now about your relations with Pasolini, about his position in those years until his death.

I've already talked about Pasolini's poetry, but Pasolini in his way was also a man of politics and an ideologue; and this, I would say parenthetically, distinguished and still distinguishes him from the great majority of Italian writers, who as a rule confine themselves to being ordinary citizens.

What do you mean?

Pasolini had at least the structure of the great writer. Without any real desire, and often even against his will, he became involved in the state of things in the world. Other writers aim only at being good writers, which is no small thing; indeed, it's a very big thing. But you must be an excellent writer to be called great, if you have no interest in the state of things in the world.

For instance?

Well, Mallarmé, for example, or Kafka.

Another Italian writer, a contemporary of Pasolini, who concerned himself greatly with social problems — I'm thinking of the fight against the Mafia — is Leonardo Sciascia.

That's not the question. Sociology isn't enough to justify an extraliterary commitment, also because it's a very debatable science. The commitment I mean, which was certainly not only Pasolini's but also Sciascia's, is rooted in something very vague but real, which must actually be called religious feeling. In fact, Pasolini wasn't a communist in the technical sense. Instead he has to be placed on the margins of what could be called Christian Marxism. For that matter, his political ideas were debatable but original: in his opinion, there was an analogy between the disciples of Christ and the subproletariat. This was all very well until the so-called boom. Pasolini sincerely believed that the subproletariat, with its freshness, ingenuousness, and authenticity, would save the world, but the boom revealed to him that his poor boys didn't want to save anyone, not even themselves. He was still suffering the blow of this disillusionment when he was killed, by one of his own heroes, in a funereal, extraurban air of reverse transformation of his values. But those who thought to see a symmetry, an analogy, between the life and work and the death of Pasolini are mistaken. It's not true that Pasolini could only die as he did. He was a man in the prime of life, full of vitality and plans. I'd call what happened to him a tragic accident, like being struck by an automobile. At this point, perhaps the idea of an accident should be probed. I want only to say that good and bad luck are a part of human life. It's as important to be lucky as to be intelligent.

Do you believe in destiny?

No, I don't believe in destiny. I believe you have to pay a great deal of attention. In the extreme, you could even say that if we "truly" paid attention we would never die.

So Pasolini sought his death through lack of attention.

In a way, yes. Especially since he was well aware of the danger involved with those boys. Once he said to me, "I risk my life every night."

Who was Pasolini really?

I got to know Pasolini well only when he had had success with his novels and his first movies. Before those fortunate years I didn't see much of him.

Why would a poet start making movies?

The vocation came to him when he worked on scripts for Fellini and others; curiously, his cinema makes good use of his poetry, his novels much less. That is because Pasolini's cinema has a greater multiplicity of interests and aspects than his novels. Pasolini's novels fall halfway between naturalism and philological aestheticism. His cinema, on the contrary, has a much greater freedom. It is variously anthropological, political, ideological, symbolic, fantastic. It's poetic, in other words. What I'm saying is that Pasolini is chiefly a poet, who expresses himself not only in verses but also in his films, his fiction, and even in his newspaper articles. Historically, Pasolini's films resolve the crisis of neorealist cinema, surpassing naturalism and the consequent mannerism of the "Italian-style comedy." I place Pasolini between Buñuel and Mizoguchi (*Ugetsu*). We are very far, as you see, from Roberto Rossellini and from Vittorio De Sica.

You still haven't described Pasolini's character.

The chief quality of his character was sweetness. A strange sweetness, partly of peasant origin, partly pedagogical: all his life Pasolini remained the schoolteacher from Friuli. Along with this sweetness, there must have been in him a capacity for hiding the wounds to his sensitivity, a characteristic of all artists and especially of those who, like Pasolini, are "different." Sexual difference is usually expressed in one of two ways: either clandestine and prudent discretion or else scandalous provocation. Pasolini knew that he possessed a scandalous sexuality and so, a bit like Genet, instead of hiding it, he flaunted it, or rather he made use of it to fight scandal with scandal. But this must have had for him a high price in self-repression. He faced various kinds of persecution, even legal, with great courage, but his health bore the brunt. He had an ulcer that one night nearly cost him his life. Dacia and I were having supper with him in a restaurant. Pasolini went to the toilet; all of a sudden the door was flung open violently and Pasolini fell to the floor, like a tree struck by a thunderbolt, in a pool of blood and vomit. I will always remember the whiteness of his face as they took him to the doctor. The white of paper, totally drained of blood.

You built a house at Sabaudia with him?

Yes, in 1972. We were very close friends, I liked the idea of living near him during the summer. We built a house on the last plot of land available. Pasolini liked Sabaudia very much, but he came there only in 1974, then in 1975 he was killed. From Sabaudia he set out every evening on homosexual raids all along the coast between Ostia and Terracina. Sometimes in my sleep I would hear him come in around three or four in the morning, stealthy as a wolf coming back from a night's hunting.

But he also owned a tower in the province of Viterbo.

Yes, he had a place at Chia, near Orte. In reality, it was a caravanserai, a girdle of mediaeval walls within which merchants used to take refuge during the night. It was dominated by a very high, pentagonal tower. It's a place that can certainly be called Dantesque: a high spur of rock between two deep chasms in whose depths two streams flow. All around, a severe forest of ilex and oak. Pasolini had the habit of going there on weekends to write his new novel, entitled *Petrolio* (Pantheon, 1997), which was never finished or published.

Have you read it?

Yes, I've read it.

What's it about?

A subject very close to that of Dostoyevsky's *The Possessed*: corruption and the catastrophe of a corrupt society. The introductory part is actually taken entirely from Dostoyevsky, with Italian names instead of Russian. But the truly successful and perhaps definitive parts are only some scenes of homosexuality, a subject that until then Pasolini had never dealt with. Though the novel supplies us with some details of the sex relations between Pasolini and the so-called *ragazzi di vita*, "boys in the life," I can't honestly say that its publication would add anything to the writer's fame. To be sure, in a very evident way it confirms the obsessive character that, toward the end, sexual life had taken on for Pasolini. That is another problem I have faced without resolving it: Pasolini's sex life was abnormal not because he was "different" but because it was obsessive. Why? Sometimes I think that "different" sex is always obsessive because it is reproached and condemned by society; that is, practically speaking, precisely because it's not normal, it can't help but be transformed into neurosis. What is certain is that it is difficult for a heterosexual to identify with the loves of a homosexual. I myself, who have many homosexual friends, feel somewhat uneasy reading novels on that subject.

Why?

I don't really know; it is very difficult for me to understand. For example, knowing for certain that Proust's Albertine was a man tempers any enjoyment of my reading. The books of Mishima and Gide bore me. Almost certainly the reason is that in books I instinctively seek that same kind of emotional relationship that I experience in my life. In other words, art, however admirable, isn't enough for me. I need a reality to follow and share, and the reality of homosexuals doesn't arouse my curiosity sufficiently; and further, I'm unable to identify with it.

How did you learn of Pasolini's death?

Early in the morning I had a phone call from Lietta Tornabuoni, who had learned about it from the police. I called the chief of police and he confirmed the truth: Pasolini had been killed. Then I got into the car and went to the Idroscalo at Ostia, where he had been murdered. The Idroscalo at Ostia is simply a stretch of scruffy, mangy beach, scattered with refuse and piles of garbage. For some unknown reason, it is fenced in with barbed wire. There was a little wooden gate, painted pink, from which it seems the murderer, Mario Pelosi, one of the usual *ragazzi di vita*, pulled loose a plank to strike Pasolini. Other pieces of wood, small and apparently inoffensive, were scattered over the sand. Pasolini's corpse was gone. It had been removed a quarter of an hour earlier. There have been many descriptions of that crime. My reconstruction of it is this: after eating supper in a trattoria that I knew because I had been there often with Pasolini, Il Biondo Tevere, Pasolini took Pelosi to the Idroscalo. There something happened, we don't know what. Perhaps Pasolini had an argument with Pelosi and struck him with a piece of wood in some painful way, provoking in him a kind of temporary insanity. Perhaps Pasolini struck him deliberately to provoke his reaction: Pasolini was a masochist. Pelosi then took a plank with nails in it and struck Pasolini on the back of the neck. Pasolini then took off his shirt or T-shirt or whatever, stanched the blood of the wound, then folded the garment and put it, rolled up, near the fence. At this point Pasolini must have threatened to report Pelosi to the police, and Pelosi gave him a terrible kick in the genitals, producing an awesome bruise noted during the autopsy.

After that kick Pasolini was finished, he didn't react, he went staggering toward the car. Pelosi followed him, striking him repeatedly with the little pieces of wood he picked up from the ground as he went along. Pasolini fainted and fell, and then Pelosi did the definitive and, at the same time, most significant thing: he knew that to kill a dog or a man you have to use a pistol or a knife, otherwise you can never be sure he's really dead. Pasolini had only fainted; he might regain consciousness and report his attacker. Without any hesitation, Pelosi got into the car, turned on the engine, and ran a wheel over Pasolini's body. This time Pasolini really died. His lungs and other internal organs exploded, as was later observed. Pelosi left the enclosure and started speeding toward Rome. But he was driving on the wrong side and was stopped by the police. At the station he said nothing of the crime but started raving about a ring he had lost, a cheap ring given him by an American soldier. Pelosi, accused of stealing the car, spent the night in a cell. At dawn a call came from the Idroscalo of Ostia saying that a body has been found and, beside it, a ring. Pelosi confessed almost at once, the ambulance took away Pasolini's body, and so ends the story of the most horrible death of an artist in all time. Perhaps with only one exception: the murder of Winckelmann in Trieste by a male lover.

What was your reaction to Pasolini's death?

He was my best friend; you can imagine the grief and the horror I felt. I have always had friends, and over the years, they have grown more and more important for me. To be someone's friend I must feel two things: cultural respect and personal fascination. For Pasolini I had both. Further, he possessed in some ways a character complementary to mine. We didn't agree on many things; perhaps this was why, finally, we got along so well. And then there was a true, sincere, profound affection, as between brothers.

While we're on the subject of friends, you've never really talked to me about your painter friends, or of your tastes in painting.

For me, painting comes after literature and before cinema. It's the art I believe I understand and love best. In fact, if I had had to choose between writing and painting, I would have picked the latter. The profession of painter fascinates me, but despite my passion for painting, it remains fairly mysterious to me. I have noticed that often painters, when they are together talking among themselves, don't give the impression of being intelligent. Then you see their paintings and you realize they are. But how does this come about? This is something I've never managed fully to understand. Further, painting is a more attractive, more fascinating, and more original profession than writing. It's more attractive because instead of battling with words, with abstractions, it has to do with something, colors and forms, that corresponds to our senses. More fascinating because it is a craft, not an intellectual exercise. Finally, more original because while we speak, that is, while we are doing something habitual, we can delude ourselves, like Molière's *bourgeois gentilhomme,* that we are making prose. Nothing in everyday life leads us to communicate with colors. Further, painting shares with sculpture, though to a lesser degree (sculpture reproduces the object), the illusion of reproducing the world as it is. Writing doesn't have this illusion, precisely because the means it uses doesn't permit it.

You still haven't told me who your favorite painters are.

I have had favorite painters, as I've had favorite writers, since I was a boy. Today I like good painting, as I like good writing.

When you were a boy, who were your favorite painters?

They differed greatly. I'll mention some at random: the surrealists, Rembrandt, Van Gogh, Piero della Francesca, Masaccio, the pre-Raphaelites, the paintings of the Villa of the Mysteries in Pompeii, Raphael, Giotto, and so on. Actually, I began liking a painter at the moment I felt his fascination. Why I felt the fascination of this painter and not of that one is another mysterious thing that doesn't have much to do with painting.

You've always had painter friends.

I've written many catalogs for shows and had a certain number of painter friends: Carlo Levi, Paolucci, Guttuso, Capogrossi, my brother-in-law Martinelli, Tornabuoni, Scialoja, Schifano, Recalcati, Cremonini, and so on. Among these the most important friendship was with Guttuso, whom I met at the end of the thirties and saw continuously until his death. With the others I have had intense friendships for defined periods, then I didn't see much of them: among these I would put Tornabuoni, with whom for a time, as I told you, I talked on the telephone every morning; or Scialoja, with whom I shared the same house at Anacapri for several summers. I like the company of painters for the same reason I prefer painting to writing. They always have something of the artisan and of the creator at the same time, whereas the writer, if he isn't a genius, is often a petty bourgeois. In short, the painter is always an artist, the writer only now and then.

What was your relationship with Guttuso?

Affectionate. I didn't like all of his painting and I didn't share his political ideas, or rather, the way he flaunted his political commitment. But on the whole he attracted me as a man. I wrote a long introduction about Guttuso and defined him in a way that I believe still works today, "a Mediterranean expressionist."

You were great friends with Carlo Levi; did you consider him more a painter or a writer?

More a painter, also of an expressionist genre, a bit in the line of Kokoschka. Carlo Levi, like Guttuso as well, for that matter, had a special personal fascination derived in part from the emblematic purity of certain ancestral features. Guttuso was charismatic in his total Sicilianness, Carlo Levi for his solar Jewishness. I always used to say to him that he had a face like certain Eastern kings, engraved on coins. He looked like a king of Cappadocia. I felt real grief on learning of his death.

And Schifano, Recalcati, Cremonini?

I could say of these three painters the same thing I said of Guttuso and Carlo Levi: namely, that my relationship with them, though influenced by my admiration for their work, was connected with a charisma, a personal fascination.

It's odd that you haven't mentioned De Chirico or Savinio.

Unfortunately I didn't see enough of them to be able to talk about them in the same way. In any case I consider De Chirico the greatest Italian painter in the heyday of the École de Paris. Curiously, his "metaphysical" painting is also in its way realistic: then the streets and squares of certain Italian cities, the "cities of silence" as D'Annunzio called them, were deserted and monumental as De Chirico painted them, and Italy was full of statues gesticulating in silence and emptiness. I knew De Chirico slightly. One day I went to supper at a house in Piazza di Spagna, and from the window I looked into the house of De Chirico across the square. De Chirico was sitting on a little chair in an odd place, by the door, his hands on his knees, and he was doing nothing. A woman friend of mine one day was surprised to hear herself asked by De Chirico, "Do I earn more, or does Moravia?" She answered, "Why you do, maestro, far more." He was a man of genius, with those moments of grouchy originality that geniuses have.

Did you consider Savinio a painter or a writer?

Savinio was a painter and a writer of equal worth. I knew him better than his brother, De Chirico; he was a likable and very intelligent man, very human. Both he and De Chirico had little that was Italian about them, in the sense of certain petty bourgeois habits. You could sense their Greek origins, their long stays in Munich and Paris. But De Chirico created a certain way of painting and Savinio didn't.

I realize we've spoken very little about the theater and about your theater. Do you feel you are also a dramatist?

I am by vocation. My first reading was, as you know, Molière, Chekhov, Goldoni, Shakespeare. My dominant idea as I was writing Gli indifferenti was to blend dramatic technique with that of the novel. My novels are plays disguised as novels. Further, I have written a dozen works for the theater. Finally, the writer who had the greatest influence on me is Dostoyevsky, no doubt the most theatrical of the Russian novelists of the nineteenth century. Why did I devote myself to the novel rather than to the theater? Because the theater is no longer as alive as it was for so many centuries; indeed, you could say it's approaching death. The theater today is an aristocratic medium of expression. It wasn't in the past; then it was like the movies, sometimes good, sometimes bad, but always for a universal public. For a great theater to exist you have to have a theatrical society, composed as it was in the days of Chekhov or Shakespeare, of directors, audience, actors, authors, critics, and so on. That society today no longer exists. Movies and TV have taken the theater's place as mass entertainment. And yet if the theater dies, some things will be impossible to say anymore. The theater is the religious place where man questions himself about the great problems of mankind: who we are, where we're going, what we're doing, and so on. You understand these things especially if you move from the novel to the theater or vice versa. The theater was born in the temples of ancient Greece; the novel, on the contrary, in the streets of Spain and England.

What is your own theater like?

Once in *Nuovi Argomenti* I published some reflections on the theater. I divided the theater into two great categories: one of the word, and the other of talk. In the theater of talk the characters say insignificant, everyday things, as in Chekhov, or else they say little or nothing, as in Beckett. The drama takes place offstage, but the everyday chatter with which the characters express themselves onstage has the quality of casting dramatic shadows, like objects seen against the light. The theater of talk inevitably ends in the theater of silence, as you can see in the Living Theater. Instead, in the theater of the word, which is the traditional theater, the drama takes place onstage, everyday speech is reduced to a minimum. My theater belongs to the second category. I think that the drama should not only not be silenced but must be louder than everyday life.

What are your plays?

I've written six plays plus some one-act works. I began with a genuine tragedy, *Beatrice Cenci,* based on the famous historical family drama of the sixteenth century. Then, a few years later, I wrote three dramas. One, *Il dio Kurt,* was a story of Jews and Nazis in a concentration camp; here I used the technique of the theater about theater; then came *Il mondo è quello che è,* a tragicomedy whose subject is taken from the linguistic philosophy of Wittgenstein. A fourth play, *La vita è gioco,* if nothing else, had the originality of dealing with the subject of political kidnapping, which didn't yet exist in Italy. A few years later I wrote *L'angelo dell'informazione,* a play about adultery and the impossibility, in fact, of being truly informed, and *La cintura,* whose subject is nothing less than the end of the world, seen through a "sadomasochistic" story. The one-act works include *L'intervista, Il colpo di stato,* and *La vergine e la droga.*

What difference is there today between the success of the novel and the success of the theater?

Theatrical success is less satisfying than success with novels. The novelist doesn't know who will read his novels; he can allow himself illusions. The playwright, on the contrary, has only to peek into the house from the wings before the curtain rises and he will see the faces of all his spectators and will immediately lose any illusions. Perhaps once it was different, when in fact there were the theatrical societies I talked about. But today, on the whole, the theater audience is very ignorant, less attached, less sensitive, more distracted than that of the movies. It is an audience that mostly goes to the theater out of social duty or because it has nothing better to do. And you have also to bear in mind a fact at once important and simple: ours is an age of the image; the word is much less communicative and immediate. Simply, the theater audience doesn't understand; the cinema audience understands.

And readers?

At least readers choose their reading; spectators obey a social reflex.

It seems to me that readers, too, are greatly influenced by the mass media.

It's true, but the theater is spectacle; reading, not. Theater is a traditional social manifestation, in other words.

So, in your opinion, the theater is obsolete?

It is certainly a form that has known better times, not because the theater of the past was really superior to today's, but because it better corresponded to a society that today no longer exists. The theater is a sublime craft, whereas the cinema is an industrial product. The modern world is industrial.

16

*A*LAIN ELKANN: *The years you lived with Dacia were the most serene years of your life and also the years of the great travels in Africa and on other continents.*

ALBERTO MORAVIA: First of all, as I said, to celebrate our union, we flew around the world: Vienna, Paris, London, New York, Los Angeles, Tahiti, Djakarta, New Delhi, Katmandu, Kabul, Athens, Rome. We did it two months, perhaps a little longer, and we actually spent some time only in New York, Tahiti, Katmandu, and Kabul. We spent a week in New York, then we stayed ten days in Tahiti, which was obligatory because there was a plane only every ten days. In Tahiti we hired a car and took a ten-day vacation. At that time Tahiti seemed to us a very beautiful place, but also very calm and, contrary to its reputation, very provincial. There were white beaches of powdered coral, enchanted lagoons filled with varicolored fish and pink coral, tall slender palms, limpid streams of fresh water, and so on. But the town of Tahiti suggested a French *sous-prefecture*. The atmosphere was announced by some big signs at the entance of the main bar, listing departures for the other Pacific islands: Easter

Island, Samoa, Bora Bora. Tahiti was peopled by natives like those painted by Gauguin. Women and men with beautiful, slightly heavy bodies and simple, dull faces. They were an indulgent people, lazy, as least in appearance: the maids in the hotel made the beds with a cigarette in their mouth, swaying their hips. Half-naked youths rode horses bareback along the beach. I remember two or three details that have remained in my mind: the fish in the lagoons are so numerous that you can catch them with your hands, and yet the Tahitians prefer canned fish. Second, there is a category of homosexuals who live, doing nothing, at the expense of the families they are living with. Third, there is the *fiù*, a kind of sudden *accidie* that attacks the Tahitian right in the middle of whatever task he may be doing. For example, a house is being built; all of a sudden a mason throws down his trowel and bucket, takes off his overalls, and announces, "I have the *fiù*," and he goes away.

The center of the island is occupied by not very high mountains, an emerald green, where nobody goes. In those picturesque mountains live chickens, pigs, and dogs, imported from other islands and completely wild. Life on Tahiti is like the air you breathe there: soft, tepid, dreamy. The philosophical mottos that explain the paintings of Gauguin are absolutely exact and relevant. We took a plane and went to Bora Bora, an island two hours by air from Tahiti. There, too, enchanting beaches of white sand as fine as face powder and tall, slender palms. Dacia took a boat and rowed out to the coral reef, about five kilometers. I had to go and get her with a motorboat, and that evening she was in bed with a temperature of 102 degrees because she had had an ultraviolet sunstroke. The return to Tahiti from Bora Bora was not without difficulties. The pilot had lingered on Bora Bora to court a girl there, so we arrived at Tahiti almost in the dark, and the airport wasn't equipped for night landings. On the runway an ambulance was already waiting for us, in case of disaster.

Our third stay was in Katmandu. Nepal wasn't yet fashionable; there were no hotels, but only a kind of hostel in a building that belonged, like everything else in Nepal, to the Rana family. Buddha was born in Nepal and died there; there is an abundance of shrines, temples, religious constructions, a bit like Franciscan Umbria. The thing that most impressed me in Nepal is that, when you first see it, it looks like a green landscape of the Appenines, but when you look closer you see a white, very high, gigantic shadow rising up, up into the sky. It is Everest, the highest mountain in the world. The second thing that impressed me was a white horse, wandering around all alone in a courtyard: it was a horse idol. The third thing was a little girl who looked out at the top of a building, she also mysteriously chosen to represent the deity. The odd thing is that, once these girls have finished their role, they have great trouble finding a husband.

In those years with Dacia, the two of you went to Cape Kennedy to witness the Apollo launching.

Yes. I was sent by *L'espresso*. Dacia also wrote some articles for *Paese sera*. First of all, we spent two weeks in New York and we went to visit the factory where they were putting the final touches on the spacecraft. Then we went on to Cape Kennedy, in Florida, to an apartment in a complex for middle-class American families, with its communal swimming pool. There I had an experience of provincial American life. They were all young families with two or three children, and they regarded us with a slight hostility. We avoided the pool and went to the beach to swim: it was the beach where, not long before, records for car racing had been made. There were huge waves ideal for surfing. Jeeps went by with armed policemen in them, a terrible wind was blowing, everything was different from Italy. On the day of the Apollo launching we were on the scene along with a million other people. I didn't know anybody, except Norman Mailer, who was there for the same reason I was. Only he wrote a book, and I wrote three articles. The sight of the Apollo rising into the sky has remained in my memory because of the slowness of the missile. It took I don't know how long to rise vertically, then it changed route, obliquely, and disappeared.

From Cape Kennedy we went to Houston, Texas, a city so American it makes New York seem a bit of Europe. We were in the

projection room of the NASA center when on the screen an enormous white worm appeared dragging itself along, erect, over a terrain all detritus and rocks, in a dark air: the first man on the moon.
He took a few steps and planted the American flag. The whole
room stood up to applaud, and immediately afterward everybody
rushed out to seek the comfort of some hot drink. In the projection
theater the air conditioning was glacial. I was particularly struck by
the contrast between these details of banal everyday life and the
absolutely fantastic and completely exceptional nature of the flight
to the moon. Probably all extraordinary events of man's history
have been accompanied by trivial little actions.

I must say at this point that, after the boldness of the venture, I
admired especially the industrial capacity of the United States,
which had employed half a million people, working in perfect
agreement, to construct the Apollo. The perfection of the missile's mechanism was revealed to me by the visit to the underground dome where the numerous computers controlling the
perfect functioning were set up: out of three million parts only
two showed some signs of irregularity. Apart from the perfection
of the preparation and the construction of the Apollo, I remember
an anecdote that in fact, though indirectly, concerned this perfection. Immediately after viewing the film of the moon I received
some phone calls from Rome, from people who knew I was there
and wanted to ask me either for information or for comments on
the event. Among the others, I heard from the receiver the
thrilled voice of a devout Italian woman: she was shouting,
"Moravia! Now isn't this a miracle?" I replied simply, "No, it's the
rational result of great industrial organization." These answers of
mine were taped and then published in Italy, but that answer was
omitted.

Tell me about Norman Mailer.

Norman Mailer was always looking for money for his numerous
families. So he accepted fifty thousand dollars to write a whole
book about witnessing the Apollo launch. Norman Mailer was
not new to this kind of novelized reporting. He wrote similar

things before and after the Apollo. I, on the contrary, confined myself to three articles in *L'espresso*, as I said; but you have to understand the difference between Norman Mailer and me in a professional and social sense. I am, or at least I believe I am, a writer whose success or lack of it depends on how the book is written. Norman Mailer, on the contrary, is a public figure, and he succeeds always. He wrote a first novel, *The Naked and the Dead*, a good book, which went well. He wrote a second, not so good, and that was all right, too. He stabbed his wife, and that was all right; he married the daughter of a lord, and that was all right, too. He ran for mayor of New York and failed, but that was all right; he wrote five hundred pages on the flight of the Apollo, and that was actually all right. This said, it must also surely be said that Norman Mailer, who defines himself as a conservative revolutionary, is one of the most likable of American public figures and the author of two or three important books.

You're also a friend of Saul Bellow?

Yes, we're friends. As I told you, I made a trip with him, for me memorable, by car from New York to Chicago. I've met him several times in the United States. I'm president of the Malaparte Prize, which was awarded him a few years ago. Saul Bellow is someone I'm very fond of for various reasons. First of all, because of his books, always extremely readable, and some of them beautiful, which afford an image of the society of the United States seen by someone who belongs to it. The novel of Saul Bellow I prefer is *Seize the Day*, the brief and moving story of a father and a son. The second reason I'm fond of Saul Bellow is something a Roman like me can't overlook: he resembles a cardinal or a bishop. He has that foresighted benevolence and also that sardonic prudence. I know he disapproves of my writing about sexuality, but this is logical in a great prelate.

What other American writers of today do you admire?

Truman Capote, Kurt Vonnegut, Raymond Carver, Tobias Wolff, Tom Wolfe, Carson McCullers, Paul Bowles, Mary McCarthy,

Henry Miller, and others. American literature, not just now but from its origins, is what can be called a literature of the far shore, Alexandrine. In American literature there is the taste for psychological sophistication and stylization characteristic of all those who have inherited a culture whose origins they care little about. In this sense, American literature seems not to favor much the institution of the so-called great writer, so frequent, on the contrary, in French, Russian, English, and other literatures.

What about Faulkner, Hemingway, Fitzgerald, and before them, Mark Twain, Thoreau, Poe, Melville?

Yes, they are great writers, but they share this characteristic, as inheritors of European culture.

What do you think of South American literature and its writers?

It is also Alexandrine, like that of the United States. Or rather, as in the case of the United States, its classics are not at home but in Europe. In this respect Borges is typical; for him the culture of the whole world, especially of Europe, is simply an immense warehouse of bric-a-brac from which to take every so often some precious curiosity. The way some people furnish their apartments with objects formerly in churches.

Did you know Borges?

I interviewed him for the *Corriere della sera*: likable, sly, a bit of a trickster. "Did you know Picasso?" I asked him. "Picasso? Never heard the name," he answered. Very Argentinian and bookish, the typical, brilliant heir of a nonnational culture.

Is Gabriel Garcia Marquez also the heir of an Alexandrine culture?

Obviously, he writes an epic using folklore as a basis. It's no accident that they compared him to Salman Rushdie, who for India has done what Marquez did for South America, but Marquez is in any case a very considerable writer, especially in the book *Chronicle of a Death Foretold*.

Getting back to Moravia, we're now in the seventies, in Italy the protest movement has generated terrorism, your relationship with Dacia Maraini is changing, and you write La vita interiore. *Shall we talk about all this?*

La vita interiore is a novel that cost me more work even than *Le ambizioni sbagliate*. Five years for *Le ambizioni sbagliate*, seven for *La vita interiore*. But whereas *Le ambizioni sbagliate* had, so to speak, a negative utility, since it enabled me to understand once and for all the kind of novel I should avoid writing (namely, the traditional novel-novel with many characters and many parallel situations), *La vita interiore* for me has a very positive value, in that it resolves a narrative problem I set myself with *Gli indifferenti* and afterward was never able to solve. It is one of those problems of ideological content to which critics attach no importance, though for writers they are basic. The problem is this: "If God doesn't exist, all is possible," Dostoyevsky said in *The Brothers Karamazov*. The sentence is reversed, but the meaning remains the same in *Gli indifferenti*, "Without an absolute moral justification nothing is possible." And in fact, Michele would like to kill his mother's lover, but he forgets to load the revolver, precisely because he lacks an absolute moral justification to act; that is to say, he is "indifferent."

Now let's jump from 1928, when I wrote the last words of the manuscript of *Gli indifferenti*, to the year 1978, when I corrected the proofs of *La vita interiore*. The heroine of *La vita interiore* is many things, but she is above all a person who shoots and kills. Why does she shoot and kill? Because, unlike Michele in *Gli indifferenti*, she has an absolute justification in carrying out the action par excellence, namely, homicide: a voice orders her to shoot. Thus, with *La vita interiore*, I resolved, fifty years afterward, the problem of *Gli indifferenti*: "The absolute justification was revolutionary duty." In other words, it had taken me half a century to acknowledge the truth of the Freudian superego. As for the voice that guides and commands my protagonist, the idea came to me as I was reading the account of the trial of Joan of Arc, who also would not have acted if she hadn't had a voice that kept telling her what she was to do. Joan of Arc all through her life remained a simple peasant girl, but at the same time she was able to act on the political and military level. This alienation fascinated me. My character also ought to remain substantially a middle-class girl from Parioli, though she supported terrorism and practiced it thanks to the external and yet inflexible voice that commanded her. As I said, the critics attach scant importance to these ideological contents, and in fact, *La vita interiore* was noticed and perhaps even praised for quite different reasons. Nevertheless, it is one of the most important novels I've written. In fact, as after *Le ambizioni sbagliate*, after *La vita interiore*, in a certain sense, my narrative has somewhat changed.

Just as it could be said that La disubbedienza *is a rather prophetic book as regards the protest of 1968, so* La vita interiore *has a bearing on terrorism.*

True, I was correcting the proofs of *La vita interiore* in that month, April 1978, when Moro was prisoner of the Red Brigades. I had had to undergo a very serious operation, I was near death, and I read the mountains of newspapers in which they discussed, basically, the subject of my novel, terrorism. A subject I had started dealing with seven years earlier, in 1971.

And was La vita interiore *a success?*

Yes, it had a success, though it wasn't understood at all. It was an attempt, I believe a successful attempt, to combine, as I said, Marx with Freud, communism and the unconscious. But in Italy, Marx, on the one hand, is confined to a public formula, while Freud, on the other, seems relegated to an exclusively private sphere. Whereas Marx should be privatized, and at the same time we should see how Freud's theories influence the life of society. In any case *La vita interiore* had a certain success. It would have sold more copies if it hadn't been twice confiscated by a particularly bigoted official.

What effects did those years of terrorism have in your life?

The Black Terrorists considered me their enemy, and they were right, but only in part: actually I am the enemy of all terrorism. In any case, one of those days, a threatening voice telephoned me with these words, "Be careful. Be very careful. New Order." Their telephone was in a café; I could hear a clink of glasses and dishes. To the second call, "Take care, companion," I replied, "Companion, my ass." Then there was a third call, really dangerous, "We have sentenced to death Alberto Moravia." This call was taken by my maid, who answered out of habit, a bit comically, "He's not in." In those days the Black Terrorists had killed a judge and various other people, so I accepted the proposal of the minister of the interior, Cossiga (now president of the republic), who said, "We belong to the same club." "What club?" "The club of those threatened by terrorists."

So for at least a year I had an armed escort: two young police agents, one with a pistol and the other with a submachine gun. They arrived each day at noon, then two others replaced them at eight in the evening. They were two Sicilian boys who had only recently enlisted and didn't know Rome. So they always made me go first through the streets. I would go to the movies, and they would wait for me outside, in the car. I invited them to come to the movies, too, and they answered, "What'll we do with the gun? What if it gets stolen?" In my opinion, an escort is useless in an assassination, as the Moro case demonstrated; the escort was promptly wiped out. It can be useful, however, in an attempted kidnapping. I went along with the escort for a few months. They followed me everywhere; it was flattering and boring at the same time. Then at a certain point I moved to Venice, and there my escort consisted of a single policeman, and a very stupid one at that, who kept losing me. This experience made one new thing clear, at least for me: faced with this kind of danger, either you give up and run or else you acquire a kind of adventurous stimulus, which, in my case, for example, gave me a great desire to write. I remember a friend said to me, "If something like that happened to me, I'd run to the far end of the United States." Probably it's a matter of the moment. In certain moments a brave man can also become cowardly, and vice versa. It depends chiefly on the spirit with which you face the frightening object.

Why is it that when everything was calm you couldn't wait to go off somewhere, but, as in the summer of 1943, when there was danger, you didn't budge?

Curiosity. But not an idle, exterior curiosity, a participating curiosity. In the summer of 1978 I was curious about what would actually happen to me as I participated, however passively, in the atmosphere of terrorism.

How do you remember the abduction and the death of Aldo Moro?

I remember chiefly that the *Corriere della sera* telephoned me in Venice at midnight to tell me they wanted an article on the kidnapping of Moro by eight the next morning. I got up at five and wrote the article I'd been asked for, in which I took the position that then was also Leonardo Sciascia's: agreeing neither with the Red Brigades nor with the government. At this point I have to make a political-historical observation. For me the Red Brigades were created by the Christian Democrats when they ceased to be a party like the others and became a regime. The Red Brigades did some very simple reasoning: against the hegemony of a democratic party you vote; against a regime you take up a gun. In fact, one of their slogans was "Never again without a gun!" In a way, the death of Moro reminds us of that of Mussolini, with the body strung up in Piazzale Loreto. Moro's death marked the end of the Christian Democrat regime and a return, even if quite relative, to parliamentary democracy. As for the Red Brigades, I've already stated the chief reason for their failure. You kill your enemies when you're in power, not when you're trying to gain power. The Red Brigades frightened the Italians both with their cruelty and with the confusion of their ideas. The majority of Italians was quickly convinced that if the Red Brigades took over, they would do more or less what the Khmer Rouge had done in Cambodia, with the same ferocity and the same ideological subculture.

How did you judge the political class with regard to the Moro case?

I was in favor of negotiation, but I don't believe the terrorists were. The terrorists had seized Moro in order to kill him; there was never any really serious talk about an exchange or negotiation. Probably they really did want power but didn't know how to move away from violence to win the recognition of their legitimacy.

In those years did you think everything would change?

Many things, as I told you, did change with the protest movement, but actual terrorism didn't change anything. And this was because the terrorists' ideas were truly confused, or rather they didn't have ideas but only a method of action, faithful, as I said, to the idea "action first and then thought." In their action you have to concede that they demonstrated a certain sinister originality, chiefly in their way of not striking isolated personalities but rather members of a given category. For example, killing Signor Rossi in order to terrorize all Signor Rossis. A Fiat worker, stopped by a journalist and asked to comment on the assassination of Casalengo, assistant editor of *La stampa*, said, "Ten, a hundred, a thousand Casalengos." In this, besides the usual thoughtlessness of the Italians, you have to see a result of the method of striking one to strike all.

Meanwhile, what was happening in your private life?

Dacia decided to leave me because, in her words, "she didn't want to be part of a couple anymore." For this reason, too, I moved to Venice and rented a very beautiful apartment: a big room on Dorsoduro near the Zattere with five windows overlooking some poetic gardens filled with birds. I lived on the second floor; on the ground floor Carlo Ripa di Meana lived with his future wife, who at that time was still called Marina Lante della Rovere. Then I went back to Rome and went to Iran with a friend of mine, Gianni Barcelloni, to shoot a film there. It was when I came back that Dacia told me definitively that she didn't want to live with me anymore. Since I loved her, I did everything to make her stay; I even tried to enlarge the apartment on Lungotevere della Vittoria so she could live in the same house and still be independent. But the condominium prevented me from carrying out this plan. Then we decided to lead a common life, only halved. Dacia came early in the morning, had breakfast with me, then went to her room and worked there till one. At one we ate together, then she left. It wasn't a very satisfactory solution. In effect she was with me only during the quarter-hour that our lunch lasted, but it was still better than nothing. At that time I suffered the anguish of abandonment, and every morning as soon as I woke up I thought of suicide. In reality, Dacia had taken with her almost twenty years of my life.

Had you expected things with Dacia to end?

Yes. More or less, I had; but since I didn't want that, I never thought about it. This arrangement of ours was naturally temporary and could last only as long as I lived alone and didn't love another woman. For four years it went on like that, and then finally I met Carmen Llera, who after two years came to live with me. Today Dacia lives completely on her own. Still, I telephone her every day, she has lunch with me once a week, and she and her present companion spend the month of August at Sabaudia.

Why do loves end?

They don't end. Once you really love a woman you love her forever, but love doesn't mean being in love. Being in love, which is at the beginning of love, lasts a relatively short time.

How did you spend the years following your separation from Dacia?

I spent them in the usual way of my life, writing on the one hand, and on the other, looking for a new companion. I believe, however, that this is more or less what everybody does, except *rentiers* and anchorites. The former don't work; the latter don't look for female partners. In this sense I'm a commonplace person, because anchorites and *rentiers* are becoming rarer all the time.

Were you alone or with another woman?
There were three other women.

Who were they?
They were three people with whom I didn't live, as I had with Elsa and Dacia, nor did I have a mere fling, as in certain brief encounters I've told you about before. They are also people I couldn't discuss without being indiscreet: I see them and spend time with them still. So I prefer not to name them.

What did you write?
In chronological order I wrote 1934, because in 1934, in fact, suicide is discussed, which was an obsessive idea in those years after the separation from Dacia.

Does 1934 mark a turning point in your writing? What is the dominant theme of the novel?
In my fiction there have never been turning points: if anything, I have taken up subjects I had previously barely hinted at without developing them fully. For example, in *La vita interiore* I took up a theme that for me was already important fifty years earlier, in *Gli indifferenti*: the absolute and moral justification of action. In 1934 I revived a theme also not fully explored in *Il conformista*: how you can become fascist. In *Il conformista* the theme was seen as the interior and insoluble problem of a Fascist; in 1934 it was, on the contrary, the problem of whole nations governed by totalitarianisms: Italy, Germany, and the Soviet Union. In this case the theme could be defined as that of schizophrenia or inevitable disassociation in totalitarian regimes divided between the values of common sense and the use that totalitarianisms make of it. Hitler, Mussolini, Stalin appealed to incontrovertible values like the fatherland or the future of mankind, but then the moment came when the Fascist,

or the Nazi, or the Communist discovered that in the name of these values horrendous crimes were being committed. Hence disassociation, the schizophrenia symbolized in 1934 by the existence of twin sisters, one a Nazi and the other an anti-Nazi, who in reality were a single person.

What made you think of the twin sisters?

They occurred to me casually. I was having dinner with a friend and, in fact, with twin sisters. For that matter the theme of twins, brothers or sisters, is a classic subject of ancient comedy, Roman and Greek, used later by Shakespeare, Goldoni, and many others...

The novel 1934 was published in 1981. What happened in your private life during the eighties?

If you asked me to talk about the novel that I'm writing, I would surely answer that I can't talk about it until it's finished. It's, as they say in English, a "work in progress," whose writing and conclusion are still susceptible to choice. But a novel, after all, is something that concerns me and only me. I can make something of it or else get it wrong. The merit or the blame will still concern me and only me. In life, on the contrary, even granting that there is a certain resemblance between life and novel and consequently the events of life can have a conclusion, still the development and the final outcome of our relationship with the people in our life doesn't depend solely on us, but also on the others, and therefore the developments are neither predictable nor due to a personal choice. So far I have talked about episodes in my life that can be considered somehow concluded because either the people involved are dead or there is no expectation of significant novelties. But there are people and relationships with people that I couldn't discuss without presumption, without being arbitrary, so at this point I will confine myself, when talking about the 1980s, to things that are really concluded, in other words, to the books that I wrote and published in that period.

But they are years that also involve your antinuclear commitment and your participation in the Parliament of Europe.

Of course, and the things I've done both in opposing the atom bomb and in taking part in the parliament of Europe belong to the category of things concluded. I have no difficulty discussing them.

But many people who have known you for years believe that, since meeting Carmen Llera, you have entered a new creative season.

Very well, I'll talk about the novels I've written in this so-called creative season. As for my relationship with Carmen Llera, others will talk about it, if they want to.

The fact remains is that the first book you published after 1934, the collection of stories entitled La cosa, *is dedicated to Carmen Llera.*

I agree. And for the same reasons, namely, because she inspired them, I should also have dedicated to her the books that came after *La cosa*. But what you might call my private autobiography stops here. From here on I will continue only with the public autobiography, primarily literary. So any question that concerns me and nobody else and only on the existential level will find me ready to answer.

Let's turn to your books, then. After 1934 you published a volume of stories, La cosa.

The stories in *La cosa* are connected with an event in my everyday life. One morning I left the house, planning to go to the beach at Sabaudia. I was driving the car and I had a dog with me, named Arancio, who was then a puppy. On the bridge nearest my house I turned to go toward Piazza Ungheria, where Carmen Llera then lived; she was to come with me to the sea. At the end of the bridge I was struck with extreme violence (I was hardly moving, because I was preparing to turn) by a car coming from the opposite direction. The impact was tremendous, but I didn't realize its violence because, thanks to that same violence, I experienced the phenomenon of retrodated memory. I can remember when I left the house and then when I woke, so to speak, seated at the wheel, looking in amazement at the completely destroyed hood of my car. The fact is that my first thought was, "Now, how will I go to the beach? I'll have to give up the outing or take a taxi." At the moment I started to get out of the car I felt a very sharp pain: my femur was fractured. Then I stayed in the car at least two hours before the ambulance arrived. My dog didn't suffer from retrodated memory, and in fact, he hid in terror under the seat. Fortunately, after a short while a woman I know came by, and I gave the dog to her to take home and at the same time asked her to call Carmen and tell her about the accident. Finally they took me to a hospital, where I spent the night in a general ward, filled with people in plaster casts in the strangest positions. All I remember of that night is that I had started reading a book and one of my companions in pain came over and asked me, "Are you the writer Moravia?" "Yes." "But do you write books or read them?"

Anyway, the next day they took me home on a stretcher and I spent three months in bed. Why have I told you about this accident? Because during those three months I wrote a majority of the stories in *La cosa*, on a lectern, on rectangular strips of paper, much as they say D'Annunzio wrote his *Notturno*. The first days I suffered very much. Writing not only distracted me from the pain but gave me the impression of a reassertion of my threatened vitality. There is something else to be said about *La cosa* on a strictly literary plane. In many of those stories there is the transparent wish to deal with the subject of sex without, however, lapsing into eroticism. In short, I thought and still think that sex begins to be interesting at the same moment it becomes insignificant. In this case, insignificant means strictly functional, lacking in any of the moral significances that have progressively been added to it by society. All this is so true that I suggested to the American publisher that *La cosa* might be called in English

Anatomic Tales, but he preferred the less exact but more commercial title of *Erotic Tales*. On other occasions I've mentioned "The Purloined Letter" by E. A. Poe. Could Poe have written that story without talking of the letter? No. And in my intention this was to happen with sex, which it was indispensable to talk about in some stories, unless I gave up the idea of writing them.

I have a feeling that you don't like eroticism.

Call it "eroticism," but it would be more precise to say "pornography," which in my view is simply the vulgar treatment of the subject of sex. There is a vulgar treatment of politics, social life, religion, and so on. So there is also a vulgar treatment of the sexual subject. And the vulgarity probably consists of isolating it from a context, making it a means for arousing the reader.

Do you consider the eroticism of Georges Bataille vulgar?

When it's not functional, yes. Anyway, you have to judge case by case. For that matter Bataille probably speaks of sex in a metaphorical sense. And besides, it's clear that though I state general ideas, I'm speaking for myself, that is, of the results I can achieve with this idea. This is to say that every writer has his own key for opening the door of reality. Balzac, for example, has money. While he talks about money, he is talking about love, politics, society, and perhaps also money. Dostoyevsky's key is homicide; Conrad's is the sea. Someone said a while ago that inspiration is talking always of the same thing and of nothing else. Well, my inspiration often leads me to talk about sex and nothing but sex: but it is a key with which I have the illusion of opening, just a little, the door of reality.

What is the meaning of the adjective "Moravian," which is frequently used?

You should probably ask that question of those who use the word. I believe a similar adjective can be coined every time we are faced with a writer who, in fact, speaks of a single thing and nothing else, but it is an adjective that cuts two ways. On the one hand, it can mean that the writer in question has created a manner that can possibly be imitated by his imitators. On the other, that in the chaos of reality, he has isolated with precision and verisimilitude a given datum. I believe I belong rather to the second category.

After La cosa *you wrote* L'uomo che guarda.

In *L'uomo che guarda* I probably bade a temporary farewell to the atmosphere of 1968. My character is called Dodo, a nickname that expresses inertia and impotence (in fact, don't the French say "faire dodo" for sleeping?). He is an intellectual, an ex-'68 protester, and is doubly a voyeur in that on the one hand he likes to watch and on the other, for social and political reasons, he can't do anything but watch. Opposite him there is a bourgeois father, authoritarian and famous, who sleeps with Dodo's wife. I said that with this novel I bade farewell to the 1968 atmosphere, but I didn't say that my character meant to indicate a complete renunciation. As long as you look, you see; and as long as you see, you judge and you can act. But besides some characters that seem to me successful, the book in my opinion is of interest because it dwells and focuses on something obvious and completely normal: the fact of looking. The relationship between father and son represents, moreover, something absolutely new in my fiction. It's the first time I created a father. Until then there had only been mothers, generally widows or with invisible husbands.

In *your latest novel*, Il viaggio a Roma, *not only do you create a second father, but the figure of the mother also returns.*

Yes, I've created many mothers. There is a mother in almost all my books; on the contrary, until these last few years, the father for me was taboo. I couldn't say why. To be sure, psychoanalysis could explain everything, saying that for me the mother is a problem and the father isn't: but what good would that do? In reality, the aesthetic result at the same moment when it achieves its fullness also annuls any explanation. Let's say then simply that in my work the figure of the mother is frequent, and that of the father is rare.

To go back to what we were saying before, that for you sex is a key, I feel that the family is a key, too. But there isn't much said about Moravia, novelist of the family.

The family is the chief subject of all Western literature: from Aeschylus on it's hard to find a writer who doesn't concern himself with the family. In this sense, I am commonplace and normal.

Why is literature so concerned with the family?

Because the family unit is the microcosm that, as they say, reflects the macrocosm. Where everything that is individual and private is forced by the nature of the family institution to cohabit with what is social and public. Cohabiting, of course, doesn't mean being in agreement; quite the contrary. On the other hand, nature makes sure that within the family it is easy to achieve the maximum of vital tension, the tragedy. Now, in my opinion, tragedy is the highest expression of literature.

What is Il viaggio a Roma *about?*

Il viaggio a Roma, which was published in 1988, tells a fable as old as the world, that of the son seeking his father, a "telemachy," in other words. I'd like to say here that all novelists and all dramatists set out telling fables, but these fables, as art demands, are driven to the extreme consequences and are inevitably in touch with the culture of the period.

What do you mean?

I'll give you a supreme example. Shakespeare tells fables that he finds in Plutarch, in Italian novellas, and so on, but as you delve into them you can only encounter the culture of the period, namely, Montaigne and generally the philosophy of the Renaissance. Now, I have told many fables in my writing, and exploring the depths of a story, I have also encountered the culture of the time, Marx, Freud, Nietzsche, Heidegger, and so forth. In the case of *Il viaggio a Roma*, precisely because I had somehow to explain the search for the father, I ended up writing a novel whose core is a perfect Freudian primal scene. But when I wrote the novel I wasn't thinking about Freud and I didn't want to be Freudian. I wanted to tell a story. In any case, the protagonist finally psychoanalyzes himself and cures himself unaided of what has to be called an Oedipus complex. In this sense it can be said that he is one of my most positive characters, but the positive aspect is Freudian, according to the idea that the roots of our psyche are to be sought in our childhood.

Yours, too, then.

Everybody's, including mine; but it is also true that these roots don't matter in artistic work except in a subordinate and not determinant way; otherwise you could end up saying that Leopardi's pessimism was determined by the fact that he had a hunchback, as I said before. If anything, the opposite is true, namely, that poetic inspiration abolishes all determination. You can't write except in complete detachment, complete freedom.

In your latest novel, Il viaggio a Roma, *and in a long story recently published,* "Il vassoio davanti alla porta," *the theme of the adolescent returns, the theme you dealt with in* Agostino *and in* La disubbedienza. *The creative results suggest that this is a very happy subject in your fiction, since these are among your best works. Do you agree?*

Yes, in a sense I agree, but you have to remember one thing: in general the heroes of fiction are always young or very young, except for King Lear, Don Quixote, and a few others. Achilles, Hamlet, and many other protagonists shouldn't be over twenty. The reason is simple and clear: the young man unites the maximum of passionate vitality with the maximum of idealism. Then there was a kind of revolution, beginning in the nineteenth century, whereby the narrator attributed a special importance to what I would call the initiation of the adolescent, and the average age of protagonists was lowered. In this sense my four novels of adolescence are four novels of initiation.

Can it be said that your fiction, from 1934 to La donna leop-ardo, *which you are currently writing, has new characteristics?*

I believe I haven't changed much since *Gli indifferenti*. Perhaps the writing has become increasingly spare, less magmatic; but the themes I deal with have remained substantially the same.

Why has your writing become so spare?

Probably because I have become more intellectualistic. In short, as the years pass, on the one hand many taboos fall away, many unconscious defenses, and on the other, consequently, there is a new impulse not to abuse the achieved freedom.

We haven't talked about your translations. Do you have clear memories of some translators?

Especially in the two foreign languages I speak, English and French. In France, René de Ceccatty and Martine Bauer. For the English-speaking countries, Angus Davidson, Ray Rosenthal, and lately, William Weaver, a friend and a truly considerable Italianist.

These years, the eighties, have been years of political commit-ment for you. You have been involved in the antinuclear struggle and have been a deputy to the Parliament of Europe. Will you talk about this?

Political commitment wasn't something new for me. On the con-trary, it may even have been greater in earlier years, as you can see from a novel like *La vita interiore*. I would say rather that the eighties, with the end of student protest and terrorism, have coin-cided with a certain lessening of my interest in politics. In fact, the novels I've written in this period have nothing political about them, except *L'uomo che guarda*, which in a certain way actually describes the death throes of political commitment. As for the European Par-liament, who ever said that parliaments mean being politically en-gaged? Parliaments are institutions meant to legislate, and politics, if it enters there, appears as party relationships. The European Parlia-ment, moreover, is the least political you can imagine, because it doesn't even have the power to make laws. The European Parliament, in reality, is concerned with economic questions. And the fact that it has no powers means that the ambitious, who often constitute the best in the political world, keep well away from it. Naturally, power, in all fields, belongs to him who wants it and aims to seize it; but this isn't the case with the European Parliament, which is fundamentally a timid institution. On the other hand, like all institutions, the European Parliament can give the impression of being useless, but that isn't the case. The day could come in which it will fill a gap, will prove not only useful but necessary.

Tell me about your personal experience there.

My personal experience is this. I had taken the antinuclear campaign very seriously. In 1984, after having twice refused to accept nomination as honorary senator in Italy, I thought that the European Parliament would offer a forum with a wider audience than the Italian Parliament, a place where I could speak out against atomic weapons. So I accepted the invitation of the Communist Party to stand as candidate for the group of the independent Left. I didn't campaign at all. I simply granted some interviews, including one with myself for the *Corriere della sera*, and I was elected with 260,000 votes. So I became a deputy and for five years I attended the Parliament in Strasbourg. I can't say that I was disappointed, because through long-standing habit when I do something, I have no illusions; I just do it, and that's that. I must admit, however, that the whole atmosphere of the European Parliament, very Nordic and very bourgeois, was not the most favorable for my antiatomic proposals. You must also consider the real procedural difficulty, not to mention the "three-minute limit" on speeches.

You said that your interest in atomic problems dates back to your visit to Hiroshima. Isn't that so?

Yes, as we said before. The only thing I'd like to add is this: for governments atomic war is like the scalpel for a surgeon. A means, that is, of solving questions that have remained insoluble at the level of persuasion. Now, as I gradually grew more and more concerned with the atomic bomb, I became aware that neither governments nor those dependent on them can be sincerely pacifist, because otherwise they would contradict themselves. Propaganda against the atomic bomb must be carried out, on the other hand, at a mass level, to create awareness and hence dissent. I wrote many articles against the atomic bomb, and I was finally elected deputy on a specifically antinuclear platform. Well, I had the constant impression that my articles in the papers and my appearances on television were more useful than my speeches to the European Parliament. For the European Parliament, however indirectly, deals with governments.

Do you have any personal memories of those years of the European Parliament?

Yes, I remember the visit of Ronald Reagan. On that occasion it was evident that, as I said, the European Parliament filled a gap, it demonstrated a real usefulness: Reagan, instead of addressing the Parliament of one of the many European countries, spoke in a Parliament that represented Europe. His reputation as a great communicator was confirmed. Taller than the officials surrounding him, he spoke unperturbed, despite the roars from the Left. In reality, thanks to a device invisible to all but himself, he read a text on an unseen screen. But on that occasion we saw why I said that the European Parliament is timid, and it represents a Europe also timid. The parliamentarians were divided into two big factions, for or against Reagan, that is, for or against America, but it can't be said that this was a point of view truly and solely European: as often happens in international politics, Europe was in hiding. This is a singular fact, which demonstrates if nothing else that Europe still has to be made, and perhaps it never will be made, in the sense of a unified and independent organism.

Why not?

The reason can be briefly stated, in these terms: organisms die of what they have lived on. Europe has lived on nationalisms, once its distinctive glory; now it could die of them.

It's still an extraordinary change, to think that nations that have always warred against each other now sit in the same Parliament.

Yes, this is true. Still, you have to remember one thing — that Europe is late with respect to the United States and the Soviet Union. If you go to New York, in the subway you will see members of every race in the world.

So in the States, as in the Soviet Union, racism can be a private matter, but never governmental or, worse still, social. Europe, precisely because of its nationalist tradition, is unprepared to create multinational societies of the American or Soviet kind. Now this, in twenty years or so, or even earlier, will be the problem that Europe will have to solve: a problem that has been partly resolved in the United States and in the Soviet Union. In Europe, in other words, the racial thrust of the Third World at least for the present seems to have no other solution but the creation of ghettos on the outskirts of the big cities. Certainly in France, Germany, England, and even in Italy, there are many people of color, but we are still in the first phase, the one that sees the nationals give up certain humiliating jobs and leave them to the people of the Third World.

Since you left the Parliament of Europe last spring, many things have changed. There has been the collapse of the Communist empire in Europe. What do you think of this?

Events in the Soviet Union and in Eastern Europe can be read in two ways: either as an overall victory of the West, which sees the East accept its values, or as a strengthening of the Communist empire, a strengthening provoked by Gorbachev and perestroika and comparable to the strengthening of a tree that in spring is pruned, its dry, useless branches lopped off. In fact, in a not too distant future I wouldn't exclude the possibility of a renewal, if not of the Cold War, at least of the historical rivalry for world hegemony between the United States and the Soviet Union. But this is already a prophecy, and I don't believe in prophets.

Have you met Gorbachev?

Yes, in the name of the association Archivio per il Disarmo, I presented him with a so-called golden dove for peace, not long ago at the Soviet embassy in Rome.

What sort of political man is he, do you think?

For the Soviet Union he has the same importance as Peter the Great, as well as the same meaning. Russia obeys a pendular movement, sometimes swinging toward the East and Asia, then toward the West and Europe. Stalin represented the movement toward the East and Asia; Gorbachev, like Peter the Great, represents the movement toward Europe and the West. As for what sort of man Gorbachev is, I can only repeat what I said in presenting him with the dove of peace, "I consider you a political man of imagination and genius." As I was speaking, I looked at him carefully; his face is actually quite singular. The eyes didn't have a definable expression. They seemed alert. The mouth, when he was serious, seemed small, with folds at the two ends, perhaps of contempt. But it became broad and cordial, even good-natured, a peasant good nature, every time he smiled.

This seems the right moment to talk about old age.

All right, let's talk about it, even though it's a subject I don't consider very interesting. Old age is a fatal disease. It isn't a question of years, but of infirmities. In this sense I don't consider myself an old man, or at least I don't "feel" an old man. The only infirmity from which I suffer greatly is having one leg weaker than the other, but I was like this when I was twelve. If anything, I seem to understand that old age could mean unlearning what one has learned during a whole life: how to live. Probably the old man unlearns how to live because he is bored with living and it seems to him that it's not worth the trouble. Between unlearning how to live and living less and less the space is brief, and death at a certain moment can also seem more attractive than life. But it is hard, at least for me, to establish at what moment old age begins, since my boredom with life began very early, like the infirmity of my leg, in other words, before I was living real life. In the end you have to admit that you're old when you start considering yourself old. Does that moment arrive? I would say sometimes it never arrives, with effects that can be both admirable and comic.

But you have always spent your time with people much younger than you, and further, you've married a woman almost half a century younger. How do you feel in their midst?

It's the confirmation of what I said, that we're not old insofar as we manage not to consider ourselves old. In my case, I think that with my vitality I manage to do what many black men do: they make you forget the color of their skin, and I, my age. Naturally, it's a matter of making others forget, not of abolishing. Anyway, I spend my time with young people because they want to be with me. The same can be said of my wife. To conclude, I have never sought out anyone, women or men. With a bit of presumption, but without vanity, I could say that success is always young.

It could be said that your success has grown very much in recent years. I think for example of your popularity in France, where they actually consider you a French writer.

The only thing I can say in reply is that nothing succeeds like success. Probably the only real success to which a writer can aspire is that of being respected and admired by fellow writers: they are the only ones who know for certain if you are a good writer or not. All the others, critics included, are unable to separate the success of the writer from that of the public figure.

What do you mean when you say you experienced boredom with life before you lived it?

It is a form of anguish that, with me, is congenital and that, in my books, at one time or another, I have called boredom, despair, lack of contact with reality, incapability of acting, and so on. I say "congenital" because I remember having suffered this anguish also as a child, when literally, as I said, I had had no experience of life. Probably this so-called boredom is the obverse of a sensitivity that is excessive and therefore easily disappointed.

Would this boredom be what the Germans call Lebenschmerz or Weltschmerz?

Yes and no. This may be presumption, but my boredom is an original boredom, and for a definition of it I refer you to the introductory part of my novel *La noia*. In my opinion, the philosopher who has spoken of a boredom similar to mine is Arthur Schopenhauer. Now *Lebenschmerz* and *Weltschmerz*, I think, have a sentimental character, which the boredom I suffer from has never had.

You are accustomed not to let yourself be carried away by your feelings. Why?

I could answer with the well-known words of Buffon, "Le style c'est l'homme," but reversing them, "The man is the style." Or rather, the complex of expressions that he succeeds in giving to his own feelings. In short, I am opposed to a style that gives a partial and distorted idea of my feelings.

Could you stop intellectualizing all your answers for a moment? You, too, must have your moments of weakness, don't you?

I have plenty of moments of weakness, perhaps more than those people who display them; but I don't see why this sort of thing has to take place in company. In my relationship with others there are no moments of weakness: there is the relationship.

Then in your life neither trust nor abandon exists?

They certainly do! But they are feelings that require a form; otherwise, they are absolutely nothing. To grasp their presence perhaps it's best to forget words, which are after all thoughts, and look at the facial expression, the tones of the voice, gestures and attitudes, everything that has to do with the unconscious. Of course, also with words you can show trust and abandon, but it will always be less direct.

What do you think of feelings?

I've already tried to explain it to you. I think that without feelings it's impossible to have any relationship with others, with reality. Feelings are the foundation of everything, the guarantee of the authenticity of the relationship.

When you finish a book, before sending it to the publisher, do you show it to someone?

No, I never have anyone read anything.

Why not? You said the best judgment is that of fellow writers.

For the same reason that I never ask advice if I have to act in one way or another.

Doesn't it seem a bit presumptuous to you?

I tried it, especially at the beginning, and it was disappointing. Probably there have been instances, for example, Ezra Pound and T. S. Eliot, where what you might call prenatal reading was useful. But frankly, it's as if a mother went around asking if the child she's about to bring into the world will have blue eyes or black.

Have you always been afraid of flattery?

It's the thing that frightens me most in the world. Obviously, there is a shameless flattering that can be identified at once, but there are also subtle forms that at first we are unable to resist. Flattery is really the most dangerous thing for an artist, also because the artist, thanks to a comprehensible weakness, tends often to flatter himself. The opposite situation, considering himself a failure, is preferable, but it, too, is no help in making him understand that really it's impossible to judge yourself; therefore we have to say stoically, with Picasso, "The work has to go well perforce."

Does old age seem a happy season to you?

I think the most unhappy age is youth, but youth tolerates, or rather ignores, solitude better than old age. When you're young it's easy to be alone, and anyway, loneliness is a challenge to be faced.

Namely?

The youth knows instinctively that the fact of not being alone depends entirely on himself. The old man knows, on the contrary, through experience, that it depends on others.

And death?

I think often of old age because, practically, it is my immediate future, if not actually my present. Of death I don't think at all, and if I do think of it, I think of it theoretically, so to speak, as the end of the temporary and senseless chaos of life. Thinking means finally feeling, however, and I simply don't feel death. Indeed, I have formed a fairly precise idea of what death is today, having been in danger of death a couple of times not so long ago. I seem to understand that either you die of a so-called stroke with a maximum rapidity and a minimum of suffering, or else you die stupefied, overcome and destroyed by a great quantity of all kinds of drugs with which modern medicine tries to delay death, thus making it simply a passage from the unconsciousness caused by the medicine to the unconsciousness caused by decease. In short, either you die suddenly or you aren't really aware of your dying. If anything, it could be said that in real old age, full of ailments and impotence, death must seem a liberation, but I obviously have not reached that point.

There's another observation to be made. Medieval works of art, both in painting and literature, speak very much of death. Today the opposite happens. The theme of death has vanished both from literature and from painting. Why is this? Because, in my opinion, in the Middle Ages they loved life much more than we love it, and this was because the duration of life in general was brief, around thirty years: mankind feared death and in fact spoke of it with terror. Today life lasts beyond seventy years, and further, there is a distressing discrepancy between the length of life and the capacity for living it to the full. Rather than live, a person survives longer than in the past. Perhaps this is the reason why people don't seem to be afraid of death and, I think, often desire it. To conclude the talk about death, I'd like to recall my joking (but not all that much) answer to the usual question, "What do you think of death?" My answer was, "If we truly paid attention we'd never die." From this remark you can sense that I think death is a mistake, an accident, perhaps avoidable though attention. It's an optimistic idea, you'll say. My reply is, "No, it is a nonidea that shows that until today I have never thought seriously about death."

Do you pay great attention?

No, not much. In fact, as little as possible.

What effect did the death of of Elsa Morante have on you, in 1984?

The same effect as the death of Pasolini. Both died a horrible death, undeserved, unjust, and decidedly unlucky. I said before that Pasolini's death has no precedents among the deaths of illustrious men in all our past. Elsa's death was not dreadful in the sense of involving criminal violence, but it was, all the same, very cruel: in reality, with ups and downs, Elsa took two years and eight months to die. What struck me most deeply in Elsa's death was that she desired to die with all the strength of her spirit, but at the same time she desired to live with her better part. In fact, a short time before dying, she told me that she had in mind a complete and very beautiful novel. Her death still resembles mysteriously her life, and so also does Pasolini's. This is something I cannot explain, which I consider unjust and against which I rebel. I think that death should not resemble life in the sense of being its negative result. It should be the end of life, nothing more than that, an end if possible not painful and, above all, normal.

How did you react to Elsa's death?

I learned of Elsa's death in Germany, in Bonn, where I was traveling for a newspaper article. It was in the dead of winter; it had snowed a great deal. I learned of her death by telephone in the hotel. Then I went out; I walked for a long time in the snow. I was moved and I tried to dispel my emotion with the chill of the winter day, but a death doesn't have just one aspect, it has many, and for this reason the death of a person, even the most humble, requires a series of ceremonies and rituals. So, that inarticulate emotion that struck me on learning the news of Elsa's death was followed by other impressions. I returned to Rome in time for the funeral; I went to see the body on view in the coffin. Elsa's face in the last years had been transformed by a somewhat grim old age. With death, it had regained an almost childish aspect, serene, perhaps smiling. With Carmen I went to the mass in the church of Santa Maria del Popolo; then we came out, got into the car, and headed for our house. Now, the hearse had to go to the cemetery of Prima Porta and the crematorium there, so it took the same direction I did, and began driving alongside my car. It was laden with wreaths, including mine and Carmen's. As it sped along, the flowers, probably carelessly fastened to the wreath, began to fly off, one after the other, and flatten on the asphalt: those flowers falling between Elsa's bier and my car made a wild, symbolic impression on me: that Elsa had flown away from my life. The last part of Elsa's death was the cremation. I went the next day to the cemetery and sat in the sun facing the crematorium, waiting for everything to be over. The crematorium is a strange building, very modern and very hermetic, not suggesting any idea of death. By chance, in that area of the cemetery there are no crosses, there is nothing to remind you that you're in a cemetery. Beyond the outer wall, I could see a Roman farm and some cows grazing on the hills. So my last impression was that Elsa had faded into the air, on a sunny day. An impression, all things considered, in harmony with Elsa's special spirituality.

Some of our most important writers have died during these past few years. Do you think there are writers worthy of taking their place?

Elsa Morante, Tommaso Landolfi, Pier Paolo Pasolini, Carlo Emilio Gadda, Italo Calvino, to mention only the most important, had the structure and probably also the ambitions of the so-called great writer. I've already said what I think a great writer is. Not necessarily the best writer, but certainly the one who manages to embody in his works a greater quantity of realities. In this sense, I wouldn't say that, at least for the present, there are great writers. On the other hand, however, it must be acknowledged that the present moment is not favorable to the human and cultural figure of the great writer. We live in an epoch of unparallelled prosperity, and we can't honestly expect this prosperity to represent a problem or something actually to be rejected. The typical great writer, if there is such a person, has not only literary ambitions but also representative, perhaps revolutionary ones; for the present, at least, it doesn't seem to me that the historical situation favors this kind of ambition. In compensation, the writers of younger generations seem more confident and more artful on the formal level than those of my generation were. I won't name names because there are so many, and all of them more or less in the phase of developing. In this respect the situation of fiction is better in Italy than in France or England. It can be compared to that of the United States.

Does this explain the success of Italian fiction abroad these last years?

Yes, in a way the moment of Italian fiction has come. I say "the moment has come" because even today this success is not yet consolidated the way that, for instance, the success of our fashion designers or our architects has been established definitively. For the present there is the recognition that Italian fiction is not inferior to any other. But this is not yet enough: we live in a global world, and all literatures now seem to be entitled to that recognition. What we still don't know is whether Italian fiction, beyond its present success, will manage to create models.

We've talked about you from your infancy to today. If you had to draw up a balance sheet of your life, what would you say?

For me, one life is much the same as another; at the level of sensitivity and in conditions of good health, there is less injustice than people believe. There are perhaps some favored people, but not those who occupy a high place in society, who have wealth, power, and so on. In my opinion, the favored are those who enjoy the privileges of having a creative or a critical relationship with art. I say this because, despite a long life full of difficulties of every sort, finally I consider myself privileged because I'm an artist; and at the same time I feel a sincere compassion for those who aren't. From this point of view I think the balance of my life has been positive. As for the products of this sensitivity of mine, I can say only that I have tried to do my best. Today's readers and, even more, tomorrow's will judge if my best was only the worst of others.

Do you regret not having done certain things, not having had certain experiences?

No, I don't regret anything, because, as I said, one life is worth much the same as another, and also because all lives, basically, can be called misguided. Life is a perfect chaos from which you can extract only some fragment, however mysterious, of order.

How do you imagine the world of the future?

My ideas are optimistic. Until yesterday men carried swords, wore wigs, traveled on horseback. In my view, mankind has just emerged from childhood and is in adolescence. Its future is that of science and the technological applications that could also transform the world completely. But it is also true that adolescence is a period of profound crisis and that the world could perish before reaching adulthood.

But hasn't the end of the world already begun, with the ecological disaster?

The ecological disaster perhaps can yet be stopped and evaded by that same technology that indicates man's definitive dominion over nature. Until yesterday the dominant idea of the relationship between man and nature was that man could draw freely and without limit on natural capital. Today this isn't possible; we've discovered that nature's resources are limited, and the terrifying aspect of this discovery is that it has taken place within a very few years. In a little more than two decades the fauna, the flora, the water of the planet have revealed a limit of exploitation, and it has often been seen that this limit has already been surpassed. There is something unspeakably dire about the idea that the ozone layer has been rent in several places, that the great forests of Latin America and Africa are destined to disappear, that rivers and seas can die, or are, indeed, already dead. The only consolation in this terrible discovery is that it corresponds, as we have already said, to the technology's domination of nature. Now, this dominion, instead of being negative, tomorrow could be positive in such a way as to reverse the race toward the end of the world. If this doesn't happen, to be sure, unlike what Ecclesiastes says in the Bible, we will be forced to see something absolutely new under the sun, something catastrophic that outstrips any imagining. Naturally, like atomic war, this new thing must be avoided. The one way to avoid it is becoming aware of it.

Assuming that the catastrophe can be avoided, what will the life and society of tomorrow be like?

I believe that science will occupy an increasingly big place in human life. I say this because if you look at the general state of things in the world, you have to grant that the only human activity that has shown undeniable progress is science, along with its technological applications. Now, what strikes me is the mysterious and probably significant contrast between the vertiginous progress of science and the equally vertiginous degradation of nature. Everything has a significance, perhaps senseless. What is the true significance of this contrast? Perhaps it isn't a contrast at all, but something logical: knowledge would lead to death.

To sum up, how should the young of today be prepared for their future life?

It's hard to answer. The fact that often their response consists in using drugs tells us that the younger generations could simply turn their back on the truth. I hope this doesn't happen and that a new relationship between knowledge and life can be found.

In what sense?

In the sense that knowledge will serve not death but life.

With this sentence do you consider the book on your life finished?

Yes.

Glossary of Names

ALBERTI, LEON BATTISTA (1404–72). Renaissance writer, humanist architect. Author of *De re aedificatoria*.

ALICATA, MARIO (1918–66). Communist leader and newspaper editor. Arrested in 1942 for engaging in underground activities while a press attaché for the Garibaldi Brigade and chief editor of *L'unità*. Member of the Communist Party central committee, the Rome City Council, and the Naples City Council, where he was director of *La voce*. Elected several times to the Chamber of Deputies from the Naples-Caserta region. Director of the National Cultural Commission of the Italian Communist Party and member of the party's nine-man directorate from 1955 until his death.

ALVARO, CORRADO (1895–1956). Poet, novelist, and journalist. Born in Santa Lucia in Calabria. Began literary career in northern Italy after fighting in World War I. Critic for the *Corriere della sera*, *La stampa*, Benedetto Croce's anti-Fascist newsletter *Mondo*, and Bontempelli's *900*. Alvaro's chief novel is *Gente in Aspromonte*.

ANGIOLETTI, GIOVANNI BATTISTA (1896–1961). Novelist and journalist. Born in Milan. Director of L'Instituto di Cultura Italiana in Prague, and professor of Italian literature in Digione, Besançon, and Paris. After returning to Italy at the end of World War II, Angioletti became editor (with Curzio Malaparte) of *Fiera letteraria*.

ARBASINO, ALBERTO (1930–). Novelist, journalist, and critic. Born in Voghera. After completing studies in languages and literature, embarked on a varied course of study, including the natural sciences, political science, and law. Contributed to literary reviews such as *Paragone* and *Il mondo* and wrote for the *Corriere della sera* and *La repubblica*.

BALBO, ITALO (1896–1940). Soldier and political figure. Born in Quartesana. Served in Italian army during World War I. Helped Mussolini seize control of the government, participating in the March on Rome in 1922. High-ranking official in the Black Shirt Militia, the Air Fleet, and the Air Ministry. Appointed governor of Libya.

BALDINI, ANTONIO (1889–1962). Novelist and critic. Born in Rome. Served in World War I. One of the founding members of *La ronda* (1920–22). Contributed to *La voce* and *Lirica* in the 1910s. His novels include *Salti di gomitolo* (1920), *Buoni incontri d'Italia* (1941), and *Rugatino* (1942). Father of Gabriele Baldini (1919–69), critic, translator, professor of English literature, and second husband of Natalia Ginzburg.

BARILLI, BRUNO (1880–1952). Journalist, novelist, and composer. Born in Fano. Obtained a degree in musical composition in Munich, but his career as a composer ended after the completion of two operas. His principal career was as a literary and music critic for Italy's major daily newspapers.

BARTOLINI, LUIGI (1892–1963). Painter, engraver, art critic, and writer. Born in Cupramontana, near Ancona. Made his debut at the Mostra Nazionale dei Grigioverdi in Naples in 1921. Considered to be one of Italy's best engravers along with Giorgio Morandi. Extensively exhibited in Italy and abroad throughout his career.

BASSANI, GIORGIO (1916–2000). Novelist and literary critic. Born in Bologna but recognized as the writer of Ferrara, the city that fed the imagination of many of his novels, which reflect the situation of the Italian Jewish population during Fascism and in the postwar period. Editor of Marguerite Caetani's review, *Botteghe oscure*. Author of *The Garden of the Finzi-Continis* (1962) and other fiction.

BAZLEN, BOBI (1902–65). Editor, critic, and translator. Born in Trieste. A seminal scout and editor for several publishing houses, including Adelphi and Einaudi. Met his contemporaries Umberto Saba and Italo Svevo in Trieste before World War II. Introduced Svevo's *Coscienza di Zeno* to Eugenio Montale, whose glowing review of the book helped launch Svevo's fame. Bazlen was crucial in introducing the culture of middle Europe to the Italian reading public.

BELLEZZA, DARIO (1944–96). Poet, dramatist, and novelist. Awarded the Viareggio Prize in 1976 for his plays. Pier Paolo Pasolini, his mentor, once called Bellezza "the best poet of the new generation."

BERENSON, BERNARD (1865–1959). Art critic and memorialist. Born near Vilnius, Lithuania. Grew up in Boston, educated at Harvard. Considered the world's foremost expert on Italian Renaissance art. Settled at Settignano, near Florence, in the Villa I Tatti, now Harvard's Center for Renaissance Studies.

BERTO, GIUSEPPE (1914–78). Novelist and screenwriter. Born in Magliano Veneto. Served in the Abyssinian War and the North African campaign before he was captured by the Allies and imprisoned at a camp in Texas. One of his first novels, *Il cielo è rosso*, was published upon his return to Italy in 1946 and established his reputation as a writer of the neorealist tradition.

BERTOLUCCI, BERNARDO (1940–). Film director and poet. Born in Parma. Assistant to Pasolini on *Accattone*. His first American art house hit *was Il conformista* (1971), awarded an Academy Award for Best Screenplay. Later directed the controversial international success *Last Tango in Paris* (1972).

BETTI, LAURA (1934–). Actress, singer, and writer. Born in Bologna. Director of the Associazione Fondo Pier Paolo Pasolini. Awarded the Coppa Volpi Award at the Venice Film Festival in 1968 for her performance in Pasolini's film *Teorema* (1969). Collaborator and close friend of Pier Paolo Pasolini, whose posthumous publications she supervised.

BONTEMPELLI, MASSIMO (1878–1960). Journalist, editor, novelist, playwright, and critic. Born in Turin. Founded 900 in 1926 with Curzio Malaparte. Also founded the literary journal *Quadrante* in 1933. Contributed to other Florentine publications such *as Il marzocco* and *La nazione*. Completed several biographical studies of Scarlatti, Verdi, Verga, Leopardi, and Pirandello. His most successful play is titled *La nostra Dea* (1925).

BORGESE, GIUSEPPE ANTONIO (1881–1952). Novelist, poet, critic, and translator. Born in Palermo. Contributed to several literary reviews, such as *Il regno* and *Leonardo*. Founded the journal *Hermes*. Assisted many young, promising Italian authors in establishing their careers, including Moravia. Married to Elisabeth Mann, daughter of the novelist Thomas Mann. Active participant in the anti-Fascist movement.

BRANCATI, VITALIANO (1907–54). Sicilian novelist, essayist, playwright, and screenwriter. Born in Pachino, near Syracuse. Brancati's first writings show interest in the Fascist movement, but this fascination disappeared when he moved to Rome and encountered Giuseppe Antonio Borgese and other anti-Fascists.

BUZZATI, DINO (1916–72). Journalist, playwright, and novelist. Born in Belluno. After establishing his reputation as a skilled journalist, embarked on a literary career that would include dozens of novels in a number of different styles and genres. Awarded the Premio Strega in 1958 for his collection *Sessanta rac-*

conti. His novel *Il deserto dei Tartari* (1940) was considered cryptically anti-Fascist.

CAETANI, MARGUERITE (1880–1963). American-born arts patron and editor. Born Marguerite Chapin; married Roffredo Caetani, Prince of Bassiano and later seventeenth Duke of Sermoneta, in 1911. In 1924 founded in Paris the review *Commerce*, which had an international scope. Founder and editor, in postwar Rome, of *Botteghe oscure*, a multilingual review that published eminent and promising writers such as Ignazio Silone, e. e. cummings, Albert Camus, Paul Valéry, and Robert Graves.

CAFFI, ANDREA (1866–1955). Political theorist and activist, and novelist. Took part in the avant-garde artistic movement as well as socialist activity in Paris at the beginning of the century. Friends with Carlo Rosselli, Malraux, Camus, and Salvemini.

CALVINO, ITALO (1923–85). Novelist. One of Italy's most highly acclaimed writers of the twentieth century. Born to Italian parents in Santiago de Las Vegas in Cuba. Spent his childhood in Liguria, later participating in the partisan movement there. Worked on the editorial staff of Einaudi publishing house in Turin, where he met Cesare Pavese and Elio Vittorini. Founded the review *Il menabò* in 1959 with Vittorini. His fiction was widely translated and admired.

CAPOGROSSI, GIUSEPPE (1900–1972). Painter. Born in Rome. Served in World War I. First exhibited his paintings in a show with his contemporaries Emanuele Cavalli and Francesco Di Cocco at the Hotel Dinesen in 1927. Included in the XVII Esposizione Biennale Internazionale D'Arte in Venice in 1930. Recognized as one of the leading artists in the revival of Roman painting.

CARDARELLI, VINCENZO (1887–1959). Poet, novelist, and editor. Born in Corneto Tarquinio. Critic for *Il marzocco, La voce,* and *Lirica.* Founded the review *La ronda* together with Riccardo

Bacchelli, Emilio Cecchi, and others in 1919. Editor of *Fiera letteraria*, a weekly literary review, between 1949 and 1955.

CARDUCCI, GIOSUÈ (1835–1907). Poet, critic, and scholar. Born in Bolgheri, south of Livorno. Considered Italy's most important poet of the second half of the nineteenth century. Professor of Italian literature at the University of Bologna from 1860 until his death. Awarded the Nobel Prize in 1906.

CAROCCI, ALBERTO (1904–72). Lawyer, critic, and journalist. Born in Florence. Important figure in the Communist Party. Took part in the flourishing, prewar literary scene in Florence, specifically as the founder of *Solaria* in 1926. Editor of several literary reviews, including *Riforma letteraria* and *Nuovi Argomenti* with Alberto Moravia and Pier Paolo Pasolini.

CASSOLA, CARLO (1917–87). Novelist, journalist, and critic. Roman-born Tuscan writer. His experience in the Resistance formed the basis of many of his novels. Member of the Partito d'Azione, an anti-Fascist coalition. Produced a number of novels and short stories, moving from a more hermetic style to one of political responsibility.

CASTELLANI, RENATO (1913–85). Screenwriter and film director. Born in Finale Ligure. In the late 1930s, wrote screenplays for Soldati, Camerini, and Blasetti. Films he directed include *Sotto il sole di Roma* (1948), *È primavera* (1949), and *Due soldi di speranza* (1952). Wrote for Italian television later in life.

CAVOUR, CAMILLO BENSO, CONTE DI (1810–61). Statesman. Born in Turin (then part of the Kingdom of Sardinia). In 1847, helped to found the newspaper *Il risorgimento*, a nationalist journal that advocated the expulsion of the Austrians from Sardinia and unification of Italy under a Sardinian constitutional monarchy. Prime minister of the Kingdom of Sardinia in 1852. Major actor in the unification of Italy in 1870.

CECCHI, EMILIO (1884–1966). Influential journalist, literary critic, art critic, and translator. Born in Florence. Wrote for *La voce, Il marzocco, Leonardo,* and *La tribuna* in Rome. Participated as one of the founding members of the literary group *La ronda.* Wrote for the *Corriere della sera* from 1927 until late in life. His *America amara* (1939) records his stay in New York City before World War II.

CERAMI, VINCENZO (1940–). Screenwriter, dramatist, and novelist. Collaborated with Roberto Benigni on several screenplays including *Johnny Stecchino* (1991), *Il mostro* (1994), and *La vita è bella* (1997). His novels include *L'ipocrita* (1991) and *Un borghese piccolo piccolo* (1995).

CHIAROMONTE, NICOLA (1905–72). Critic, editor, political activist, and writer. Born in Rapolla, near Potenza. Outspoken anti-Fascist, then blacklisted. Published work in the Reviews *Il mondo, Coscientia, Solaria,* and literary and film reviews in *Fiera letteraria.* Collaboration with the activist group Giustizia e Libertà prompted his move to Paris in 1934 to flee Fascist authorities. Fought in Spanish Civil War as a pilot in the squadron commanded by André Malraux. Coedited *Tempo presente* with Ignazio Silone from 1956 to 1968. Frequent contributor to *Partisan Review* and *Dissent.*

CIANO, GALEAZZO COUNT (1903–44). Marriage to Edda Mussolini, the dictator's daughter, helped gain him promotion to Foreign Minister in 1936, in which capacity he signed the Pact of Steel with Germany in May 1939. He gradually fell out of favor with Benito Mussolini and resigned from his post in February 1943. Remained a member of the Fascist Grand Council and voted for Mussolini's removal on July 25, 1943. The following month, Ciano was imprisoned and later executed by the German firing squad.

CITATI, PIETRO (1930–). Novelist, journalist, translator, and influential critic. Born in Florence. Contributor to *Il giorno* and the *Corriere della sera.* One of his principal works is the novel *Goethe* (1970).

COLOMBO, FURIO (1931–). Journalist, political scientist, and television writer. Born in Chatillon. Awarded the Premio Tevere for literature in 1987 for *Cosa farò da grande*, the Premio Amalfi for television writing in 1988, and the Premio Capri for journalism in the same year. Has written for *La stampa* since 1972. Visiting professor of political science at several universities, including Yale University and New York University. Member of the executive committee of the International Scholarly Exchange Center at Columbia University. Coauthored *Il nuovo medioevo* (1972) with Umberto Eco.

CONTINI, GIANFRANCO (1912–90). Scholar, linguist, and critic. Born in Domodossola. Professor of philology in universities in Germany, Switzerland, and Italy. Respected for studies of thirteenth- and fourteenth-century Italian poets, especially Dante and Petrarch.

CREMONINI, LEONARDO RAFAELLO (1925–). Visual artist. Born in Bologna. Began studying art in Bologna in 1940 under the guidance of Guglielmo Pizzirani. An early success in 1952 at the Catherine Viviano Gallery in New York City launched his reputation in America. Awarded the Manotto prize in 1967. Many modern authors have written about his work, including Moravia in the catalog to a 1972 exhibit at the Galleria Gabbiano in Rome.

CROCE, BENEDETTO (1866–1952). Philosopher and scholar. Born in Pescasseroli in Abruzzo. Famous for his reinterpretation of Hegel and Marx as an opposing ideology to the Fascist movement. Founder of the journal *La critica*, which he used as a personal forum for his opinions. Author of a great number of works. His teaching heavily influenced many intellectuals of the first half of the twentieth century. His quiet but firm opposition to the Fascist regime also had a profound influence on his younger contemporaries.

D'ANNUNZIO, GABRIELE (1863–1938). One of the most influential and prolific writers in the Italian tradition. Born in Pescara. Wrote in many genres; his poetry, like his personality, was characterized by decadentism. Fought in World War I and was heavily involved in the politics of his times; an early supporter of Mussolini.

DEBENEDETTI, GIACOMO (1901–67). Journalist and critic. Born in Biella. Along with Romano Bilenchi, was an important writer in the neorealist movement. Noted for his portrayal of the situation of the Jewish people in Italy during World War II, particularly of the ghettoization of Roman Jews by Nazi soldiers. Also an influential critic.

DE CHIRICO, GIORGIO (1888–1978). Painter. Born in Vólos, Greece. Famous for his paintings of deserted cityscapes such as *Enigma of an Autumn Night* (1910). Founded the magazine *Pittura metafisica* together with futurist painter Carlo Carrà in 1920. Influenced surrealists such as Yves Tanguy and Salvador Dalí.

DE FEO, SANDRO (1905–). Screenwriter and journalist. Born in Modugno. Cowrote several films, including *La provinciâle* in 1953.

DE GASPERI, ALCIDE (1881–1954). Political leader. Born in Terino, South Tyrol. Opposed to communism as well as collaboration with Western democracies. Imprisoned in 1926 for opposing Mussolini's dictatorship. Active in the Resistance (1939–45). One of the founding members of the Christian Democratic Party. Prime minister from 1944 to 1953.

DEKOBRA, MAURICE (1885–1973). French novelist and journalist whose works were very popular in the 1920s and 1930s. His novels include *La gondole aux chimères: Roman cosmopolite* (1926), *La madone des sleepings* (1925), and *Á Paris tous les deux . . . Journal d'un Yankee entre deux guerres* (1945).

DELFINI, ANTONIO (1907–63). Experimental novelist, poet, and journalist. Born in Modena. Founded literary reviews such as *Ariete-Riforma*. Coedited the literary review *Oggi* with Pannunzio, Chiaromonte, and others, as well as *Caratteri*, a Roman publication. Frequented European literary circles in Paris (where he met Pannunzio, Angioletti, and Malaparte) and Florence (where he met Montale, Landolfi, Bonsanti, and others). Politically active, especially as a member of the Communist Party.

DE SICA, VITTORIO (1902–74). Film director, producer, and actor. Born in Sora. Started his career as a singer and comic stage and film actor. One of his most famous films, *Ladri di biciclette* (1948), was awarded a special Academy Award for best foreign-language film before the category was created. Considered a major neorealist filmmaker, De Sica collaborated with screenwriter Cesare Zavattini.

ECO, UMBERTO (1932–   ). Novelist and scholar. Born in Alessandria (Piedmont). Considered the most important writer on semiotics since Roland Barthes. Has written numerous critical works on language, aesthetics, and popular culture as well. As a novelist, achieved international commercial success with *Il nome della rosa* (for which he was awarded the Strega Prize in 1981). Professor of semiotics at the University of Bologna since 1971.

FARGUE, LÉON-PAUL (1876–1947). Poet and journalist. Born in Paris. Collaborated with Marguerite Caetani on the review *Commerce*.

FENOGLIO, BEPPE (1922–63). Novelist, critic, and translator. Born in Alba. Served in the military and fought in the partisan movement. Known for his portrayal of the partisan movement and for the Anglomania apparent in his works, especially in his posthumous publication, *Il partigiano Johnny* (1968).

FLAIANO, ENNIO (1920–72). Novelist, playwright, screenwriter, journalist, critic, and writer. Born in Pescara. Frequented the Caffè Aragno in Rome, along with Cardarelli, Pannunzio, Brancati, De Feo, and Savinio. Coeditor with Pannunzio of *Il mondo*. Collaborated extensively with Fellini and a number of other Italian film directors. Theater critic for Benedetti's and Pannunzio's *Oggi* and the periodical *Europeo*.

FOGAZZARO, ANTONIO (1842–1911). Novelist. Born in Vicenza. Contemporary of realist Giovanni Verga; represented the opposition to decadentism in Italian literature. Two of his most noted novels are titled *Malombra* (1881) and *Daniele Cortis* (1885).

FOSCOLO, UGO (1778–1827). Poet, novelist, critic, and translator. Born on the island of Zákinthos, Greece. Considered the most famous poet of the eighteenth-century Italian neoclassical movement as well as early romanticism. Joined the French in 1799 against the Austrian invasion of Italy. After the success of the Austrian forces, went into exile in England, where he remained until his death.

GADDA, CARLO EMILIO (1893–1973). Novelist and critic. Born in Milan. Fought in World War I. Worked as an engineer until 1931, then at RAI, the Italian state radio. Awarded several literary prizes, including the Premio Viareggio in 1953. Famous for his unique narrative, which experiments with regional dialects and with technical and academic language. His most celebrated novels are *Quer pasticciaccio bruto de Via Merulana* (1957, translated as *That Awful Mess on Via Merulana*, 1965) and *La cognizione del dolore* (1963, translated as *Acquainted with Grief*, published in 1969).

GARBOLI, CESARE (1928–). Literary critic and editor. Born in Viareggio (Lucca). Among his recent publications are *Penna Papers* (1984), essays on Sandro Penna, and *Il gioco segreto: Nove immagini di Elsa Morante* (1995). Editor of the review *Paragone letterario*.

GARIBALDI, GIUSEPPE (1807–82). Political leader. Born in Nice, France. Member of Mazzini's Giovane Italia Society for the unification of Italy. During his career he led many revolutionary expeditions against French and Austrian forces. Garibaldi's men, known as the "Red Shirts" and also as "The Thousand," conquered Sicily and Naples in the early 1860s. This victory allowed for the establishment of a united Italy in 1861 with Victor Emmanuel as king.

GENINA, AUGUSTO (1892–1957). Catholic screenwriter and film director. Born in Rome. Directed more than 150 films during forty years and wrote the screenplays to nearly all of them. His films deal with subjects ranging from melodrama to Fascist propaganda. Cousin of the director Mario Camerini and husband of the actress Carmen Boni.

GINZBURG, NATALIA (1916–91). Novelist, critic, and dramatist. Born in Palermo, grew up in Turin. Member of the Einaudi group since its beginnings in Turin. One of Italy's most famous writers from the twentieth century, known for her incisive portraits of everyday, domestic life.

GIONO, JEAN (1895–1970). Novelist, poet, and playwright. Born in Manosque, Alpes-de-Haute Provence, France. His novel *Regain* (1930) inspired the classic film *Harvest,* directed by Marcel Pagnol in 1937.

GOTTA, SALVATORE (1887–1980). Popular novelist and short story writer of the Fascist period. Born in Ivrea. His works were concerned with the fortunes of the middle class in rural settings. Author of more than seventy novels, including *Il figlio inquieto* (1917), *L'amante provinciale* (1920), *Lilith* (1934), and *Tre donne innamorate* (1938).

GUGLIEMI, ANGELO (1929–). Literary critic, novelist, poet, and television writer. Born in Arona. Wrote extensively on Italian avant-garde poetry, especially Gruppo 63, in volumes such as *Avanguardia e sperimentalismo* (1964) and *Gruppo 63: Critica e teoria* (coedited with Renato Barilli, 1976). Literary critic for *Paese sera* and *Corriere della sera.*

GUTTUSO, RENATO (1912–87). Painter. Born in Bagheria, near Palermo. Opposed to Fascism and the Mafia, as reflected in the paintings *Flight from Etna* (1938–39) and *Assassination* (1948). Member of the Communist Party. Awarded the Lenin Peace Prize in 1972.

INGRAO, PIETRO (1915–). Communist leader, journalist, and screenwriter. Born in Lenola (Latina). As a young man, studied film at the Experimental Center for Cinema in Rome and collaborated with Luchino Visconti on *Ossessione* (1941). Active in the anti-Fascist student movement in Rome. Joined the Communist Party in 1940. Editor of Milan-based party newspaper *L'Unità* for ten years. One of the first Communists to be elected to Parliament (1948). Named to party secretariat in 1956 and also elected to the Executive Committee.

LA CAPRIA, RAFFAELE (1922–). Novelist, journalist, editor, and screenwriter. Born in Naples. Coeditor of the literary review *Nuovi Argomenti*. Writer for the *Corriere della sera*. Awarded the Strega Prize in 1961 for *Ferito a morte*. Collaborated with film director Francesco Rosi on several films, including *Mani sulla città* and *Uomini contro*.

LA CAVA, MARIO (1908–88). Novelist and critic. Born in Bovalino Marina in Reggio Calabria. Wrote for several literary reviews and newspapers, including Longanesi's *L'Italiano* and *Omnibus* and Bonsanti's *Letteratura*. His first novel was *Caratteri* (1939).

LANDOLFI, TOMMASO (1916–79). Experimental novelist. Born in Pico, near Frosinone. Contributed to the Florentine literary journals *Campo di marte* and *Letteratura*. Critic for *Mondo* and *Corriere della sera*. Awarded the Viareggio Prize for *Ottavio di Saint-Vincent* in 1958.

LARBAUD, VALÉRY (1881–1957). Translator, poet, and novelist. Born in Vichy. Responsible for introducing seminal works of world literature to France, having translated Conrad, Hardy, Butler, Whitman, and Joyce along with many other authors.

LATTUADA, ALBERTO (1914–). Film director, novelist, and poet. Born in Milan. Active contributor to anti-Fascist publications in his late teens. Established his reputation as a neorealist filmmaker with such films as *Il bandito* (1946) *and Luci di Varietà* (1950, in collaboration with Fellini). His first commercial success was *Anna*, starring Silvana Mangano.

LEOPARDI, GIACOMO, CONTE (1798–1837). Poet. Born in Recanati. First attracted public notice with his patriotic ode "All'Italia" and "Sopra il monumento di Dante" (1818). Universally considered Italy's greatest modern poet, whose more private, lyrical expressions of grief have gained him a position as one of the nation's most important existential poets.

LEVI, CARLO (1902–77). Novelist, journalist, and visual artist. Born in Turin. Studied medicine. Active in the Resistance. Member of two anti-Fascist groups: Piero Gobetti's Rivoluzione Liberale in Turin and, later, Carlo and Nello Rosselli's Giustizia e Libertà. Imprisoned and sent into exile for anti-fascist activity; recorded his confinement in the internationally acclaimed *Cristo si è fermato a Eboli* (1947, revised 1963). Other works include *L'orologio* (1951), *Le parole sono pietre: Tre giornate in Sicilia* (1956), and *Doppia notte dei tigli* (1959).

LONGANESI, LEO (1905–57). Painter, novelist, editor, and critic. Born in Ravenna. A dissenting Fascist. Edited many provocative literary reviews, the most important of which is *L'Italiano* (1937–39), which primarily addressed the issue of art and Fascism. Coedited *Il selvaggio* with Mino Maccari. Giorgio Morandi was his friend and mentor.

MACCARI, MINO (1898–1989). Painter, journalist, and editor. Born in Siena. Illustrated numerous periodicals, including *Il selvaggio*, *L'Italiano*, *Omnibus*, and *Il mondo*. Editor of Malaparte's *La stampa*. Awarded the Premio Internazionale dell'Incisione at the 1948 Venice Biennial.

MALAPARTE, CURZIO *(pseudonym for Kurt Erich Sukert)* (1898–1957). Journalist and novelist. Born in Prato. Served in World War I and later in World War II as a liasion officer; experiences recorded in his novel *Kaputt* (1944). Editor with G. B. Angioletti of *Fiera letteraria* and *La stampa* of Turin. Politically ambiguous, he was arrested for anti-Fascist activity, including the publication in France of his book *Technique du coup d'etat*. Founded the newspaper *Prospettive*. Later became a Communist and, shortly before his death, visited China.

MALERBA, LUIGI *(pseudonym for Luigi Bonardi)* (1927–   ). Novelist and screenwriter. Born in Berceto, Parma. Best known for his two early avant-garde novels, *Il serpente* (1966, translated as *The Serpent*), for which he was awarded the Premio Sila and the Priz Medicis, and *Salto mortale* (1968, translated as *What Is This Buzzing, Do You Hear It Too?*), for which he won the Premio Selezione Campiello.

MANZONI, ALESSANDRO (1785–1873). Novelist, poet, playwright, and critic. Born in Milan. Writer of romanticism who embraced Roman Catholicism. Senator of the new Kingdom of Italy in 1860. His classic novel *I promessi sposi* (1827) describes life in Milan under Spanish rule in the seventeenth century.

MARAINI, DACIA (1936–   ). Novelist, poet, playwright, and journalist. Born in Florence. Daughter of the orientalist Fosco Maraini. Her family was imprisoned in a concentration camp in Japan for two years during World War II. Her first novel, *La vacanza* (1962), explores the situation of women in modern society, a concern that would enter her other critical works as well. Cofounded the feminist theater group La Maddalena in 1973. Former companion of Alberto Moravia.

MARINETTI, FILIPPO TOMMASO (1876-1944). Writer. Born in Alexandria, Egypt. Founded the avant-garde Futurist movement, which he championed from 1909 until the end of World War II. Futurism attacked traditionalism in every aspect of Italian life and culture and was the ancestor of other counterculture artistic movements, such as Dada and Surrealism. A full-fledged Fascist, fought as a volunteer in Mussolini's Ethiopian campaign and again in 1942 at the Russian front.

MARTINELLI, ONOFRIO (1900–1966). Painter and arts administrator. Born in Mola di Bari. Member of the group Les Italiens de Paris with De Chirico, Savinio, Tozzi, and others. Regularly exhibited his works at the Quadriennali di Roma and the Biennali di Venezia. Professor at the Accademia di Belle Arti in Florence. Married to painter Adriana Pincherle, sister of Alberto Moravia.

MATTEOTTI, GIACOMO (1885–1924). Socialist leader. Born in Fratta Polesine. Elected general secretary of the Chamber of Deputies in 1924 around the time that Mussolini began to conduct terrorist attacks on leftists. Matteoti denounced the Fascist Party to the chamber on 30 May 1924 and was murdered by the *squadristi* less than two weeks later. The issue of his murder, called the Matteoti Crisis, marks a turning point in the history of Fascism.

MAURIAC, FRANCOIS (1885–1970). Novelist, poet, playwright, essayist, and journalist. Born in Bordeaux, France. A devout Catholic, he aimed at reviving faith and worldly life. Novels include *Le Baiser au lepreux* (1922).

MAZZINI, GIUSEPPE (1805–72). Political leader and theorist. Born in Genoa. Advocated the unification of Italy and the expulsion of Austrians from the peninsula. Established the Giovane Italia Society in 1834. Imprisoned and sent into exile various times because of his attempts to spark republican uprisings.

MILANO, PAOLO (1904–88). Critic, translator, author, and editor. Born in Rome. Prominent literary critic in Italy and, during his exile, in the United States. Contributed to literary and theater reviews such as *Italia letteraria* and edited *Scenario* (1932–38). In exile, after Italy's anti-Semitic laws were espoused, he taught at the New School and Queens College in New York City. After his return to Italy, critic for *L'espresso* (1957–86).

MONDADORI, ALBERTO (1914–76). Publisher, journalist, editor, and poet. Born in Verona. Worked as a film producer during his early adulthood. Founder and director of *Epoca* and *Tempo*, the first Italian magazine in color. Member of the family publishing house Mondadori Editore from 1945 to 1968. Awarded the Viareggio prize for poetry.

MONTALE, EUGENIO (1896–1981). Poet, critic, and political activist. Born in Genoa. One of the main forerunners of the Italian hermetic movement. Principal member of literary and intellectual circles in Florence, such as le Giubbe Rosse group and the circle of Bernard Berenson. Editor of many journals, including *Vieusseux, Letteratura, Campo di Marte, Pegaso,* and *Solaria.* Awarded the Nobel Prize for literature in 1975.

MONTANELLI, INDRO (1908–). Journalist and screenwriter. Born in Fucechio, near Florence. Foreign correspondent. Editor of several newspapers and, in old age, columnist for *Corriere della sera.* Cowriter of several films, including *Pian delle stelle* (1946), *Tombolo, paradiso nero* (1947), and *Il generale Della Rovere* (1959). Codirector with Enrico Gras of *I sogni muiono all'alba.*

MORANTE, ELSA (1912–85). Novelist and poet. Born in Rome. Awarded the Strega Prize in 1957 and the Viareggio Prize in 1948 for *Menzogna e sortilegio.* Married to Alberto Moravia in 1941. Other important works include the novels *La storia* (1974) and *Aracoeli* (1982).

MORO, ALDO (1916–78). Prime minister of Italy. Born in southern Italy. Secretary of the Christian Democratic Party from 1959 to 1963. Responsible for the inclusion of the Socialist Party in a coalition with the Christian Democrats, thus dissolving a threatening tension in the government. Kidnapped and murdered by the Red Brigades, a group of left-wing terrorists, in 1978.

NIEVO, IPPOLITO (1831–61). Poet and novelist. Born in Padua. Principal work is the novel *Le confessioni d'un ottuagenario.* A celebrated patriot; participated in Garibaldi's campaign in 1859, as one of "The Thousand" in Sicily.

NOVENTA, GIACOMO *(pseudonym for Giacomo Ca'Zorzi)* (1898–1960). Dialect poet and journalist. Born in Venice. Volunteered in World War I. Friend of several anti-Fascist leaders including Gobetti, Rosselli, and Carlo Levi. Critic for *La gazzetta del Nord, Il socialista moderno,* and *L'Italia socialista.*

ORIANI, ALFREDO (1852–1909). Born in Faenza. Once-popular novelist whose reputation was boosted by Fascist support of his work. In 1924 a national edition of Oriani's works (edited by Benito Mussolini) was commissioned. His three principals works are the novels *Gelosia, La disfatta,* and *Vortice.*

PALAZZESCHI, ALDO (1885–1974). Poet and novelist. Born in Florence. Palazzeschi's career spanned many generations and reflected changes in style from turn-of-the-century *crespuscolari* poets, futurism, and the experimentalists of the latter half of the twentieth century.

PANCRAZI, PIETRO (1893–1952). Literary critic, novelist, poet, journalist, and editor. Born in Cortona. Important literary critic of the twentieth century, whose works include *Scrittori italiani dal Carducci al D'Annunzio, Scrittori d'oggi,* and *Nel giardino di Candido.* Contributed to a variety of newspapers, including the *Gazzetta di Venezia, Il resto del carlino,* and *Corriere della sera,* and also to the literary review *Pegaso.*

PANNUNZIO, MARIO (1910–68). Journalist and political activist. Born in Lucca. Prominent anti-Fascist and anticommunist during the years of Mussolini's regime. Staunch follower of Benedetto Croce. Founder and editor-in-chief of the authoritative weekly newspaper *Il mondo* from 1949 to 1966. Member of the Partito Liberale, which he left in 1955 to help found the Partito Radicale.

PAPINI, GIOVANNI (1881–1956). Poet, novelist, editor, and journalist. Born in Florence. His unorthodox *Storia di Cristo* (1921, translated as *Life of Christ*) provoked censorship. His outspoken and often unpopular political and intellectual views isolated him. One of the founders of *La Voce* in Florence and cofounder with Giuseppe Prezzolini of *Leonardo.*

PARISE, GOFFREDO (1929–86). Novelist and journalist. Born in Vicenza. His most widely known work is his first novel, *Il ragazzo morto e le comete* (1951). Also worked in the cinema. Foreign correspondent from China, Biafra, and Vietnam for Italy's major daily newspapers. His most important later work is the series of short pieces collected in the two volumes titled *Sillabario*, published in the early 1970s.

PASOLINI, PIER PAOLO (1922–75). Poet, novelist, critic, and film director. Born in Bologna. One of the most important cultural figures in twentieth-century Italy. Influenced by the theories of Antonio Gramsci and Marx. Made fundamental (and often controversial) contributions to cinema and literature as well as the fields of semiotics and film theory. His most important works are *Le ceneri di Gramsci* (1957), a collection of poems, and *Ragazzi di vita* (1955) and *Una vita violenta* (1959), two novels.

PAVESE, CESARE (1908–50). Novelist, poet, and editor, and winner of the Strega Prize. Born in Santo Stefano Belbo in the region of Cuneo. Collaborated with Cesare de Lollis on the political newsletter *Cultura*, for which he was arrested and confined for three years. Member of the editorial staff at the Einaudi publishing house in Turin. Translated works from English to Italian. His novels include *La luna e i falò* and *La bell'estate*. Committed suicide in 1950; his moving diaries were published posthumously.

PENNA, SANDRO (1906–77). Poet. Born in Perugia. First published in journals such as *Letteratura, Botteghe oscure,* and *Paragone.* Awarded the Viareggio Prize in 1957 for his (not numerous) collected works.

PEREC, GEORGES (1936–82). Novelist, poet, dramatist, and essayist. Born in Paris. Awarded the Prix Theophraste Renaudot in 1965 for *Les choses: Une histoire des années soixante* and the Prix Medicis in 1978 for *La vie mode d'emploi.* Member of the Ouvroir de litterature potentielle, also known as the Oulipo group, from 1967 to 1982. The Oulipo writers were dedicated to the pursuit of form in literature, especially toward a union of literature and mathematics.

PINCHERLE, ADRIANA (1909–96). Painter. Born in Rome. First exhibited her work in 1931 in the Prima Mostra Romana d'Arte Femminile in the Galleria di Roma, and thereafter extensively exhibited in Europe and abroad. Sister of Alberto Moravia and wife of Onofrio Martinelli.

PINCHERLE ROSSELLI, AMELIA (1870–1954). Playwright and writer of children's stories. Born in Venice. Aunt of Alberto Moravia. Remembered as a writer and as the mother of anti-Fascists Carlo and Nello Rosselli, whom she encouraged in their political activities. Her play *Anima* (1901) won the Teatro d'arte Award in 1898.

PIOVENE, GUIDO (1907–75). Novelist, critic, and journalist. Born in Vicenza. Foreign correspondent for several periodicals, including *La stampa*. Awarded the Strega Prize in 1970 for his last novel, *Le stelle fredde*. Also worked for the RAI, Italy's television and radio programming center.

PIRANDELLO, LUIGI (1867–1936). Playwright, novelist, poet, critic, and editor. Born near Agrigento. One of Italy's most important authors of the twentieth century. Won international acclaim for the play *Sei personaggi in cerca d'autore* (*Six Characters in Search of an Author*), written in 1922. Cofounder with Bontempelli, Oriani, and Prezzolini of the theater group Compagnia del Teatro d'Arte in 1925. Awarded the Nobel Prize for Literature in 1934.

PONTIGGIA, GIUSEPPE (1934–   ). Novelist and critic. Born in Como. Editor of *Verri* from 1956 to 1961 and since 1972 contributes to the *Almanacco dello Specchio*. His literary essays (on a variety of authors, from Pindar to Gadda) have been collected in the volume *Il giardino degli Esperidi* (1984). Awarded the Selezione Campiello prize in 1978 for his novel *Il giocatore invisibile* (1978).

PRATOLINI, VASCO (1913–91). Novelist, poet, critic, and editor. Born in Florence. Editor of *Letteratura* and coeditor with Alfonso Gatto of *Campo di marte*. Participated in the Resistance. Honored by the Accademia dei Lincei for his collected works. His most successful novel, *Cronache di poveri amanti* (1947), was translated into English as *Tales of Poor Lovers*.

PREZZOLINI, GIUSEPPE (1882–1982). Scholar and professor. Born in Perugia. Edited *Leonardo* with Giovanni Papini and founded *La voce,* a journal that gave rise to a literary circle among early twentieth-century Italian poets. Professor of Italian at Columbia University, New York, where, a Fascist sympathizer, he lived during the years of the regime.

QUASIMODO, SALVATORE (1901–68). Poet, journalist, and editor. Born in Modica, Sicily. Professor of Italian literature at the Conservatorio di Musica in Milan. Edited the weekly periodical *Il tempo.* Awarded the Etna-Taormina Prize for Poetry in 1953 (which he shared with poet Dylan Thomas) and the Nobel Prize in 1959.

QUENEAU, RAYMOND (1903–76). Novelist, poet, and publisher. Born in Le Havre, France. Involved early in his career with André Breton and the Surrealist movement, produced work that reflects a contemporary concern with the efficacy of written language in representing the irrational forces of the mind. Founder with Francois Le Lionnais of Ouvroir de litterature potentielle (the Oulipo group).

RECALCATI, ANTONIO (1938–). Painter. Born in Milan. Famous for his works in ceramic, which have been exhibited in museums throughout Italy.

REMARQUE, ERICH MARIA (1898–1970). Novelist and playwright. Born in Osnabrueck, Germany. His most famous novel *Im Westen nichts Neues* (*All Quiet on the Western Front,* 1928) reveals his strong reservations about the military and led to the author's exile by the Nazis.

ROSSELLI, CARLO (1899–1937). Political activist, theorist, and journalist. Born in Rome. A founder of the anti-Fascist group Giustizia e Libertà in Paris in 1929. Editor of several political newsletters with anti-Fascist agendas, including *Non mollare* and *Quarto stato.* Wrote *Socialismo liberale* (1930) while in political confine in Lipari. In 1937 assassinated in Paris with his brother Nello by the *cagoule,* a group of French fascist hitmen.

ROSSELLI, NELLO (1900–1937). Political activist and historian. Born in Rome. Participated in Giustizia e Libertà, an anti-Fascist group in Paris founded by his brother, Carlo. Published many books on Italian history, including *Mazzini e Bakunin: Dodici anni di movimento operario in Italia* (1927). Assassinated in France with his brother Carlo in 1937.

ROSSELLINI, ROBERTO (1906–77). Leader of neorealist movement in Italian cinema. Born in Rome. The films *Roma, città aperta* (1945), *Paisà* (1946), and *Germania anno zero* (1947) brought the neorealist style to international attention. Rossellini's films are characterized by their use of amateur actors, authentic settings, partly improvised scripts, and documentary footage.

SABA, UMBERTO (1883–1957). Poet and novelist. Born in Trieste. Served in World War I as an airfield inspector. Close friends with Italo Svevo, who was also born in Trieste. Moved to France and then Florence and Rome during the German occupation of his native city.

SANGUINETI, EDOARDO (1930–). Novelist, poet, scholar, and critic. Born in Genoa. Belonged to the avant-garde literary group called Gruppo 63 together with Giuliani and Anceschi. Edited the influential anthology *Poesia italiania del novecento*, seen by some critics as responsible for revising the Italian canon of contemporary works. Noted as a scholar of Dante and of twentieth-century poetry.

SARFATTI, MARGHERITA GRASSINI (1883–1961). Art critic, journalist, and novelist. Born in Venice. One of the leading art critics of this century. Editor of the artistic review *Avanti* and critic for several newspapers, including *La stampa* and *Popolo d'Italia*. Responsible for bringing together the artists of the Novecento group. Mussolini's mistress for more than twenty years, and a lively cultural figure during Fascism.

SAVINIO, ALBERTO *(pseudonym for Andrea De Chirico)* (1891–1952). Poet, novelist, painter, set designer, and musician. Born in Athens. Contributed to the journals *La voce* and *La* *ronda.* Included by Breton in the community of surrealists in Paris. Cited by Sciascia as "the greatest Italian writer since Pirandello." Younger brother of painter Giorgio De Chirico.

SCHIFANO, MARIO (1934–98). Painter. Born in Homs, Libya. His works rely on images often found in popular culture, such as poster and television advertisements.

SCIALOJA, TOTI (1914–98). Painter, journalist, and poet. Born in Rome. Exhibited works at the third and fourth Quadriennale di Roma. Participated in the Resistance. Art critic for *Il selvaggio* and *Mercurio*.

SCIASCIA, LEONARDO (1921–89). One of Sicily's most noted novelists. Born in Racalmuto, in the province of Agrigento. Used the detective novel form to explore the hidden workings of the Mafia, as in *Il giorno della civetta* (1961). Published critical work on the island's other great author, Luigi Pirandello.

SICILIANO, ENZO (1934–). Novelist, critic, journalist, biographer, and playwright. Born in Rome. Editor of the literary review *Nuovi Argomenti*. Contributes to numerous periodicals, especially the *Corriere della sera*. Wrote a biography of Pasolini and essays on Moravia, Guccione, and Puccini. Awarded the Viareggio Prize in 1981 for his historic fiction *La principessa e l'antiquario* (1980).

SILONE, IGNAZIO *(pseudonym for Secondino Tranquilli)* (1900–1978). Novelist and journalist. Born in Pescina dei Marsi in the region of Abruzzi. Wrote for the socialist newspaper *Avanti!* and was one of the founders of the Italian Communist Party in 1921. Later broke with the Party. Editor of *Avanguardia* and *Il lavoratore*. Moved to Switzerland in 1929 to escape persecution by the Fascist regime. His novels, especially *Fontamara* and *Bread and Wine*, which won an international audience, were first published outside of Italy.

SOFFICI, ARDENGO (1879–1964). Painter, poet, critic, and novelist. Born in Rignano sull'Arno, near Florence. In contact with Picasso, Max Jacob, Apollinaire, Braque, and Giovanni Papini during his years in Paris. Art critic for *Leonardo* and contributer to *La voce*. Wrote critically on Futurism and Cubism.

SOLDATI, MARIO (1906–99). Novelist, journalist, critic, and film director. Born in Turin. His first work, *America, primo amore* (1935), describes his experience of America while on a fellowship at Columbia University. Worked as a film director and screenwriter, often collaborating with Mario Camerini. His novels include *Lettere da Capri* and *Los marldo*.

SVEVO, ITALO *(pseudonym for Ettore Schmitz)* (1861–1928). Playwright, novelist, and journalist. Born in Trieste. For much of his life a successful businessman. His most famous novel, *La coscienza di Zeno*, was published in 1923 and attracted international attention thanks to his friend James Joyce, who during his stay in Trieste had taught Svevo English.

TOGLIATTI, PALMIRO (1893–1964). Political leader, journalist, and editor. Born in Genoa. Cofounder of the Italian Communist Party in 1921 and director of political operations abroad while in exile. One of the leading western Communists of his generation. Made significant contributions to international communist theory, particularly through his writings on polycentralism, the concept that Communist parties must adapt their strategies to different national conditions, independent of the movement in Moscow.

TURATI, FILIPPO (1857–1932). Leading socialist, writer, and journalist. Born in Canzo, near Como. General secretary of the Partito Socialista dei Lavoratori Italiani (PSLI) from 1921. Founder of the socialist journal *Critica sociale* together with Anna Kuliscoff. Fled Italy for France in 1926, where he became president of the Concentrazione di Azioni Antifascista, a coalition of noncommunist groups of Italian emigrants in Paris.

UNGARETTI, GIUSEPPE (1888–1970). Poet. Born in Alexandria, Egypt. Fought in World War I. Ungaretti's poetry bridges the gap between the schools of Futurism and *La voce* with the lyric modes of the latter half of the century. Appointed professor of contemporary Italian literature at the University of Rome in 1942, where he remained for the rest of his life. His fame was rivaled only by that of Montale.

VERGA, GIOVANNI (1840–1922). Sicilian novelist and playwright. Born in Catania. Leading writer in the *verismo* movement. One of his most famous novels, *I malavoglia* (1881), depicts the class struggle inherent in many realist works. The libretto for Mascagni's opera *Cavalleria rusticana* was based on Verga's short story and play of the same title, and *I Malavoglia* inspired Luchino Visconti's great film *La terra trema* (1948).

VISCONTI, LUCHINO (1906–76). Film, opera, ballet, and stage director. Born in Milan. Worked as an assistant to director Jean Renoir. His debut film *Ossessione* (1942) is often considered the first example of Italian neorealism. His work profoundly influenced later neorealist directors Rossellini and De Sica. Active opponent of Fascism.

VITTORINI, ELIO (1908–66). Novelist, journalist, and translator. Born in Syracuse, Sicily. Editor of the Florentine journal *Solaria*. Translated major works of American literature into Italian. Most famous novel is *Conversazione in Sicilia* (1941), strongly influenced by Hemingway. Fought in the Resistance.

VOLPONI, PAOLO (1924–94). Poet and editor. Born in Urbino. Contributed to the journal *Officina*, founded by his friend Pasolini. Published several volumes of verse and prose, many of which received literary awards. His first novel, *Il memoriale*, is considered his best work.

ZAMPA, LUIGI (1905–91). Actor, playwright, screenwriter, and film director. Born in Rome. Trained at the Centro Sperimentale between 1935 and 1938. Entered Italian film industry as a screenwriter in 1938. Established career as neorealist filmmaker with the film *Vivere in pace* (1946). In collaboration with Moravia,

Bassani, and Flaiano, made the film *La romana* (1954, starring Gina Lollobrigida), based on Moravia's novel.

ZUCCOLI, LUCIANO (1870–1930). Journalist, popular novelist, and editor. Born in Calprino. Wrote several novels, including *L'amore di Loredana* and *La volpe di Sparta*. Contributed to the periodicals *Provincia di Modena* and *Gazzetta di Venezia*.

Selected Bibliography

NOVELS

Gli indifferenti, Alpes, 1929, translation by Aida Mastrangelo of original edition published as *The Indifferent Ones*, Dutton, 1932; translation by Angus Davidson published as *The Time of Indifference*, Farrar, Straus, 1953; translation by Tami Calliope published as *The Time of Indifference*, Steerforth Press, 2000.

Le ambizioni sbagliate, Mondadori, 1935, translation by Arthur Livington published as *The Wheel of Fortune*, Viking, 1937, translation by Angus Davidson as *Mistaken Ambitions*, Farrar, Straus, 1955.

La mascherata, Bompiani, 1941, translation by Angus Davidson published as *The Fancy Dress Party*, Secker & Warburg, 1947.

Agostino: Romanzo, Documento, 1944, translation by Beryl de Zoete published in *Two Adolescents: The Stories of Agostino and Luca*, Farrar, Straus, 1950 (published in England as *Two Adolescents: Agostino and Disobedience*, Secker & Warburg, 1952). See also *La disubbidienza*.

La romana, Bompiani, 1948, translation by Lydia Holland published as *The Woman of Rome*, Farrar, Straus, 1949; that translation was updated and revised by Tami Calliope and published by Steerforth Press, 1999.

La disubbidienza, Bompiani, 1948, translation by Angus Davidson of original edition published as *Disobedience*, Secker & Warburg, 1950; translation also published in *Two Adolescents: The Stories of Agostino and Luca*, Farrar, Straus, 1950 (published in England as *Two Adolescents: Agostino and Disobedience*, Secker & Warburg, 1952). See also *Agostino: Romanzo.*

Il conformista, Bompiani, 1951, translation by Angus Davidson published as *The Conformist*, Farrar, Straus, 1951; translation by Tami Calliope published by Steerforth Press, 1999.

Il disprezzo, Bompiani, 1954, translation by Angus Davidson published as *A Ghost at Noon*, Farrar, Straus, 1955; translation published as *Contempt*, New York Review Books, 1999.

La ciociara, Bompiani, 1957, translation by Angus Davidson published as *Two Women*, Farrar, Straus, 1958.

La noia, Bompiani, 1963, translation by Angus Davidson published as *The Empty Canvas*, Farrar, Straus, 1965; translation published as *Boredom*, New York Review Books, 1999.

L'attenzione: Romanzo, Bompiani, 1965, translation by Angus Davidson published as *The Lie*, Farrar, Straus, 1966.

Io et lui, Bompiani, translation by Angus Davidson published as *Two: A phallic novel*, Farrar, Straus, 1972 (published in England as *The Two of Us*, Secker & Warburg, 1972).

La vita interiore, Bompiani, 1978, translation by Angus Davidson published as *Time of Desecration*, Farrar, Straus, 1980.

1934, Bompiani, 1982, translation by WIlliam Weaver published under same title, Farrar, Straus, 1980.

L'uomo che guarda, Bompiani, 1985, translation by Tim Parks published as *The Voyeur: A Novel*, Secker & Warburg, 1990.

Il viaggio a Roma, Bompiani, 1988. translation by Tim Parks published as *The Journey to Rome*, Secker & Warburg, 1988.

La donna leopardo (literally, The Leopard Woman), Bompiani, 1991. As yet untranslated into English.

SHORT STORIES

L'amore coniugale, e altri racconti, Bompiani, 1949, translation by Angus Davidson of long story entitled "L'amore coniugale" published as *Conjugal Love*, Secker & Warburg, 1951.

I racconti, Bompiani, 1952. Selected stories, including "Inverno di malato"

(A Sick Boy's Winter), "L'imbroglio" (The Imbroglio), and "L'amante infelice" (The Unfortunate Lover), were translated by Frances Frenaye, Baptista Gilliat Smith, and Bernard Wall and published as *Bitter Honeymoon and Other Stories*, Secker & Warburg, 1960. Selections from *I racconti*, including "La provinciale" (The Wayward Wife), were also translated by Angus Davidson and published as *The Wayward Wife and Other Stories*, Secker & Warburg, 1960. Stories from *I racconti* that have not been transltated include "La tempesta" (literally, The Storm), "L'architetto" (The Architect), and "La casa è sacra" (The Home Is Sacred).

Racconti romani (originally pubished in *Corriere della sera*), Bompiani, 1954; selected stories translated by Angus Davidson and published as *Roman Tales*, Secker & Warburg, 1956; Farrar, Straus, 1957.

L'epidemia; racconti surrealisti e satirici (literally, The Epidemic, Surrealistic, and Satircal Tales), Bompiani, 1956 is a short story collection that has not yet been translated into English.

Nuovi racconti romani (originally published in *Corriere della sera*), Bompiani, 1959; selected stories, including "Io et Lui" (He and I), translated by Angus Davidson and published as *More Roman Tales*, Secker & Warburg, 1963.

L'automa, Bompiani, 1963, translation by Angus Davidson published as *The Fetish*, Secker & Warburg, 1964; published as *The Fetish and Other Stories*, Farrar, Straus, 1965. This collection includes a short-story version of *L'uomo che guarda* (see Novels), translated here as "The Man Who Watched."

Una cosa è una cosa, Bompiani, 1967, translation by Angus Davidson of selections published as *Command and I Will Obey You*, Farrar, Straus, 1969.

Il paradiso, Bompiani, 1970, translation by Angus Davidson published as *Paradise and Other Stories*, Secker & Warburg, 1971; published as *Bought and Sold*, Farrar, Straus, 1973.

Un'altra vita, Bompiani, 1973, translation by Angus Davidson published as *Lady Godiva and Other Stories*, Secker & Warburg, 1975; translation published as *Mother Love*, Panther, 1976.

Boh, Bompiani, 1976, translation by Angus Davidson published as *The Voice of the Sea and Other Stories*, Secker & Warburg, 1978; includes "La vergine e la droga" (The Virgin and the Drug).

La cosa e altri racconti, Bompiani, 1983, translation by Tim Parks published as *Erotic Tales*, Secker & Warburg, 1985; includes "La cintura" (The Belt) and "La cosa" (The Thing).

PLAYS

Beatrice Cenci (published in *Botteghe oscure*, 1955), translation by Angus Davidson, Secker & Warburg, 1965; Farrar, Straus, 1966.

Teatro, Bompiani, 1976, is a collection of plays that has not been translated. It includes *Il dio Kurt* (literally, The God Kurt), *Il mondo è quello che è* (The World Is What It Is), *La vita è gioco* (Life Is a Game) and *L'intervista* (The Interview).

L'angelo dell'informazione e altri testi teatrali, Bompiani, 1986, is another untranslated collection of theatrical pieces. It includes *L'angelo dell'informazione* (literally, The Angel of Information) and *Il colpo di stato* (The Coup d'Etat).

Unpublished plays and screenplays include *Il cielo sulla palude* (literally, The Sky over the Swamp), *Il colpo di pistola* (The Gunshot), *La freccia nel fianco* (Arrow in the Hip), *Senza cielo* (Without Heaven), (The Trap), and *Zazà*.

OTHER WORKS

Un mese in URSS (literally, A Month in the USSR), Bompiani, 1958, is a travel memoir that has not yet been translated.

L'uomo come fine e altri saggi (essays), Bompiani, 1964; selected essays translation by Bernard Wall and published as *Man as an End—A Defense of Humanism: Literary, Social, and Political Essays*, Farrar, Straus, 1965.

La rivoluzione culturale in Cina occero il convitato di pietra, Bompiani, 1967, translation published as *The Red Book and the Great Wall: An Impression of Mao's China*, Farrar, Straus, 1968.

A quale tribù appartieni? Bompiani, 1972, translation by Angus Davidson published as *Which Tribe Do You Belong To?*, Farrar, Straus, 1974.

TRANSLATED TITLES OF
WORKS BY OTHER AUTHORS

Alcools (Alcohols), Guillaume Apollinaire

L'allegria (Happiness), Giuseppe Ungaretti

Americana, edited by Elio Vittorini

L'amour est mon péché (Love Is My Sin), Anonymous

La bellissime avventure di Caterina dalla Trecciolina (The Lovely Adventures of Caterina of the Little Braid), Elsa Morante

Le Bourgeois gentilhomme (The Would-be Gentleman), Jean-Baptiste Molière

Bouvard et Pécuchet (Bouvard and Pécuchet), Gustave Flaubert

Il bugiardo (The Liar), Carlo Goldoni

"Le ceneri di Gramsci" ("Gramsci's Ashes"), Pier Paolo Pasolini

La coda di paglia (literally, The Straw Tail, but it really an idiomatic expression that means "hypersensitive"), Guido Piovene

La cognizione del dolore (Acquainted with Grief), Carlo Emilio Gadda

Colline, Jean Giono

Il deserto dei tartari (The Tartar Steppe), Dino Buzzati

Le donne di Messina (The Women of Messina), Elio Vittorini

L'Étranger (The Stranger), Albert Camus

Faux monnaieurs (The Counterfeiters), Andre Gidé

Fontamara, Ignazio Silone

"Gli occhiali d'oro ("The Gold-rimmed Spectacles"), Giorgio Bassani

Gli ultimi giorni di Alba (Twenty-three Days in the City of Alba), Beppe Fenoglio

I nostri antenati (Our Predecessors), a collection of three short novels by Italo Calvino

L'isola di Arturo (Arturo's Island), Elsa Morante

Kaputt, Curzio Malaparte

La lunga vita di Marianna Ucrìa (The Silent Duchess), Dacia Maraini

Manon Lescaut, Antoine Francois Prevost

Menzogna e sortilegio (House of Liars), Elsa Morante

Il mondo salvato dai ragazzini (The World Saved by Little Children), Elsa Morante

La Nausée (Nausea), Jean-Paul Satre

Il nome della rosa (The Name of the Rose), Umberto Eco

Operetta morali (Moral Operas), Giacomo Conte Leopardi

Ossi di seppia (Cuttlefish Bones), Eugenio Montale

Il partigiano Johnny (Johnny the Partisan), Beppe Fenoglio

La pelle (Skin), Curzio Malaparte

Il piacere (The Child of Pleasure), Gabriele D'Annunzio

Père Goriot, Honoré de Balzac

Les Précieuses ridicules (The Foolish Ladies), Jean-Baptiste Molière

Il ragazzo morto e le comete (The Dead Boy and the Comets), Goffredo Parise

Le rouge et le noir (The Red and the Black), Stendahl

Roma città aperta (Open City), directed by Roberto Rossellini

Sei personaggi in cerca d'autore (Six Characters in Search of an Author), Luigi Pirandello

Il sentiero dei nidi di ragno (The Path to the Nest of Spiders), Italo Calvino

Senza i conforti della religione (Without the Comforts of Religion), Silvio Guarnieri

Il sillabario (The Abecedary), Goffredo Parise

La storia (History), Elsa Morante

Symbolik des Geistes (Psyche & Symbol), Carl G. Jung

Ugetsu, a film directed by Kenji Mizoguchi

Uscita di sicurezza (Emergency Exit), Ignazio Silone

La vita intensa (The Intense Life), Massimo Bontempelli

La vita operosa (The Hard-working Life), Massimo Bontempelli

La voce (The Voice), edited by Giuseppe Prezzolini

Voyage au bout de la nuit (Journey to the End of the Night), Louis-Ferdinand Céline

Index